A Self-Made Nation

A Self-Made Nation

THE PEOPLE AND PRINCIPLES THAT BUILT AMERICA

———

Al Fuller

Wilbrad Publishing - Kirkland

Wilbrad Publishing
Kirkland, Washington
United States of America
Copyright © 2016 Al Fuller
All Rights Reserved, including in whole or in part in any form.

ISBN-13: 9780997836707
ISBN-10: 0997836709
Includes bibliographical references and index.
Library of Congress Control Number: 2016915691
Wilbrad Publishing, Kirkland, WA

*To the people profiled in this book, for giving me hope
when I needed it.*

Table of Contents

Preface: Why I Wrote This Book· · · · · · · · · · · · · · · · ix

Chapter 1   A Nation of Nonconformists. 1
Chapter 2   Benjamin Franklin 8
Chapter 3   John Jacob Astor 30
Chapter 4   Eli Whitney. 41
Chapter 5   Free States and Free Enterprise 55
Chapter 6   Robert Fulton and His Steamboat. 71
Chapter 7   Cornelius Vanderbilt 80
Chapter 8   A Brief History of Railroading in the United States. . .105
Chapter 9   The Mellons 128
Chapter 10 Andrew Carnegie 148
Chapter 11 John D. Rockefeller. 168
Chapter 12 Thomas Edison. 184
Chapter 13 Diamond Jim Brady 208
Chapter 14 How They Did It 231
Chapter 15 Final Word 260

Notes. 263
Index· 301
Author Biography 309

PREFACE

Why I Wrote This Book

———

*Living the American dream has been intense, difficult
work, but I couldn't have hoped for a more satisfying life.*

E S T E E   L A U D E R

I WROTE THIS BOOK TO encourage young Americans to believe in themselves and in the opportunities available to them. From its founding the United States has been a nation where the future is unlimited for a person who believes in the power of his own efforts, and as long as young Americans continue to understand this their future, and the nation's future as well, will continue to be unlimited.

The history of the American nation itself is a rags-to-riches story. In the 1780s the United States was a small, poor country with no non-human resources to speak of. The U.S. of that time had no factories, no technology, no transportation infrastructure, and very little hard money; and was regularly insulted and oppressed by both England and France. Yet that same country was the richest and most powerful nation on Earth by the end of the next century. No other nation or empire in history has ever thrust itself onto the world scene with that kind of speed; not the Romans, not the Greeks, no one. And the engine that drove this unprecedented growth was ordinary

Americans, most of whom started out in life with nothing but determination, self-reliance, and freedom.

The true story of this wonderful self-made nation is inspiring and encouraging; it edifies and gives hope. There can't be many things more satisfying than overcoming obstacles to achieve success, and our history clearly shows not only that success of that kind is attainable for any ordinary American, but that the greatness of the nation itself was built almost exclusively by people who started out in life with nothing.

Going from poverty to the middle class or beyond has been so common in American history that there was a time when no one even tried to deny that such opportunities were available. At one time a dirt-poor teenager like Andrew Carnegie, working as a messenger boy in the streets of Pittsburgh, could plan on succeeding in business and be so confident about it that he could say, as Carnegie did, "If I don't, it will be my own fault, for anyone can get along in this country."[1]

Today the opportunities are still here, but the hope is too often missing. In recent years it seems to have become fashionable among the self-proclaimed "elite" who populate our news media and college faculties to try to take hope away from supposedly "disadvantaged" young Americans by portraying the United States as a country where success has always been reserved for those who are born to wealth and power. This portrayal of our nation's history is as poisonous as it is inaccurate. Nothing could be further from the truth, and nothing could be more damaging to the self-confidence and hope of modern-day Americans who happen to grow up in difficult circumstances.

Two centuries of good examples show that the only disadvantage that can stop a person from making progress in America is despair, yet despair seems to be the very thing that many wealthy, educated opinion leaders are peddling to our poor and working class citizens. One college history textbook, for example, has this to say about the faith that nineteenth century Americans like Carnegie had in themselves and their country: "The *unrealistic expectations* inspired by *the rags-to-riches myth* more than the absence of real opportunity probably explains why so many workers, even when expressing dissatisfaction with life as it was, continued to subscribe to such middle-class values as hard work and thrift – that is, they continued to hope." (Italics added)[2]

Hard work, thrift, and hope. These are the very cornerstones of the typical American success story, yet the professors who wrote this history textbook mock them as "unrealistic" and a "myth." Disparaging these crucial principles can only do harm to the students who read these texts. When a young person is told that his own efforts can have no value in overcoming a "disadvantaged" background, he is likely to start believing that pernicious message, and quit trying. Killing a person's belief in his own ability to create a better life for himself is just about the cruelest thing anyone could ever do, yet there are college professors doing it in their classrooms and textbooks.

I once heard a scientist say that the only way to win an argument with a credentialed authority in his field is to "drown him in data." That's what this book was written to do. The purpose of this book is to overcome the soul-killing propaganda of so many figures in academia and the media by drowning them in true stories of early Americans who went from poverty or near-poverty to success and wealth. To keep the book down to a reasonable size I have restricted the list of subjects to people who started their careers in the nation's first hundred years or so. Most of the self-made men mentioned in this book are described only in passing, with just a very brief biographical sketch to show the disadvantages that each of them had to overcome. Only a few famous names like Rockefeller and Carnegie get whole chapters, and I have tried to make these chapters as short as possible while doing justice to these men's remarkable stories.

CHAPTER 1

A Nation of Nonconformists

———

The welfare of the nation is squarely up to us as individuals.

HENRY FORD

THE AMAZINGLY RAPID RISE OF the United States from poor backwater to leading world power was fueled by the equally amazing achievements of ordinary people who started their careers without wealth, connections, status, or "privilege." Some of the people profiled in these pages have names like Astor, Vanderbilt, Carnegie, Mellon, and Rockefeller; names not commonly associated with poverty, but made famous by men who started out with nothing. Some are famous for reasons other than the financial success they achieved, although all of them did achieve financial success.

Many of these people never got much formal education. Many were told in childhood that they were idiots or losers. (Thomas Edison's first grade teacher, for example, told Edison's mother that her son was mentally defective.)[3] Many belonged to unpopular ethnic or religious groups. They all grew up in a time when there were no governmental welfare programs to fall back on if their efforts failed.

The things that allowed these ordinary folks to achieve such extraordinary success, other than having the good fortune to live in

America's free states, are habits and character qualities that anyone can emulate. None of the things that made these people so successful are out of the reach of any ordinary American today. In fact self-made success is in many ways easier today than it was in the nation's early years, particularly for members of ethnic minorities who, today, don't have to contend with the kinds of government-imposed discrimination that afflicted minority members so shamefully in the nation's early years. The critical habits and characteristics that create success in America will be abundantly illustrated in the pages that follow.

First among these characteristics, and absolutely indispensable for success, is a belief in the efficacy of effort. Great success requires great effort, and only the person who expects his efforts to yield results will work as hard as the people profiled in this book.

Other traits characteristic of these upwardly mobile individuals are tenacity, a passion for their work, foresight strengthened by objectivity, and a commitment to self-education. They filled other people's needs. They honed their people skills and developed, in most cases, at least a basic understanding of salesmanship. Most of them started their careers working for someone else, and when they did they focused on developing their own skills to meet the needs of their employers, so as to make themselves valuable human resources. When in a position to hire employees of their own, these individuals all, without exception, put a very high priority on identifying, attracting, retaining, developing and motivating the best human resources they could find. All of these principles will be illustrated in detail in this book.

Another key characteristic of all these individuals is that they truly were individuals, in every possible sense of the word. A self-made man is not a herding animal. Each of these people marched to the beat of his own drum; each made his own decisions according to his own judgment. All of them were, in one way or another, non-conformists.

It is significant that all of these stories take place in America's Northern states. The stories in this book all come from the eighteenth and nineteenth centuries, and America's title as the "land of opportunity" did not really apply in the Southern states until the South finally got rid of the old "Jim Crow" culture of government-imposed racism during the 1960s. In the early years of the republic the culture of self-reliant individualism that gave rise to so many rags-to-riches stories was common only in the Northern states. The origins of this cultural trait go back to colonial times. When the United States declared independence and created a constitution, the Founders' determination to protect each individual's right to non-conformity played a huge role in determining the kind of nation that America was to become.

Non-Conformity in Religion
In the early 1830s a French nobleman named Alexis de Tocqueville traveled through the U.S. and wrote up his observations in the now classic book *Democracy in America.*

Tocqueville made it clear that while religion was an important part of the American character, religious conformity was not. The Americans he met approached God as individuals. Unlike Europe, where citizens passively accepted whatever religious denomination their rulers might impose on them, Americans citizens chose their own churches. "The sects which exist in the United States are innumerable." said Tocqueville, "They all differ in respect to the worship which is due from man to his Creator, but they all agree in respect to the duties which are due from man to man."[4] He made these observations while traveling in the Northern states, not the Southern ones. During the time of his visit there was still very little religious diversity in the South.

From their earliest days, the British colonies in the Northern part of North America attracted large numbers of religious dissidents. Most of the Northern colonies, in fact, were actually founded by religious dissidents.[5] These religious non-conformists were a rare breed, very different from the great majority of Europeans in their individualism, independence, and plain stubbornness. It was the descendants of people like this who became the self-made millionaires of later generations.

In contrast, the four original Southern colonies were all founded as purely economic ventures. All four of them were founded with the support of the English government and named after English monarchs,[6] and all four of them retained the Church of England as the official state religion. It's worth noting that none of the nine Northern colonies were named after government leaders.

Today we take for granted that each of us can attend any church we like, or no church at all, according to our own choice; but things were very different in seventeenth century Europe. The king of England was the head not just of the national government, but also of the national church, and membership in his church was mandatory. England was far from unique in this respect; each European government imposed a mandatory state religion on its citizens.

What is significant for the purposes of this book is that most Englishmen were willing to worship the way the government told them to worship. Going along with the herd comes naturally to most humans, and this is especially true when more than just peer pressure is involved. It is a rare individual who will stick to his own beliefs when he is told to change them by an authority structure with the power to inflict severe penalties for non-conformity. Most of the early immigrants to the Northern colonies were individuals of this rare kind.

Once the northern British colonies were established, they attracted religious dissidents from all around Europe. The Pilgrims who crossed the Atlantic in the Mayflower in 1620 were English "separatists;" people who were so offended by corruption in the Church of England that they felt they had no choice but to completely separate themselves from it. This was criminal behavior in England at that time; in 1558 parliament had passed a law making weekly attendance at Church of England services mandatory. Merely missing a Sunday service was punishable by a fine. During the late 1500s, prominent separatist leaders were often jailed, and at least two were put to death.[7] The Separatists were willing to endure this kind of persecution because they put a higher value on serving God according to their own beliefs than on popularity, comfort, or even life itself.

When they fled to the New World the original Pilgrims found the religious freedom they were seeking, but at a steep cost. Half of them died of starvation and disease in the first year. None of them returned to England or renounced their Separatist faith. Despite the dangers, separatists continued to travel to Plymouth and the population of the colony grew rapidly.

In 1629 a new group of religious non-conformists, known as Puritans, established a colony not far from Plymouth, at Massachusetts Bay. The two colonies would merge in 1691 to form the Colony of Massachusetts.

Like the Separatists, the Puritans came to North America to gain the freedom to worship God as they believed He wanted to be worshiped. All these new immigrants did what they could to succeed financially in the New World, but they were not fortune-seeking adventurers. Most would have very much preferred to stay in England if they could have done so without betraying their faith or facing persecution. Persecution at the hands of King Charles I drove Puritans to North America in large numbers from 1630 through the first part of 1642, but the wave of immigration stopped abruptly in '42 when Oliver Cromwell, a Puritan himself, overthrew Charles and ended the persecution.[8] When persecution resumed under Charles II, so did the Puritan immigrations to North America.

The colonies of Rhode Island and Connecticut were founded by colonists who had been driven out of Massachusetts because their religious beliefs differed from those of the Puritans. The colonies of

Maine, New Hampshire, and Vermont all allowed a degree of religious freedom that attracted non-conformists from Britain and the European continent.

In 1682 William Penn founded a colony he called "Sylvania" as a refuge for persecuted English Quakers. The colony was later renamed Pennsylvania in his honor. Unlike the Mayflower Pilgrims and the Puritans, Penn and his followers allowed complete religious liberty from the day the colony was founded. Soon Pennsylvania attracted large numbers of German religious non-conformists and Scots-Irish Presbyterians, along with Jews, English Catholics, French Protestants, et al. In 1704 Penn founded the adjacent colony of Delaware, again instituting a policy of freedom of religion that attracted persecuted religious minorities from various European countries.

New York was founded by the Dutch and then taken over by England. The original colonists were not religious pilgrims, but Dutch policies aimed at increasing the number of colonists in the area attracted a highly diverse population, and when England took possession of the territory they continued those policies. Maryland, which fought with the Union against the Confederacy during the Civil War, despite being a slave state, was founded specifically as a haven for persecuted English Catholics.

Clearly (and ironically, as it turns out), the primary motive for moving to northern North America in the seventeenth century was religious, not financial.

FOUNDING PRINCIPLES

In the 1780s, when the United States had just won its independence and the Founders were debating how to constitute a government for the new nation, creating a dynamic economic system was the last thing on any of their minds. Because repressive governments had made non-conformity so painful for the colonists and their ancestors, religious and political freedoms were the Founders' top priorities. Their shared obsession was to limit the power and reach of the central government and protect the rights and freedoms of every individual.

In their determination to protect American individuals from arbitrary government power, the Founders built economic freedom into the United States' political system without much conscious effort. The result, almost by accident, was a perfect recipe for national growth: a population of individualistic citizens and a government that left them alone to pursue their dreams.

That the free enterprise system they created quickly became a wellspring of new technologies and unprecedented economic growth was an unexpected side effect of the Founders' desire to protect religious and political freedoms.

The Southern states, unfortunately, did not fully participate in the freedom, nor in the growth, until late in the twentieth century.

CHAPTER 2

Benjamin Franklin

———

*By perseverance, study, and eternal
desire, any man can become great.*

GEORGE PATTON

WHEN BENJAMIN FRANKLIN WAS 65 years old he started writing an autobiography that he never got around to finishing. The purpose of the book, as he explained on the first page, was to share with his heirs an account of how he had "emerged from the poverty and obscurity in which I was born" to become accomplished and wealthy. He worked at the book off and on over the years, but at the time of his death the manuscript covered only the first 52 years of his life. To this day the book has no ending; it simply stops in the middle of a chapter.

Eventually his heirs published what he had written, just as it was. The autobiography became an instant classic. Although the book is not well known today, Franklin's account of the steps he took to rise from rags to riches inspired several generations of young Americans, including some who overcame similar "poverty and obscurity" to achieve even greater financial success.

Thomas Mellon said in his own autobiography, "I regard the reading of Franklin's autobiography as the turning point of my life."[9]

John D. Rockefeller, when he was well on his way to becoming the world's richest man, often read excerpts from Franklin's book to children in the Sunday school class he taught, using his own well-known financial success to justify the faith he had always had in Franklin's principles.[10]

The autobiography was so well-known in the nineteenth century that Mark Twain once wrote a tongue-in-cheek article in which he complained that his boyhood had been scarred by the expectations his father put on him after reading Franklin's book.[11]

It seems appropriate to start a book about American success stories with the one that established the pattern.

COMING TO AMERICA

Benjamin Franklin's grandfather, Thomas Franklin, was an English blacksmith who had four sons. The two older sons, as loyal subjects of King Charles II, were willing to attend the king's church in conformance with English law. They lived in peace in England all their lives. Thomas' two younger sons converted to the Puritan faith, refused to compromise, and had to flee to the colonies to avoid persecution. Josiah, the youngest son, made a life for himself in Boston, became a pillar of his neighborhood church, and worked very hard to put food on the table for his ever-growing family.[12] On January 17 of 1706, Josiah's fifteenth child was born, and Josiah named the boy Benjamin after his Puritan older brother.

The younger Benjamin Franklin received no formal education until he was eight years old, but he was an avid reader before he ever set foot in a classroom. His parents taught him to read and write when he was still very young; so young that he would later say "I do not remember when I could not read."[13] From early childhood Benjamin believed that his mind was the most important resource he had, and he worked constantly to increase the value of that resource.

Josiah Franklin owned enough books to cover a small shelf in his home, an unusual thing for an eighteenth century tradesman, and Benjamin took full advantage of this asset. Some of the books were heavy tomes on serious subjects, but the boy worked his way through all of them. Exercising his brain with intellectual challenges seems to have been Franklin's favorite activity, from early childhood until the day of his death.

When Benjamin was 10 years old his father, who was then self-employed as a candle-maker, took him out of school and put him to work in the shop. Despite getting only two years of formal education, Franklin eventually did such a good job of educating himself that he would become world famous for his intellectual achievements, and come to be known internationally by the title "Dr. Franklin."

Benjamin continued to spend every spare minute improving his mind. He read every book he could borrow or buy. He spent nearly every penny his father paid him for books, which he would read and then sell to raise money for still more books.[14]

When he wasn't working or reading, young Benjamin enjoyed physical exercise, especially swimming. The Benjamin Franklin we see today on the hundred dollar bill is a chubby old fellow, but that portrait was painted in France in 1785 when Franklin was a wealthy, well-fed 79-year-old. Franklin the boy was full of energy and physically very fit.

Benjamin's older brother James had set up a printing shop in Boston and in 1718 Josiah arranged for 12-year-old Benjamin to become James' apprentice. A typical apprenticeship in the early eighteenth century was a legal contract in which the apprentice agreed to be "indentured," i.e. committed to a state of near-slavery, for a period of several years in exchange for room, board, and the opportunity to learn a valuable skill. Benjamin's contract was for nine years. Benjamin, ever the eager student, managed to learn everything his brother could teach him about the printing business within the first few years.

Benjamin continued to take advantage of every opportunity to sharpen his intellect. After making the acquaintance of another boy in Boston who was of an intellectual bent, ("another bookish lad in the town,") he started a debate with the youngster about the question of education for women, which his young friend opposed. After an initial face-to-face conversation, the two young philosophers continued the debate by mail. Benjamin's father, after reading all the letters, offered some constructive criticism:

> Without entering into the discussion, he took occasion to talk to me about the manner of my writing; observing that, though I had the advantage of my antagonist in spelling... I fell far short in elegance of expression, in method and in perspicuity, of which he convinced me by several instances. I saw the justice of his remarks, and thence grew more attentive to the manner in writing, and determined to endeavor at improvement.[15]

Teenage boys are not always this willing to accept criticism from their parents, but for Franklin the opportunity to improve his writing was more important than any tendency he might have had toward teen rebellion. He responded to his father's critique by putting himself through a series of exercises aimed at honing his writing skills.[16] In later years his skills as a writer would become one of his greatest assets.

To increase his access to books, young Franklin formed friendships with adults who had personal libraries. He also took advantage of his job in a print shop by forming friendships with booksellers' apprentices, whom he would persuade to lend him books from the sellers' stock. He would read a book at night and return it to the sale shelf the next morning.[17]

At 16 Benjamin read a book about vegetarianism. James was obligated to provide all his meals, so Benjamin asked James to figure out what the monthly cost of his food was and give him half as much in cash. The older brother accepted the deal right away, for obvious reasons, and Benjamin managed to feed himself a cheap, vegetarian diet on half the money his brother gave him, i.e. one quarter of what his original food budget had been. The remaining cash he spent on books. When James was taking his other employees out for dinner, Benjamin would stay behind, eating a piece of bread and reading.[18]

Literature was not the future inventor's only interest. During the two years he spent in elementary school he had flunked arithmetic twice, so during his apprenticeship he made a point of making up for his earlier failures by working his way through the exercises in a math book in his spare time. During this period he also studied science and philosophy.[19] He learned the Socratic Method and practiced it in debates with friends and family members.[20] He indulged an interest in things nautical by reading books on navigation, from which he learned the fundamentals of geometry.

It was during this period that he began to reject the Puritan faith of his parents. He had the same independent streak his father had shown in rejecting the Church of England, and in the case of the younger Franklin that independent streak led to even more unorthodox views in religion. When he was 15 years old he read some books on the subject of Deism, a sort of philosophical precursor to atheism, written by a Christian author who opposed it. The effect these books had on Franklin was "quite contrary to what was intended," because "the arguments of the Deists, which were quoted to be refuted, appeared to me much stronger than the refutations."[21] He declared himself a Deist, and even persuaded a couple of his friends to join the unpopular sect.

He would renounce Deism a few years later, but he never returned to Puritanism. When he was in his early thirties and living in Philadelphia his parents wrote to him, urging him to return to the faith of his youth, and his reply was revealing. "If it were a thing possible," he said, "for one to alter his opinions in order to please another, I know none whom I ought more willingly to oblige in that respect than yourselves. But," he went on, it is "not in a man's power" to change his beliefs to please another person.[22]

That statement tells us a great deal about Benjamin Franklin, and about upwardly mobile people in general.

Franklin seems to have genuinely believed that it is "not in a man's power" to change what he believes in response to external pressure, but he was clearly wrong. Most people, then as now, were willing to change their beliefs in response to peer pressure, or in response to pressure from authority figures, or for any number of other reasons unrelated to evidence and reason. People like Franklin, who form their beliefs strictly by using their own judgment to evaluate the available data, are the exception rather than the rule.

A willingness to believe something "not because it's true, but for some other reason"[23] has always been a human characteristic. Things are no different today. On most college campuses, professors and administrators pressure their students to conform to a code of "politically correct" thinking on social and political subjects, and most students conform to it without putting up much of a fight. It's a rare student who is brave enough to choose his own beliefs, in that environment, in defiance of powers that be. Franklin's approach might not be the best way to achieve short-term popularity, but it's the way all the successful people profiled in this book approached life, and Franklin doesn't seem to have been able to conceive of any other way of thinking. Franklin was unwilling to believe anything that did not appear to him to actually be true.

In his later years, Franklin would give consistent financial support to a Presbyterian church in Philadelphia, although he rarely attended services. In the autobiography he claimed he "never was without some religions principles," and specifically said that he believed God "made the world, and govern'd it by his Providence," and that each man will be rewarded or punished for his deeds in the afterlife. Serving one's fellow man, he often said, was the best way to serve God.[24]

Franklin generally showed respect for the Bible, and quoted from it fairly often. One biblical passage in particular was an inspiration to him from early childhood. The passage is from Proverbs chapter 22, verse 29: "Seest thou a man diligent in his calling? He will stand before kings, he will not stand before mean men." Franklin had faith in this principle and made it the theme of his career, and in his case the proverb proved to be true, not just figuratively, but literally. In the autobiography he described how this passage encouraged him to be industrious in his work and his studies, and the results he achieved:

> I from thence considered industry as a means of obtaining wealth and distinction, which encourag'd me, tho' I did not think that I should ever literally *stand before kings*, which, however, has since happened; for I have stood before *five*, and even had the honor of sitting down with one, the King of Denmark, to dinner.[25]

At work in his brother's print ship, Benjamin studiously applied himself to the technical aspects of work; operating and maintaining the machinery, making ink, procuring and managing the necessary materials, etc. And despite growing friction with his brother he found a way to contribute actual content to the newspaper James was printing.

James Franklin's shop was typical of early eighteenth century print shops in that it did contract work for anyone who wanted something printed, and it also published a newspaper. James was the primary writer for his newspaper, which he called the *New England Courant*. Several volunteers also contributed content to the paper, some of them using assumed names. In 1722 16-year-old Benjamin disguised his handwriting and slipped an essay under the print shop door, in which a fictitious character named Silence Dogood introduced herself to readers as the farm-dwelling widow of a deceased minister. She was, as one Franklin biographer puts it, "a slightly prudish widowed woman from a rural area, created by a spunky unmarried Boston teenager who had never spent a night outside of the city."[26] James printed the piece and it got rave reviews. The younger Franklin submitted 13 more essays in Mrs. Dogood's name before the game lost its charm. In the last essay Benjamin revealed his real identity. He reveled in the attention the pieces brought him, but his increasingly resentful older brother accused him of being "vain" about his literary success.

The friction between James and Benjamin often took physical form. In the autobiography Benjamin records that "my brother was passionate, and had often beaten me, which I took extreamly amiss; and, thinking my apprenticeship very tedious, I was continually wishing for some opportunity of shortening it." Eventually he would get his chance.

During that same year James' newspaper printed a piece about the ruling assembly's efforts to protect the coast from pirates. The assembly took the view that James was mocking them, and jailed him for a month. During James' incarceration Benjamin published the paper himself. In one of the three issues he published, Benjamin ran a Silence Dogood essay in which the feisty old widow condemned government restrictions on freedom of speech. "Whoever would overthrow the liberty of a nation," his alter ego said, "must begin by subduing the freeness of speech."[27]

In January of 1723 James again angered the local authorities, and they issued an order forbidding him to publish the *Courant* "or any other pamphlet or paper of like nature" without prior approval. James consulted with several friends and decided to transfer control of the paper, at least officially, to his younger brother. To maintain the fiction that Benjamin was the real publisher and not under James' management, James signed papers liberating Benjamin from the remaining years of his apprenticeship contract. The two of them signed a separate, secret contract indenturing Benjamin for the remaining years of the original pact. The first *Courant* issue officially published by the younger Franklin went out on February 11 of 1723.[28]

Benjamin's new role was more than just a fiction for public consumption; he actually did take on a larger role in the management of the paper. Knowing that James could not go public with the new contract of indenture, he took full advantage of the situation.

Unwilling to be a mere figurehead, as James had intended, Benjamin wrote and published much of the content of the paper, and even changed the editorial approach. In that first issue in February of 1723 he informed readers that the new policy of the *Courant* would be "to entertain the town with the most comical and diverting incidents of humane life." James continued to have input of course, and the paper continued to touch on politically sensitive subjects, but the politics would be wrapped in humor for as long as Benjamin stayed involved.

The *Courant* prospered under the younger Franklin's management. Circulation increased and the Franklins were able to raise the price they charged.[29] With Benjamin's compensation still limited to room and board by the contract, James reaped all the financial benefits of the paper's increasing popularity, but despite the financial benefits to himself he grew increasingly resentful of his upstart younger brother. The beatings continued.[30]

In 1723 Benjamin made up his mind to run away. Quietly and carefully he planned his escape. To raise a little travelling money he sold all the books he could bring himself to part with. Although Boston was the largest "city" in the colonies, it was a small town of only about 12,000 people; hardly the sort of place where a fugitive could melt into the crowd. It would be necessary to leave Boston. With the help of a friend, Benjamin arranged passage on a ship to New York. He boarded the ship under cover of darkness.

Franklin got off the ship in New York City on October 5 of 1723. With a population of only 7,000 souls, New York was the third largest city in the colonies, behind Boston and Philadelphia. There was only one print shop in New York, and it was not hiring, so he resolved to move on to Philadelphia. He spent the next several days making his way to the City of Brotherly Love on foot and in small boats. He arrived on a Sunday morning; tired, bedraggled, and not looking at all like a man who had success in his future:

> I was dirty from the journey; my pockets were stuff'd out with shirts and stockings, and I knew no soul nor where to look for lodging. I was fatigued with traveling, rowing, and want of rest, I was very hungry; and my whole stock of cash consisted of a Dutch dollar, and about a shilling in copper.[31]

He found a bakery and bought some cheap bread, which he ate on his feet as he continued to explore the city. As he walked around he happened to pass the home of a teenage girl named Deborah Read who "thought I made, as I certainly did, a most awkward, ridiculous appearance."[32] First impressions may be lasting, but they are not irreversible. Miss Read would eventually become Mrs. Benjamin Franklin.

Exhausted from his days and nights on the road, he asked around until he found an inn he could afford. In the morning he did what he could to make himself look presentable and went to the city's two print shops to apply for a job. The proprietor of the city's one well-established print shop was one Andrew Bradford, whose father operated the New York shop Franklin had visited several days earlier. Bradford had very little work for him at that time, but offered to rent him a room. A man named Samuel Keimer was in the process of opening Philadelphia's second printing business, and he had a crying need for someone with Franklin's skills.

Franklin soon proved to be indispensable to Keimer. During his five years in James' shop, and despite the personal friction between the two brothers, Benjamin had adhered to his biblical principle of being "diligent in his calling." He'd worked very hard and always applied his keen and curious mind to every detail of the printing business, and by the time he ran away to Philadelphia he was an old pro. With the youngster's help Keimer was able to start putting out work of decent quality despite the poor condition of his press and other equipment.

Once Franklin started working for Keimer on a steady basis, Keimer insisted that he move out of Bradford's house and find a new place to live. Keimer had no accommodations to offer, but arranged for his new employee to lodge with an acquaintance named John Read, whose teenage daughter Deborah had been so amused at Franklin's appearance on his first day in town. With gainful employment and a place to live, Benjamin "lived very agreeably" in his new home town. He spent his spare time reading, studying, and socializing with literate young people like himself.

When Franklin had been enjoying his new life for several months one of his brothers-in-law, a man named Robert Holmes, who lived in Delaware, heard something of Franklin's activities in Philadelphia and exchanged letters with him. Holmes happened to be an acquaintance of William Keith, the territorial governor, and he showed the governor his young brother-in-law's letter.

Governor Keith was impressed, both with Benjamin's story of self-made success and with his skills as a writer. Soon after that he stopped in at Keimer's shop for a visit. Over a glass of Madeira the governor told the Benjamin that he considered both Bradford and Keimer less than competent, that the colony needed someone better to handle its printing needs, and that he believed the teenage runaway was just the man for the job. After an abortive effort to persuade Josiah to help fund Benjamin's shop (Josiah judged that the governor must be a man "of small discretion" if he would try to set up a boy of 18 in business), the governor promised to fund the venture himself, by providing Benjamin with letters of credit that Benjamin would use in London to acquire all the capital goods he'd need to set up shop.

In November of 1724 18-year-old Benjamin spent a considerable part of his savings on a ticket for London. He quit his job at Keimer's shop and packed his meager possessions in a chest. When the ship landed in London on the day before Christmas, 1724, Benjamin learned a hard lesson about believing the promises that politicians make. There were no letters of credit from the governor.

Bewildered, he approached a man who had befriended him during the voyage and asked for advice. His new friend, a Quaker merchant named Thomas Denham, knew the governor well. He told Benjamin that Governor Keith was in the habit of making himself popular (at least temporarily) by making promises he couldn't or wouldn't keep. As for Keith giving anyone letters of credit, Denham told Benjamin that Keith could not have plausibly written any, "having, as he said, no credit to give." Because of Governor Keith's dishonesty, the young would-be entrepreneur had quit his job and spent a month at sea. He now found himself unemployed, financially and personally embarrassed, and nearly friendless in a strange town.

Franklin didn't waste any time hating the governor or feeling sorry for himself. Self-pity is the quickest road to Hell, and people who are determined to succeed know that problems are to be overcome, not wallowed in. Franklin focused on coming up with a plan for making the best of his disagreeable circumstances. As a first step, he asked his older and wiser friend for advice. Denham gave him some good counsel.

Denham, who would play a significant role in Franklin's life, had a rags-to-riches story of his own. Years earlier he'd been a businessman in London whose business failed, leaving him with debts he couldn't pay to several different creditors. He'd avoided debtors' prison by negotiating with his creditors, who accepted less than full payment and allowed him to leave the country. In Pennsylvania he had started over with nothing and managed to build a business and a substantial fortune. When he travelled to London with Benjamin in 1724 he carried with him enough money to pay off the unpaid balances he felt he still owed to his creditors. He invited them to a dinner, expressed his appreciation, and presented each of them with a bank draft for the unpaid sum with interest.[33]

Denham suggested that Benjamin try to get a job with one of the large printing companies in the city, where he could learn skills and methods he hadn't seen in his brother's small shop in Boston. Franklin agreed that this was his best course of action, and spent the next 18 months working at two large printing houses in the city. He earned a journeyman's wages but bad company and bad habits prevented him from accumulating enough money to pay for his passage back to Philadelphia. A friend named James Ralph had come across on this ship with him, and lived with him during that first year. Ralph was unemployed for most of the year, so he "borrowed" regularly from Franklin for his subsistence, and often persuaded his meal ticket to buy tickets for both of them to plays and other expensive entertainments. After a year of this, the two of them had a falling out over a woman, and Ralph unilaterally declared that Franklin's bad behavior in the matter cancelled the financial debt. By this time Benjamin had come to regard Ralph's friendship as a burden, so he was satisfied to write off the money and the friendship.

At work he soon distinguished himself by his skill and speed. His employer began giving him all the rush jobs to do, and increased his pay. Liberated from James Ralph's influence, he began to live more thriftily and save up some money. He also supplemented his income by lending drinking money to some of his beer-loving coworkers, who would have to pay him back with interest on payday.

During his spare time he read and studied, and supplemented the physical exercise he got at the print shop by swimming in the Thames.

As in Boston and Philadelphia, he struck up friendships with people who could lend him books.

In the summer of 1726 Thomas Denham, who like Franklin had been in England for a year and a half, was making preparations to return to Philadelphia. He persuaded Franklin to make the return trip with him, promising him a job in the general store he planned to open. Their ship sailed in July and arrived in Philadelphia in mid-October. Franklin, always hungry for learning, spent the six-week voyage filling up his journal with scientific observations about the seaweeds and marine creatures he encountered, and notes on the social and psychological effects of the voyage on his fellow passengers.[34]

Denham opened his general store in Philadelphia in the autumn of 1726. This was Franklin's first chance to get some mercantile experience, and he took advantage of the opportunity to develop some new skills. In his autobiography he gives himself credit for having become "expert in selling" during the few months he worked in Denham's store. Unfortunately he and Denham came down with unrelated serious illnesses in February of 1727. Franklin was ill for a long time but recovered; Denham died. Franklin was once again unemployed.

Samuel Keimer's printing business had expanded in Franklin's absence, but none of Keimer's five new workers had the skills Franklin had, so Keimer offered him good wages to come back and manage the printing operations for him while Keimer opened a stationary store. Franklin was not particularly fond of Keimer, and would have accepted lower wages to work as a clerk in any general store in the area, but no other job was available and he accepted Keimer's offer.

He soon came to understand that Keimer intended to pay him at such a lavish rate only temporarily, for a year or two, until Franklin had put the print shop in good working order and taught the essential skills of running a print shop to the other five workers. Nevertheless Franklin applied himself to the job wholeheartedly, consistent with that biblical principle of being "diligent in his calling." He treated the inexperienced workers with respect and soon earned theirs. He worked to teach them everything he knew without reservation.

In addition to the skills and practices he taught the other employees, Franklin made his own direct contributions to Keimer's business. Typeface had to be imported from England in this era, and Franklin devised a method for molding typeface in the shop; the first typeface founding operation in the New World.[35] Producing typeface in-house gave Keimer an advantage over every other print shop owner in the New World. This was the first of many useful things Franklin would invent during his long career.

In 21st century corporate America, where silly jargon is far too common, and taken far too seriously, there is one bit of corporate-speak that is actually meaningful. Nobody really knows what it means to "leverage a platform to maximize impactfulness," but it was a wise person who first called a company's personnel department the Human Resources Department. Human beings really are important resources, the most important resources any company has, and some human resources are more valuable than others. The wages and benefits a company is willing to pay a worker are directly related to how valuable a resource that worker is, although the correlation is not a perfect one.

Franklin's relationship with Keimer is illustrative. When Franklin came back to Pennsylvania in 1726, Keimer's business was in disarray and in debt. Keimer had used borrowed money to expand his operations, and the low wages he offered only allowed him to hire inexperienced and unskilled workers. When Franklin came back onto the job early in 1727 Keimer needed him, and offered him pay commensurate with his value to the operation, although the expense taxed Keimer's resources severely. As the other five employees increased their skills under Franklin's tutelage, Franklin's relative value gradually declined. After six months Keimer began to pressure Franklin to accept a pay cut, something Franklin emphatically (and wisely) refused to do. As time went on and Franklin continued imparting valuable skills to his young co-workers, Keimer became more and more resentful of the wages he had agreed to pay his foreman. After a few more months Keimer was rude to Franklin in front of the other workers and Franklin promptly resigned.

One of Keimer's other employees was a personable but irresponsible 30-year-old named Hugh Meredith. The day Franklin resigned, Meredith came to his home when the office closed and proposed a partnership. Meredith believed he could persuade his father to front the money they'd need to open a print shop of their own, Franklin would provide the expertise, and the two of them would be equal partners. Franklin quickly agreed to the deal, and they ordered the equipment they would need for the shop.

While Franklin and Meredith were waiting for their equipment to arrive, Keimer found that losing his most important human resource had left him between the horns of a dilemma. He'd managed to secure a contract to print some paper money for the New Jersey colony, but the job was complicated and he knew he couldn't complete the work without Franklin. Worse, Andrew Bradford was still operating a competing print shop in Philadelphia and Keimer (who had no idea that Franklin and Meredith were about to go into business for themselves) was afraid that Bradford would hire Franklin and take the money-printing job away from him. His need for Franklin's skills outweighed his ego; he swallowed his pride and asked Franklin to forget their recent disagreement and come back to work. For the right salary, Franklin accepted the offer.[36]

The money-printing contract gave Franklin the opportunity to form relationships with several important figures in the New Jersey government, relationships that would come in handy later, when he was running his own business. By the time the New Jersey project was done, early in 1728, Franklin's equipment from London had arrived. Franklin and Meredith collected their pay and told Keimer that they were leaving him. They let him find out for himself that they were going into business in competition with him. Within a couple years Keimer would be out of business.[37]

Franklin attracted business away from his two rivals the way successful competitors always do; he worked harder and did better work. He worked long hours and went out of his way to make sure that people in the community knew about it, believing that a reputation for industriousness would be something he could trade on. He also continued to widen his circle of friends.

Around this time he first organized what he called a "Junta," a group of poor but enterprising young men like himself who wanted to improve their minds. The group met on Friday evenings. Franklin wrote up a set of rules for their discussions; each man was required to take his turn providing a thesis for an evening's discussion "on any topic of Morals, Politics, or Natural Philosophy (science)." A moderator controlled the debates to keep them civil and constructive.

Remarkably, the group continued to meet regularly for 30 years. During Franklin's long absences in Europe he continued corresponding with the other Junta members by letter. When the group was formed all the members were poor working class tradesmen; over the years many of them became financially successful and took on prominent roles in Philadelphia society.[38]

The remarkable success of so many Junta members, all of whom were as poor and obscure as Franklin when the group was formed, clearly cannot be the result of some sort of in-born genetic superiority that all of them had. It would be a very great coincidence if all the poor tradesmen who joined the Junta were blessed by birth with some sort of special genius that allowed them to be so successful in life. What the success of these men shows is that any ordinary American who makes an effort to develop his own mental powers will reap rewards.

Many of the discussion questions Franklin presented to the group give insight into his interests and agenda. Some of them show us pretty clearly what his career philosophy was. For example: "Does it not, in a general way, require great study and intense application for a poor man to become rich and powerful, if he would do it without the forfeiture of honesty?"[39] Franklin clearly believed that the answer to that question was "yes."

From early childhood through old age, Franklin was constantly trying to increase his knowledge and improve his skills. In this he has much in common with most of the other upwardly mobile Americans profiled in this book. Andrew Carnegie, to cite just one example, was as avid a reader as Franklin in his youth and pulled together a mutual improvement group patterned after Franklin's Junta, although Carnegie's club didn't last several decades the way Franklin's did.

Franklin also developed a flair for publicity and showmanship that pre-shadowed P.T. Barnum's career in amusing ways. Bradford printed a newspaper in his shop, much as James Franklin had during Benjamin's apprentice days, and when Franklin planned to start publishing a newspaper, Keimer got wind of his plan and rushed into production with a newspaper of his own. Franklin put his own newspaper plans on hold until he could put Keimer's paper, and Keimer's shop, out of business. He resolved to undermine Keimer's dull and badly-written newspaper as a way of reducing Keimer's revenue stream and exacerbating his debt problems. In a Machiavellian move that Barnum would have loved, Franklin resolved to prop up Bradford's equally pedestrian newspaper by contributing some content that people would actually want to read.

Using a variety of pen names, Franklin began contributing essays to Bradford's paper. In one of the early essays Franklin, under the pen name "Busy-Body" announced that Bradford's paper had been "frequently very dull" up to this time, and announced his intention to make it more interesting. If Bradford knew who was providing the columns it didn't prevent him from printing them; he knew good writing when he saw it and he loved the circulation increases that

Franklin's pieces were bringing him.[40] In many of the essays Franklin poked fun at Keimer and his writing. Keimer tried to respond to Franklin's witty barbs in kind, but he hadn't spent years honing his skills as a writer, and he was no match for a rival who had. Sales of Bradford's paper soared while Keimer's paper went nowhere.

In October of 1729 Keimer sold his newspaper to Franklin for next to nothing, and moved to Barbados. By his conspicuous hard work and his ever-growing business sense, Franklin was able pick up most of the business Keimer had been getting, putting himself on a roughly equal basis with Bradford. From now on anything interesting he wrote, under his own name or a pseudonym, would be printed in his own paper, which he re-named the Pennsylvania Gazette.

Shortly after Franklin was able to buy out Keimer, he found a way to escape his partnership with Meredith. Meredith was a heavy drinker who did very little useful work, leaving virtually everything up to Franklin and a raw apprentice or two. To make matters worse, Meredith's father failed to provide some of the start-up funding he'd promised. Franklin struggled to make payments on the equipment he'd bought on credit while fighting for market share with Bradford and Keimer in a city that was arguably too small for even two printers. Two of Franklin's other friends came to the rescue, lending him the money to buy out Meredith's interest, which he did near the end of 1729. Through constant hard work and thrifty living he soon repaid his friends, after which he owned the business unencumbered.

Circulation of his newspaper soared, bringing him welcome revenue and publicity. To attract more printing business, Franklin targeted the government contracts that Bradford had been getting, and soon made some inroads there; getting contracts to print meeting minutes and some of the colony's money. To supplement the printing and newspaper revenues, he opened a stationary store that soon grew into a general store carrying all sorts of products. When Deborah Read, whose husband had abandoned her, became Franklin's common-law wife in September of 1730, she quickly proved to be a helpmate in every sense of the word. In addition to keeping house, she minded the store while he worked in his print shop.

Almanacs were an important source of revenue for printers in that era, and in 1732 the ambitious 26-year-old Franklin decided to start editing and printing an almanac of his own. *Poor Richard's Almanack* went into print before the end of the year. Filled with Franklin's clever insights and homespun wit, it soon became the biggest selling almanac in the colonies. Many of the maxims we associate with Franklin (e.g. "Early to bed and early to rise makes a man healthy, wealthy, and wise") were first printed in *Poor Richard's*.

Bradford's print shop went out of business just a few years after Keimer's, leaving Franklin with the only newspaper and the only printing house in town. Between his newspaper, his almanac, his print shop, and his retail store Franklin was well on his way to prosperity by the time he was in his late twenties. He'd learned to put a high value on thrift while struggling to build a business and pay off his debts, but as his success grew he and Deborah began to be able to afford luxuries that neither of them had experienced in their youth. Silver replaced pewter and fine china replaced cheap earthenware. Franklin also developed a taste for rich foods and fine wine, which would eventually cost him the athletic shape of his youth and produce the chubby balding figure we see today in portraits of him.

Prosperity did not lessen his desire for learning. At the age of 27 he added foreign languages to the list of subjects he studied. Over the next few years he taught himself to read and write French, Italian, Spanish, and Latin; in that order. He also grew ever more interested in what was then called "Natural Philosophy," i.e. science.

By his thirtieth birthday Franklin was becoming quite influential in the city. As he continued to hone his people skills and demonstrate his enthusiasm and wisdom, he began to be able to rally his fellow Philadelphians to important causes. He led the movements that created the city's first lending library, its first fire department, and its first university. He also helped reform the city's "night watch" of frequently drunk and poorly supervised men into a true police department.

Eventually his influence in the city was so great that his support became indispensable, even for good causes that should have been able to attract public support without his help. When a public-spirited doctor tried to solicit donations for the construction of the city's first hospital, he had very little success. He came to Franklin and informed him that "I am often ask'd by those to whom I propose subscribing 'Have you consulted Franklin upon this business? And what does he think of it?'" After making a few inquiries, Franklin very publicly made a contribution to the hospital fund, and urged his friends and readers to do likewise. Donations started rolling in and the hospital was soon built.[41]

In 1733, upon hearing that the City of Charleston had no print shop, Franklin formed a partnership with one of his more promising apprentices. Franklin funded the start-up of a print shop in Charleston, which his protégé would operate, with one third of the profits going to Franklin. Over the ensuing years Franklin initiated many more of these partnerships, most of which turned out to be quite profitable for him. In 1748 Franklin, at the age of 42, was able to turn his Philadelphia business interests over to one of his partners and effectively retire. For the remaining half of his 84 year life he was able to focus his energies on study, scientific experiments, invention, philanthropy, and public service.

With the exception of *Poor Richard's Almanack* and the Franklin Stove, all the things for which Franklin is famous happened after he'd gotten rich enough to retire from active business. It was in retirement that he conducted his famous experiments with electricity, which proved that lightning was an electrical phenomenon and led to his invention of the lightning rod. He was chosen by the colony of Pennsylvania, and later by all the colonies collectively, to represent their interests before the English government. Later he represented Pennsylvania in the Continental Congress and helped Thomas Jefferson write the Declaration of Independence. After that he traveled to France and persuaded King Louis to provide crucial assistance to America in her war of independence, then came home and played an instrumental role in the Constitutional Convention.

The methods and habits Franklin used to progress from penniless runaway to honored statesman have been emulated by any number of poor youngsters throughout American history. America is, as Franklin once said, "a place where it is asked of stranger not 'what is he?' but 'what can he do?'"[42] For two centuries young Americans have been proving the truth of that statement by following Franklin's example.

CHAPTER 3

John Jacob Astor

———

In Europe we are wont to look upon a restless disposition,
an unbounded desire of riches, and an excessive love of
independence, as propensities very formidable to society.
Yet these are the very elements which ensure a long
and peaceful duration to the republics of America.

ALEXIS DE TOCQUEVILLE

JOHN JACOB ASTOR WAS THE first poor American to leave his family an enormous fortune when he died. He wouldn't be the last.

By the end of the nineteenth century Caroline Astor, the wife of one of John Jacob's grandsons, was the reigning diva of East Coast high society. The elite of New York social circles were known as "The 400" because that's how many people she invited to the annual ball she hosted in her Rhode Island summer house.[43] The coveted invitations were sent only to snobbish "old money" families like hers; self-made millionaires like Diamond Jim Brady waited in vain for an invitation.

In the early twentieth century Caroline's nephew, William Waldorf Astor, set his heart on becoming a titled English Lord. He moved to Britain and effectively bought a title by donating vast amounts of money to charities favored by King George V. The king made him "Baron Astor" in 1916 and upgraded his status to "Viscount Astor" in 1917, a title his great-grandson holds today.

The Astor family fortune was founded by a man who left Germany at the age of 16 with nothing but a bag of clothes on his shoulder and a few small coins in his pocket.

THE YANKEE PEDDLER TRADITION

The United States had just won its independence from England when Astor arrived on American shores, but the tradition of poor itinerant peddlers earning their fortunes in the American colonies goes back to the mid-1600s.

Boston was the primary seaport of the northern colonies in the seventeenth century, and when ships from England docked there, merchants large and small purchased manufactured products which they would then sell or trade to white colonists and Indians. Products like metal cooking pots, sewing needles, metal tools and weapons, and woven cloth were in such demand in the colonies that even ordinary sailors would often buy a few odds and ends before leaving England, and sell them profitably on the docks of Boston. Many young Bostonians got their start in business by working for wages until they had a few shillings, buying manufactured trade goods on the docks, and then travelling the rivers and trails in search of customers for their goods.

Those who were industrious and thrifty could increase their inventory of trade goods with each trip. Many made the progression from traveling on foot with a backpack full of goods, to paddling a canoe full of products up and down some frontier stream, to driving a peddler's wagon or poling a whole raft of products up a river to the settlements along the shores. The next stage, which many traveling peddlers eventually reached, was opening a store in a town and doing business indoors.[44]

What businesses in England wanted from the colonies was raw materials: agricultural products, timber, salted fish, and the furs of various animals. Gold and silver had not yet been discovered in North America, and furs were the most valuable product the English colonies had to offer throughout the seventeenth and eighteenth centuries. When Indians or frontier settlers traded with itinerant peddlers, the wilderness product that gave them the most bargaining power was furs. When the wandering merchant returned to the Boston docks to trade for manufactured goods, a bundle of furs was more valuable than anything else he might bring in.

By the time the United States achieved independence the fur trade was big business, but it was still open to small independent operators; even to a poor German immigrant fresh off the boat from London. Astor got his start in America as one of these travelling fur traders.

Astor's Birth and Childhood

John Jacob Astor was born Johann Jakob Astor in Walldorf, Germany in 1763. His father Jakob, the town butcher, was reputedly a descendent of French Protestants who had fled religious persecution in France in the late 1600s. His mother, of whom little is known, died when he was only three years old.

Most of Walldorf's residents couldn't afford meat in their diet on a regular basis, so Jakob's business was somewhat seasonal. He would have plenty of work in the fall when the farmers around the town butchered a steer or hog for winter consumption, and around major holidays and festivals, but for much of each year he was idle. Jakob was an improvident man who during the good times tended to save little and spend much, primarily on beer, so his children frequently went hungry when he wasn't working.[45] Kind-hearted neighbors sometimes gave Johann food when his mother was unable to feed him.[46]

Johann had little in common with his irresponsible father. Like Benjamin Franklin before him, he was an avid reader from early childhood. He was disciplined, curious, and ambitious. Johann was encouraged in his reading and studying by the village schoolteacher and the pastor of his family's church. He read all the books and newspapers he could get his hands on, and with his teacher's encouragement he learned everything he could about the world outside of Walldorf.[47]

He had two older brothers, both of whom had left Germany by the time Johann was a teenager. One lived in London and started a company that manufactured musical instruments, the other made his living as a butcher in New York City. Henry Astor, the New York brother, stimulated Johann's imagination with his letters home, in which he described the colonies as a land of opportunity where a hard-working boy could achieve far more than was possible in Germany.

When Johann was 13 years old his father pulled him out of school and put him to work in the butcher shop. Although his formal schooling was over, he continued to be inquisitive, open-minded, and an avid reader. His old schoolteacher continued to give him advice and moral support, as did his pastor. He continued to dream of making his fortune in the colonies, which by that time were calling themselves the United States of America and fighting desperately to achieve independence from England. Acting on advice from his two mentors, he resolved to make his way to London to live with his brother George for a time and learn to speak English, then move to America as soon as the Revolutionary War, and its wartime travel restrictions, came to an end.

In 1779, at the age of 16, Johann left home with his few possessions in a bag on his shoulder. He hiked to the banks of the Rhine River, where he managed to get a temporary job for a timber company that was floating a log raft downstream to the North Sea. He'd left home without enough money for boat fare,[48] but he earned enough during his 14 days on the log raft to pay for a ticket to London, where his older brother George immediately gave him a job and a place to stay.

In London he changed his name from Johann Jakob to the more English-sounding John Jacob. He focused all his energies on working, saving money, and learning to speak English. In September of 1783 Benjamin Franklin and two other American diplomats signed the treaty that ended the Revolutionary War. Astor immediately made plans to immigrate to the new nation.

Like Franklin, Astor started his career believing that hard work and thrift were the keys to success. Determined to succeed, he worked very hard and saved his pennies. In his four and a half years in the musical instrument shop he managed to save up enough money to buy one nice suit of clothes, seven flutes from the shop, and a steerage class ticket to Baltimore, with around five English pounds left over.[49] He left England on the ship *North Carolina* in late November or early December of 1783, just a couple months after the peace treaty was signed.

On the ship with Astor were several men who were active in the fur trade, most of whom were wealthy men with first class berths. Whenever any of these men would venture into parts of the ship where steerage class passengers were allowed, Astor would discreetly position himself close to them to listen in on their conversations. Very soon he made up his mind that the fur business would be his road to riches.

An even better source of information on America's most lucrative business was a young German-born fur trader who was traveling in steerage with him. The trader was a wealth of information about every aspect of the business and Astor, who at that early stage in his career had already developed a knack for making people like him, spent hours in conversation with his new friend. His curiosity about the fur business knew no bounds, and he remembered everything he heard.

The trip to Baltimore took nearly four months and ended with the *North Carolina* getting stuck in the ice in Chesapeake Bay miles away from the city. All the other passengers on the ship passively waited for help to come, or for the ice to break up,[50] but Astor took matters into his own hands. He crawled out of the ship and hiked across the ice to land. Fortunately for him he had so few possessions that he could carry all his baggage with him, flutes included, in one trip.[51] From Baltimore he quickly made his way to New York, to the home of his brother Henry.

Henry had just gotten married, and the house where he and his new bride were living was small, so he was reluctant to take his brother in as a long term boarder. John soon found a job with a German baker named Dieterich for room and board plus a small stipend. The job involved roaming the streets of the city selling bread and cakes. It gave young Astor a chance to sharpen his people skills, learn the geography and culture of the city, and find buyers for all but one of his flutes. He'd learned to play the flute in England, and he kept one of the instruments for his own amusement.

New York had only about 20,000 residents at that time, so learning to navigate her streets didn't take long. By the time Astor died, in 1848, the city would have a population of half a million people and Astor would own so much of it that people called him "The Landlord of New York." In 1784 he was still peddling loaves of bread in the streets and saving his pennies.

After a short tenure at the bakery Astor was able to find a fur trader who was willing to give him a job. Robert Bowne, a Quaker trader with an established shop in the city, agreed to give him room and board plus two dollars a week. Initially Astor spent much of each working day beating furs with a stick to keep moths from infesting them. Astor embraced the work enthusiastically, determined to be the best pelt-beater Bowne had ever seen. Thrilled to be working in a shop where he could learn more about the fur business, he focused on making himself as valuable a human resource as possible. His attitude and work habits impressed Bowne, who soon gave him more demanding duties and a raise in pay.[52]

While working for Bowne, and with Bowne's knowledge and approval, Astor spent virtually every penny of his wages buying furs. The revenue he got from selling his flutes similarly went for furs. In the autumn of 1784, after just a few months in New York, Astor had acquired enough pelts to make it worth his while to travel to London to dispose of them in person. He knew that in London fur prices were higher, and the prices of manufactured goods lower, than in the colonies; the larger profits he made on his trades justified the time he spent traveling. While he was in the city he also negotiated contracts with two musical instrument companies, one of them his brother's, to be their representative in New York.

As soon as he got back to New York Bowne re-hired him, once again with the mutual understanding that Astor would give Bowne his complete loyalty and do excellent work for him, while spending his spare time and his personal monies developing his own businesses. Bowne also provided his protégé with a place to store his furs and access to the company strongbox, in which Astor kept his stash of cash side by side with Bowne's. Astor was such a valuable employee that sometime in 1785 Bowne presented him in with an inscribed silver watch.[53]

In the spring of 1785 Bowne sent Astor up the Hudson River into Iroquois Indian territory to trade directly with the Indians on their own ground. It was a tough and dangerous assignment; traders who ventured into Indian country alone didn't always come back alive. On this first wilderness trip Astor didn't bring any of his own trade goods; he went purely as Bowne's agent. Bowne was paying the transportation and living expenses, and for obvious reasons he didn't want to pay for an extra horse or mule to carry Astor's personal goods. Astor's first trip was a great success, and Bowne sent him on a second such trip before the two of them amicably parted company and Astor went into business for himself on a full time basis.

For the next few years Astor made regular trips into Indian territory. Any number of other small scale traders were doing the same thing, but Astor prospered faster than anyone else. The things that set Astor apart from other itinerant fur traders of the late 1780s, aside from his education and intelligence, were his personal discipline and drive and his constant focus on the long term. While he didn't enjoy living in the wilderness for long periods, he proved to be just as physically strong and tough as any other backwoodsman. He faced the same dangers and hardships the other traders faced with the same calm demeanor. But in other ways he was unusual.

The typical wilderness trader of that era was a crude man who accepted sexual favors from Indian women as readily as furs in exchange for his trade goods. It was not uncommon for a mountain man who had accumulated a little money to go on a long drinking binge and find himself broke when he finally sobered up. Personal discipline and delayed gratification were not popular concepts in the fur trading business.

Astor had no interest in liaisons with Indian women, even before he was married at the age of 22, and once he and his wife Sarah were married he remained devoted to her for the rest of his life. Nor was he ever interesting in dulling his faculties with over-priced frontier whiskey. Other than the money he and Sarah spent on the bare necessities of life in those early days, he saved every penny he earned for trade goods, which he used to barter for ever-increasing quantities of furs. In modern parlance he "plowed the profits back into the business." Astor was also different from other frontier traders in his insatiable desire for knowledge. In every crossroads tavern and Indian village he would talk much, listen more, and remember everything he heard. Throughout the trading areas he was known for his inquisitiveness.[54]

Sarah was a good helpmate to Astor. She kept house on a very tight budget in the early years of their marriage, and during his frequent business trips she profitably managed the music store they'd opened shortly after their wedding. John and Sarah had eight children together, five of whom survived to adulthood. As their family and their wealth increased, Sarah focused more and more of her time on managing their household and raising her children. Employees handled the day-to-day affairs of the music store, which grew to be one of the largest music distributors in New York before Astor sold the company in 1803 to focus on his other business interests.

Astor's capacity for near-constant hard work allowed him to postpone the day when he had to start delegating duties to employees, but the business grew so fast that becoming an employer soon became unavoidable. He made his last trip into the wilderness during the winter of 1788-89; after that he procured all his pelts via employees and from independent agents. Eventually he would have teams of people trading for furs all across North America.

In the summer of 1789 Astor, who by now was earning money hand over fist from his dealings in the fur business, made his first commercial real estate purchase. As his income from the fur trade continued to increase, he continued to make wise and careful choices in the purchase of real estate. Predicting the continued growth of New York City, Astor spent years buying land on the outskirts of the city, wherever the outskirts might be at any point in time; then watching the city borders move outward to encompass his properties. As the city kept expanding he used the ever-increasing rental revenues from the properties he owned to buy new properties on the new outskirts.

By 1800, the year Astor celebrated his thirty-seventh birthday, his net worth was somewhere over a quarter of a million dollars,[55] making him one of the wealthiest men in the city.[56] He had an army of fur traders sending him pelts from Canada and the northern United States all the way from the Atlantic coast to the Eastern slopes of the Rocky Mountains. He began to look enviously at the profits that ship owners were making transporting his products to Europe and China.

Early in that year he formed a partnership with several other wealthy investors for the purpose of buying an ocean-going ship called the *Severn*. In April it sailed for China with a cargo of furs and other products. In 1804 Astor bought out his partners and became sole proprietor of the *Severn*. By the end of 1806 he owned three ships, which he kept in constant motion transporting his trade goods between Europe, China, and the U.S.

Astor and his family lived well, but they didn't flaunt their wealth. His wife had no ambitions to be the social director of the entire eastern seaboard, as her grandson's wife would be less than a hundred years later. They lived in a nice house, but didn't build the kind of palace they could have afforded. Meanwhile Astor used his ever-growing profits from the fur trade to buy and build more ships, and buy and hold more real estate. His real estate deals numbered in the hundreds. Soon he was sending ships all around the world to transport every kind of product; many of them didn't even carry furs as part of their regular cargo.[57]

In the early 1820s the Astor family picked up its first European title. During a trip to Paris Astor's youngest daughter Eliza met and married a Swiss Count, becoming Countess Eliza Rumpff. Her grandson, who inherited the title Count Rumpff from her son upon his death, may have inspired some envy in the heart of his second cousin William Waldorf Astor, who went to such extremes to procure a title of his own in the early twentieth century.

Astor never tired of hard work. He continued to actively manage his business affairs until ill health forced him to retire at the age of 70. John Jacob's retirement was the end of Astor family involvement in the fur trade. The population of fur-bearing animals in North America was being depleted by all the trapping that had been going on, and silk was displacing fur in European and American fashion. By the time of Astor's retirement the rents his New York properties were yielding were enormous, and they would only grow as the city's population grew. When Astor died in 1848 he was the wealthiest man in the United States, and one of the richest people in the world.

By that time up-from-poverty stories like his were commonplace in the U.S., but Astor's career, which started the same year the colonies won their independence from England, could be considered the first truly American rags-to-riches success story.

CHAPTER 4

Eli Whitney

———

It's hard to beat a person who never gives up.

BABE RUTH

AT THE DAWN OF THE Iron Age, around 1,200 BC, living conditions for the human race were grim. Most children died before reaching adulthood, often of hunger-related illnesses. Cloth garments were so rare and expensive that most people only owned one suit of clothes. The only modes of transportation were sail-powered boats and ships, saddle horses, and wheeled carts pulled by horses or other beasts of burden. The rich and powerful could afford to light their homes with oil lamps at night, but the great majority of people went to bed in the dark.

Amazingly, things hadn't changed much when English entrepreneurs and inventors launched the Industrial Revolution nearly three thousand years later. Sailing ships and horse-drawn carts were still the best vehicles for transporting goods. Cloth and clothing were still rare and expensive. Oil lamps were still being used by those wealthy enough to afford them, but most people still went to bed in the dark. As many as half of all children died before the age of ten, and hunger-related diseases were a primary cause of death.[58] Around the world adults and children worked from dawn to dusk to produce enough food, or to earn the money to buy enough food, to avoid starving to death. Wrought iron was still used for tools and weapons; steel still was, as it had been for all those centuries, a specialty product made only with great difficulty and in small quantities.

In the eighteenth century most people could still only afford one suit of clothes, and lived in them night and day. Bathing or washing would force people to expend precious resources making or buying soap, and gathering or buying fuel for use in heating water; more resources than most people could afford to spare on a regular basis. Open fires were the only way to heat people's homes in winter, and fuel was not very affordable for anyone but the rich, so people shivered in the dark, sleeping in their filthy clothes in their small homes, whenever the weather was cold.

In nearly 30 centuries the human race did very little to improve its living conditions. Other than gunpowder and the printing press there was very little world-changing technology introduced over that long span. Then American entrepreneurs came on the scene, and in the blink of an eye the pace of human progress accelerated wildly, far beyond anything the world had ever seen.

The revolution actually started in Britain. Technology and prosperity grew faster in eighteenth century England than any other nation because English law enforced contracts impartially, and because England did less than any other nation to impair the creation of small businesses, or interfere with the rights of small property holders. England's political system allowed ambitious commoners some freedom of action; while in other European nations "an hereditary aristocracy hindered or stifled the spirit of enterprise, thereby holding back national economic development."[59] In the 1700s, inventors in Great Britain developed the steam engine and harnessed it to drive textile mills that made clothing and blankets more affordable to the masses. In 1829 English engineer George Stephenson deployed the world's first commercially viable railroad train.

But American entrepreneurs and inventors would soon put their British brethren to shame. As soon as the United States became an independent nation American inventors, driven by ambition and allowed to pursue their dreams with minimal government interference, began to make the world a vastly better place. In a little over 200 years Americans would give the world the telegraph; the telephone; the steamship; viable automobiles; machine tools; the assembly line; the modern corporation; photographic film; flush toilets; skyscrapers; the electric light; polyphase electric generation, distribution, and motors; television; the recording and motion picture industries; powered flight; the computer; and any number of other game-changing inventions, along with most of the improvements in these technologies over time. Nothing comparable has ever happened anywhere else in the world.

Most of the Americans who created these miracles were self-made men who started out in life with nothing but ambition and good ideas. Eli Whitney was typical of these. Whitney is best known as the inventor of the "cotton gin;" a relatively simple device that made large scale cotton production possible for the first time in history. But his contributions to the science of mass production were even more significant. The cotton gin played a huge role in America's economic development, and dramatically raised worldwide standards of living by making clothing and other necessities more affordable for the masses, but the impact of Whitney's role in promoting the concept, and developing the science, of mass production through the use of interchangeable parts has been even greater.

Whitney invented and marketed his products because he believed he could make a lot of money by doing so, and he was right. After some initial struggles his mass production technologies were a great financial success; during the later years of his life he was a wealthy man. The large and long-lasting benefits that his work yielded for the rest of the human race were a happy side effect.

Eli Whitney was born and raised on a small farm near Westborough, Massachusetts. He was born on December 8 of 1765, the first of four children. His mother died when he was 11 years old. According to the memoirs written by Eli's sister Elizabeth after her brother had become rich and famous, Eli took on the responsibility of helping his father care for his three younger siblings from the time his mother became ill. Like all self-made men, he was an independent thinker. "He was remarkable," his sister said, "for thinking and acting for himself at the age of 10 or 12 years."[60]

Eli worked hard on the farm, as all farm children of that era did,[61] but his parents did allow him to go to school. He loved learning and applied himself to all his studies, distinguishing himself in mathematics in particular.[62] He also loved tinkering with the tools in his father's workshop. "As soon as he could handle tools," according to Elizabeth, "he was always making something in the shop."[63] At first his father showed little appreciation for Eli's various projects. The elder Whitney seems to have assumed that Eli was destined to be a farmer, and viewed the boy's eternal tinkering as a distraction from more important things. Eventually his attitude would change.

When Eli was 14 years old and Elizabeth was about 12, their father re-married. According to Elizabeth's account their stepmother was always cold toward the Whitney children, reserving her maternal affections for her own children by a previous marriage. Their stepmother's aloofness may have bothered Elizabeth more than it bothered Eli; by this time he was a very independent boy who didn't need much maternal nurturing.

Right around the time his father remarried Eli came up with an idea that allowed him to use his mechanical skills to earn the Whitney family some much-needed money. The Revolutionary War had been going on for several years at this point and manufactured products from Europe were extremely scarce. One of the products in short supply was nails. Using a forge that he'd persuaded his father to install in the workshop, the boy began producing and selling nails. He soon branched out into other products like knife blades. Eager to improve his products and his profitability, he traveled around visiting workshops in the area; on one occasion he disappeared for three days on a fact-finding trip that his father had not authorized.

Young Whitney ran his nail business for roughly two years before the end of the war, and a flood of cheap English nails, made the business unprofitable. He continued to make and sell hat pins, knife blades, and various other goods; but his wartime cash cow was dead.

By the time he was in his late teens Eli had set his heart on going to college. Life on his father's small farm had not prepared him academically or financially for college, and his stepmother tried to dissuade his father from assisting him in any way, but Eli refused to give up his dream. He procured a job teaching school at a village near his family's farm, struggling to stay ahead of his pupils in some of the subjects he was hired to teach.[64] His compensation was room and board plus seven dollars a month, which he scrupulously saved, and spent on tuition for the college-prep classes he took each summer.[65]

At the advanced age of 23 Whitney, who had managed to save a small amount of money through years of hard work and thrifty living, took and passed the entrance exam for Yale College. A family friend lamented Eli's decision to pursue a higher education, opining that "it was a pity that such a fine mechanical genius as his should be wasted." Eli's father belatedly agreed to provide his son with some financial assistance, although the farm didn't produce enough hard currency to support the Whitney family and pay all of Eli's educational expenses. Eli used up his meager savings, worked at what odd jobs he could get, borrowed what he could, and took advantage of whatever assistance his father could provide. According to at least one account, Eli kept records of the money his father was able to send him during his college years and eventually repaid the debt in full.[66]

Eli graduated from Yale in September of 1792 at the age of 26. He wanted to study law, but he was in debt and needed to find employment right away. The only job offer he could get was from a man named Phineas Miller, a fellow Yale graduate who hired him on behalf of a South Carolina plantation owner named Dupont, who had commissioned Miller to find him a suitable private tutor for his children. Miller was the business manager of another plantation owner, a widow named Catharine Greene, and he had agreed to try to find a tutor for Mr. Dupont's children while accompanying Mrs. Greene on a trip to New England.

Whitney was to meet Phineas Miller and Mrs. Greene in New York, then sail with them to Savannah, Georgia before striking out overland for Mr. Dupont's plantation in South Carolina. Whitney was plagued with bad luck. The ship that was to take him from Connecticut to New York was shipwrecked several miles from the city. Whitney was able to get off the wrecked ship safely, but he had to dip into his meager traveling fund to pay for transportation the rest of the way into New York. In the city he was exposed to smallpox and had to be inoculated as a precaution; the inoculation caused him to break out in pocks.[67] Between his medical bills and his other expenses he soon went through the money he'd planned on using to book his fare to Savannah, but Mrs. Greene graciously lent him the money for his fare. The voyage to Savannah took six days, and Whitney was seasick the whole time.

When they all got to Georgia, Catharine Greene invited Whitney to stay at her estate while he continued his convalescence. Soon he got the bad news that Mr. Dupont had grown tired of waiting for Whitney and hired someone else to tutor his children, leaving Whitney broke and unemployed a thousand miles from home.[68]

During his stay at the Greene plantation Whitney had opportunity to show off his skills as a mechanic and inventor, and when several Southern businessmen were visiting one day Mrs. Greene boasted to them that her houseguest was a man who could "do anything." Her visitors challenged Whitney to come up with an efficient way to separate cottonseeds from cotton fibers.

The Southern states had already begun to lag behind the North economically. Southern culture was not conducive to the kind of entrepreneurial enterprise and "Yankee ingenuity" that was already transforming the economies of most of the Northern states. The Southern economy was almost exclusively agrarian, and farming methods were relatively primitive. The primary cash crops were tobacco, rice, and indigo. Rice, being a perishable foodstuff, was difficult to export over long distances. Tobacco grew well only in Virginia and the Carolinas.

By the time Whitney arrived in Georgia it had been determined that cotton grew very well in the southernmost of the Southern states, and was an extremely valuable product both in the North and in England, where the Industrial Revolution was rapidly making textile production more efficient. The problem that the Southern planters presented to Whitney at Mrs. Greene's dinner party was cottonseed removal. Cotton fibers clung so tenaciously to their seeds that it took a worker (usually a black slave) a whole day to de-seed a single pound of the precious product.[69] The planters told Whitney that if they could get their hands on an efficient means of seed removal it would make cotton growing far more lucrative than anything else they could do with their land.

After their guests left, Phineas Miller and Catharine Greene (who by this time were engaged to be married) discussed the issue with Whitney. It was determined that Whitney would stay with them until he could produce a machine that efficiently separated cotton from its seeds. The Millers would be his partners, and profits would be shared 50-50.[70] Free room and board was necessarily a part of the deal, for Whitney didn't have a dollar to his name.

After six months of night and day tinkering in a closed room on the Greene/Miller estate, using bits of wire and other odds and ends that he could find on the estate or buy cheaply with his partners' money, Whitney demonstrated a small hand-cranked rotary machine that could clean cotton at an unheard-of rate. By the time he submitted his patent application, he'd built a slightly larger version that could still be operated by a single person, and could clean 50 pounds per day; 50 times the rate of a person working with bare hands.[71]

The "cotton gin" Whitney invented transformed the Southern economy almost overnight. In 1793, the year Whitney produced his first crude prototype, U.S. cotton production was five million pounds. By 1820 production had increased thirtyfold, to 170 million pounds.[72] This explosion in production didn't suppress prices as one might expect, because demand kept pace with the skyrocketing supply as textile manufacturers switched from wool and flax to cotton, and ramped up their productive capacities.[73]

Whitney and the Millers moved as quickly as they could to build a cotton gin factory in New Haven, Connecticut. At the same time, Whitney applied to the U.S. patent office for his patent, which was granted early in 1794. Their plan was to install the gins they were producing up North in facilities all throughout the South, and charge the growers a fee for cleaning their cotton. They borrowed this business model from the grist mill operators of that era, who ground farmers' grain into flour for a fee.

Unfortunately for the partners, having a patent on the device that was causing this great economic expansion was not as profitable for them as they expected it to be. The cotton gin was a fairly simple device that any decent mechanic could copy. Many plantation owners built their own gins based on Whitney's design rather than pay Whitney and Miller for the use of theirs. Slaves were not allowed to give testimony in court, so plantation owners put their slaves to work in windowless buildings, making and operating cotton gins, and Whitney had no way to prove that his patent rights were being infringed.

Any moral principles of the kind that might restrain a person from intellectual property piracy were scarce among the slave-owning planters of the South. People who didn't scruple to inflict all the horrors of human slavery on their fellow man apparently didn't lose much sleep over patent infringements. Indeed, as far back as 1792, even before Whitney had invented his cotton gin and been victimized by the patent infringers, he had lamented in a letter to a friend that "as for the moral world I do not believe it exists so far South."[74]

WHITNEY LEAVES THE SOUTH

By the end of 1797 the cotton gin business had become so frustrating that Whitney left it largely in Miller's hands. The challenges the partners faced by this time were legal rather than mechanical, and Miller continued to pursue their interests in court while Whitney set his mind on finding a more reliably lucrative business. Having had his fill of trying to do business in the slave states, he resolved to stay in Connecticut full time. The workers in his New Haven factory, all of whom had been trained by him personally, were a human resource he didn't want to lose; so he focused his mind on finding a new product to manufacture on a large scale. In May of 1798 he made a formal proposal to U.S. Treasury Secretary Oliver Wolcott, offering to sell the federal government 10,000 muskets, with accessories, over the next few years.

The government had reason to find his proposal attractive. The U.S. was still far behind countries like England and France in every kind of manufacturing in 1798, and domestic firearms production was next to nil. America couldn't count on purchasing the military weapons it needed from either France or England, because both of these nations were so belligerent toward the U.S. that war with one or the other of them was a real and imminent danger. The U.S. government had already tried to address the problem by establishing two government-run armories, but one of them had been able to produce only a thousand muskets in three years, and the other had not yet succeeded in producing a single gun by the time Whitney made his proposal.

In 1798 the government contracted with 27 different U.S. manufacturers to produce a total of 40,000 muskets with their various accessories (bayonet, ramrod, etc.) over the next two or three years. Whitney had by this time developed a plan to assemble muskets from interchangeable parts; a radical idea in the 1790s. Whitney was the only contractor audacious enough to commit to producing several thousand guns; the other 26 parties were to produce a total of only 30,000 weapons between them.

Whitney's achievements up to that point made Wolcott less skeptical than he might otherwise have been of Whitney's vision. Whitney had by this time not only invented a world-changing new technology, he'd put together a factory and workforce that produced cotton gins in impressive volumes (albeit without the interchangeable parts concept) before unlawful competitors made cotton gin production unprofitable. Even though no one else in the U.S. was claiming to be able to produce weapons on the scale that Whitney envisioned, his claims carried weight.

Whitney insisted that the government make partial payment for the weapons in advance, to cover the costs of hiring and training new employees and procuring the materials he'd need for such a large scale undertaking. Secretary Wolcott agreed to Whitney's terms; partly because the government was so desperate to get the guns, and partly because he and President Adams were eager to encourage the kind of large scale U.S. manufacturing that Whitney had described in his proposal. "Besides obtaining an immediate supply of arms," Wolcott wrote in one of his letters on the subject, "it is the wish of the Government to diffuse such a degree of skill in the manufacture of Musquets as will exempt this country from the necessity of arranging further importations."[75]

Whitney and the other contractors all failed to meet their quotas in the allotted time. At the end of the contract period the government had received only about a thousand of the 40,000 muskets that were supposed to have been delivered.[76] None of those had come from Whitney's factory, which was still making and stockpiling individual gun parts in large quantities but which had not yet produced all of the parts necessary for the mass production of weapons. Manufacturing something as complicated as firearms in the United States, where production of materials like iron and steel was still in its infancy and mechanics and engineers were scarce, turned out to be a lot more difficult than Whitney, Wolcott, or any of the other weapons contractors had realized.

Fortunately for the United States, Adams and his administration managed to avoid a land war with France, although there were a few naval skirmishes between 1798 and 1800. England functioned as an ally of sorts during this period, albeit an unfriendly and unreliable one. When the naval "Half War" with France ended in 1800 Britain resumed her bellicose attitude toward the U.S., but the Jefferson and Madison administrations managed to stave off open warfare with the mother country for several more years.

By the end of 1800 Whitney realized he would have to persuade the government to grant him more time and money if he was to make the project a success. In early January of 1801 the inventor went to Washington, DC, the nation's new capital, to ask for an extension and another cash advance. Because there had just been a presidential election, Whitney had to plead his case both with lame duck President John Adams and with President-Elect Thomas Jefferson.

Whitney came to Washington armed with letters testifying to the quality of the few prototypical muskets he had produced up to that time. A Connecticut congressman wrote, in reference to Whitney's muskets:

They have met universal approbation and are considered as evidence that this Country need not depend on a disgraceful recourse to foreign Markets for this primary means of defense. All Judges and Inspectors unite in a declaration that they are superior to any that the artists of this Country, or importation have brought into the Arsenals of the United States – and all Men of all parties agree that his talents are of immense importance, and must be exclusively secured by and devoted to the means of defense.[77]

The government's official Inspector of Small Arms likewise wrote a letter endorsing the quality of Whitney's muskets. More important than the letters were the samples Whitney brought with him that January. He brought a large number of interchangeable musket parts and demonstrated how the parts could be mixed and matched at will, and a completed gun assembled from any combination. Showing a knack for marketing, Whitney then invited various government officials to take the musket apart, choose new parts at random, and re-assemble the weapon with their own hands. The demonstration was a complete success. The government extended Whitney's deadline and gave him another advance payment. Eight months later Whitney delivered the first 500 muskets, which were duly examined, tested, and accepted by government inspectors.

It should be noted that many modern day historians suspect that Whitney fudged that all-important 1801 product demonstration by practicing in advance with the components he brought to Washington, and tweaking many of them with a file to make them more easily interchangeable. Whether that is true or not, Whitney did eventually deliver the 10,000 guns his contract called for, and the overall quality of his weapons was generally applauded by government inspectors. Weapons from other sources, including those from a government-run armory, which were hand-crafted in the traditional way, were found to contain greater numbers of defects than Whitney's guns. And over time he did undeniably develop a system that produced large volumes of truly identical, interchangeable parts.

Whitney finally concluded his initial musket contract with the federal government in January of 1809. By that time the State of New York had given him a new contract for a thousand muskets for its state militia. Other state contracts would follow. By this time his philosophy of interchangeability was a proven technology and his factory was operating efficiently. There would be no need to ask the states for extensions; all the weapons were delivered on time.

In June of 1812 the United States declared war on England, and Whitney's business boomed. When the war ended the government continued to order arms, and Whitney's company continued to thrive. For as long as he lived Whitney continued to innovate; year by year he developed new machines and methods to improve the quality of his product and reduce the production costs.

When Whitney died in 1825 he left his wife and children a considerable fortune.[78] His son, Eli Whitney Jr., was too young to take over the business right away, but the elder Whitney had trained two of his nephews to run the company. The two nephews were paid well to manage the company and did so without help until Eli Jr. was ready to take on an active role in the business.

In 1843 Whitney's company, under the leadership of Eli Whitney Jr., signed a contract with Samuel Colt to produce the famous Colt revolver, the so-called "gun that won the West," in large quantities.[79]

Colt, of course, was the usual American rags-to-riches story. His mother died when he was very young and his struggling father couldn't support the family properly, so Samuel had to spend much of his childhood earning his own living as a farmhand on other families' farms.[80]

Through the Civil War the Whitney armory sold rifles and revolvers to the Union side. In 1888 Eli Whitney Jr., at the age of 68, sold the gun factory to the Winchester Repeating Arms Company so he could concentrate on his other business interests.

By this time John D. Rockefeller and his Standard Oil Company had made lamp oil affordable for ordinary working people. Mass production according to the principles Eli Whitney Sr. had pioneered had made all sorts of consumer products similarly affordable for the masses. Owning more than one suit of clothing was no longer a luxury that only the rich could afford. Steam engines powered ships and trains that moved people and products more rapidly and safely than anyone could have imagined in 1765 when Eli Sr. was born. The telegraph made it possible to send a message hundreds of miles in an instant. Food production had increased so rapidly that death by starvation was no longer a danger in the Western world. The food supply in America was so plentiful that much of each year's crop was exported overseas.

And virtually all of this miraculous progress was engineered by people who started out with nothing; people like Eli Whitney Sr.

CHAPTER 5

Free States and Free Enterprise

———

We will win our freedom because the sacred
heritage of our nation and the eternal will of
God are embodied in our echoing demands.

MARTIN LUTHER KING, JR. – FROM HIS 1963
"LETTER FROM A BIRMINGHAM JAIL"

TODAY, WHEN AMERICA'S SOUTHERN STATES are leading the nation in job creation and economic growth, it might be hard to envision a time when the opposite was true, but this was the case for almost the first 200 years of our nation's history. When Eli Whitney fled the South for Connecticut he left a dysfunctional, broken society defined by moral bankruptcy and economic poverty. When he returned to the North he re-entered the Land of Opportunity.

It is truly remarkable, in view of the way new technologies were always springing up like mushrooms in the Northern states in America's early years, that only two innovations of any real value came out of the South between the nation's founding and the end of the Jim Crow era in the late 1960s. One was Whitney's cotton gin. The other was Cyrus McCormick's mechanical harvester, which was introduced roughly half a century later. McCormick started out with nothing, just as Whitney had, and, like Whitney, he had to flee the South to make his fortune.

Other than these two innovations, the only thing of any great value that came out of the South during this long period was a huge quantity of cotton, which was America's most valuable export product for many years. Intellectual property, the kind of property that can only be created by skilled and motivated human beings, was almost exclusively a Northern product. The economic history of the South illustrates unmistakably the link between freedom and prosperity. Free enterprise only thrived in the "free" states, and it was free enterprise that created prosperity.

Most of today's younger Americans, who grew up in an era when economic growth in the 11 states of the old Confederacy was racing ahead of that in the North, may have a hard time believing that the South was ever economically, technologically, and culturally backward; but the South was just that until the last vestiges of government-imposed racial segregation were finally eliminated in the late 1960s.

Free and Enslaved Economies

In his famous and influential book 1835 book *Democracy in America,* French nobleman Alexis de Tocqueville described the United States as a nation where the average citizen "is taught from his earliest infancy to rely upon his own exertions…"[81] The result of this philosophy was that "America is a land of wonders, in which everything is in constant motion, and every movement seems an improvement…No natural boundary seems to be set to the efforts of man; and what is not yet done is only what he has not yet attempted to do."[82]

But Tocqueville made it clear that this attitude was only observable in the Northern states. The culture of the Southern states was dramatically different. His explanation was that the institution of slavery had a corrosive effect on the character of the white residents of the slave states; that it "enervates the mind, and benumbs the activity of man." Slavery, he said, "dishonors labor," and "introduces idleness into society."[83] Because Southern whites looked down on hard work as something degrading, and nearly two thirds of the Southern population was white, the productivity of the Southern work force was always grossly inferior to that of the North.

To illustrate his point, Tocqueville describes the contrast he observed during a trip down the Ohio River. With the slave state of Kentucky on his left and the free state of Ohio on his right, he observed that all the productive activity seemed to be going on to his right:

> Upon the left bank of the Ohio labor is confounded with the idea of slavery, upon the right bank it is identified with that of prosperity and improvement; on the one side it is degraded, on the other it is honored; on the former territory no white laborers can be found…on the latter no one is idle, for the white population extends its activity and its intelligence to every kind of employment. Thus the men whose task it is to cultivate the rich soil of Kentucky are ignorant and lukewarm, whilst those who are active and enlightened either do nothing or pass over to the state of Ohio, where they may work without dishonor.[84]

Tocqueville wrote in detail of the dilapidated condition of the buildings and yards he saw on the Southern side of the river, with everything falling into apparent disrepair. In the free state, in contrast, buildings were freshly painted and neatly kept.

Booker T. Washington, who founded Tuskegee University and became the nation's foremost civil rights advocate in the early twentieth century, saw the South's dysfunctional culture at close range in his childhood. Washington was a slave until he and his family were freed by the advancing Union Army in 1865, when Washington was nine years old. His first-hand observations of the institution of slavery matched Tocqueville's more detached perspective exactly:

> The hurtful influences of the institution were by not by any means confined to the Negro. This was fully illustrated by the life upon our own plantation. The whole machinery of slavery was so constructed as to cause labour, as a rule, to be looked upon as a badge of degradation, of inferiority...The slave system on our place, in a large measure, took the spirit of self-reliance and self-help out of the white people...As a result of the system, fences were out of repair, gates were hanging half off the hinges, doors creaked, window-panes were out, plaster had fallen but was not replaced, weeds grew in the yard. When freedom came, the slaves were almost as well fitted to begin life anew as the master, except in the matter of book-learning and ownership of property. The slave owner and his sons had mastered no special industry. They unconsciously had imbibed the feeling that manual labour was not the proper thing for them. On the other hand, the slaves, in many cases, had mastered some handicraft, and none were ashamed, and few unwilling, to labour.[85]

First Lady Abigail Adams made similar observations in 1800, when the Capitol and White House were moved from Philadelphia to Washington, DC. Mrs. Adams had lived in Massachusetts for most of her life, and Washington was the first place where she was directly exposed to the institution of slavery. As construction on the new White House was going on she watched a team of 12 slaves doing their work each day, while the owners of the slaves stood around doing nothing. In a letter to a friend she expressed her contempt for the laziness of the slave owners. She could not understand, she said, how a slave-owning white man could "walk about idle, though one slave is all the property he can boast."[86]

A really comprehensive look at the financial and cultural poverty of the antebellum South is a book called *The Cotton Kingdom*, by Frederick Law Olmsted. Olmsted was a modestly successful New York farmer who in his late twenties began a career as a freelance journalist. In the late 1850s he traveled through the Southern United States, describing everything he saw in great detail. The expenses of his trips through Dixie were under-written by a couple of New York newspapers, and his observations were initially published in the papers in serial form. *The Cotton Kingdom*, which was first published in book form in 1861, is an exhaustive account of his Southern U.S. travels. (Later Olmsted would change careers again and become the nation's most prominent landscape architect. His works include New York's Central Park and the grounds of the U.S. Capitol and the White House.)

In the book Olmsted documents in painstaking detail the technological and economic backwardness he encountered throughout the slave states. He cites economic statistics from government and other sources, and recounts numerous personal anecdotes from his own travels to confirm what those government statistics showed.

Everywhere he saw poor or non-existent transportation and communication infrastructure. Telegraph lines were virtually nonexistent. Homes and other buildings were in disrepair; the kind of decay Tocqueville had observed on the left side of the Ohio River was everywhere Olmsted traveled. Property values were a fraction of those up North.[87] Roads were terrible. Bridges were few and far between. Train and steamship service, where it existed at all, was unreliable.

Olmsted's research into the culture of the South was exhaustive. "At least five hundred white men," he says, "told me something of their own lives and fortunes, across their own tables, and with the means of measuring the weight of their words before my eyes…"

What he heard and saw was not pretty.

> I know that while men seldom want an abundance of course
> food in the cotton states, the proportion of free white men
> who live as well in any respect as our working classes at the
> North, on an average, is small, and the citizens of the cotton
> States, as a whole, are poor. They work little, and that little,
> badly; they earn little, they sell little; they buy little, and they
> have little – very little – of the common comforts and conso-
> lations of civilized life. Their destitution is not material only;
> it is intellectual and it is moral.[88]

The South's problems had nothing to do with a lack of physical
resources; the Southern states had plenty of fertile soil and a longer
growing season than the North. It also had navigable rivers and good
ports; it had all the non-human resources the North had, and then
some. The problem was the culture.

SLAVE-OWNING WHITES
The great majority of Southern whites were poor, and poor whites
were kept poor by an inverted value system that viewed hard work
as degrading. Only around a third of white Southern families owned
slaves in the antebellum years, and most of those families owned
fewer than six.[89] The number of planters who owned enough land
and slaves to be considered truly wealthy was always tiny. Plantation
owners large and small believed that it was beneath their dignity to
do any kind of work with their own hands. The richest planters were
able to spend their time gambling (a Southern passion), riding, and
entertaining guests. Conspicuous consumption was much admired
and widely practiced. The wealthiest planters tended to live beyond

their means, so many of them borrowed against future crop harvests and lived in a constant state of debt.

The smaller planters tried to live the same way, although they had a harder time persuading banks to lend them money against their meager crops. Hunting, fishing, racing horses, and gambling were the pastimes of the smaller planters. Meanwhile their children dressed in rags and their homes lacked furniture. As Mrs. Adams had observed in 1800, owning even a single slave would make a Southern white man feel like he was "above" doing any kind of useful work for himself or his family; in that scenario the lone slave would have to earn enough income by his labor to support himself, his owner, and the owner's entire family.

Olmsted gives an insightful economic analysis of the smaller plantations in his book, based on government statistics about cotton production and prices. He reviews the costs associated with transporting cotton to market via the South's primitive roads and ports, the average production of cotton per slave in the cotton-intensive states, and other relevant factors; then subtracts the cost of food and other necessities for the slaves themselves. Olmsted calculates that a typical small-scale cotton planter made a profit of only about 25 dollars per year from the labor of each slave. A family that owned four slaves would have to live on an income after expenses of around a hundred dollars per annum.[90]

By comparison, an unskilled laborer in any part of the United States in those days could earn between 100 and 200 dollars per year in wages. Slave-owners like the ones Mrs. Adams observed, who "rented" their slaves to outside employers, could typically earn an income of between $110 and $140 per year per unskilled slave, in addition, in many cases, to the slaves' room and board.[91]

The larger plantation owners benefited from certain economies of scale, and could earn a somewhat larger profit than the smaller planters on a per-slave basis.

Poor White "Crackers"

Two thirds of the Southern white population did not own slaves. With the exception of first generation white immigrants from Europe (chiefly Germans and Irish) most of the slave-less whites in the region lived a lifestyle that Olmsted described as "lazy poverty."[92] Few outside of the larger cities held full time jobs for any length of time. While self-discipline, self-reliance, and hard work were admired in the North, Southern culture perversely assigned higher status to the man who did nothing for himself. Hard work was considered demeaning. "To work industriously and steadily, especially under the direction of another man," was denigrated.[93]

These Southern "crackers," as native-born poor whites were called, tended to avoid the embarrassment of working full time for a paycheck, although they would take temporary jobs for a few days at a time when forced to do so by severe financial need.[94] The South was overwhelmingly rural in that era, and most poor whites obtained at least some of their food supply by hunting and fishing; activities that looked like recreation and were therefore held in high esteem in that culture. Most poor whites either owned or "squatted" on little plots of land where they would grow a few food crops for home consumption.

They also stole. Poor whites who owned plots of land near large plantations were a constant annoyance to the wealthy planters, largely because of their never-ending theft of livestock, food crops, and anything else of value. "In no single instance," said Olmsted, did he speak to a wealthy planter who didn't express his irritation with his poor white neighbors.[95] Some planters went so far as to buy up the farms of their poor neighbors and leave them fallow, as a buffer zone.[96]

The Southern aversion to disciplined effort applied to academics as well. The illiteracy rate was high[97] and the percentage of white children who regularly attended school was low.[98] Books, magazines and newspapers were scarce or completely absent in the great majority of homes Olmsted visited during his extensive travels. Large plantation owners would often hire private tutors for their children, but poor white children tended to grow up without much education.

SLAVES AND SLAVE LABOR

Nearly 40 percent of the people in the Confederate states just before the start of the Civil War were slaves.[99] Most of the work that got done was done by slaves, and that includes both skilled and unskilled labor. Contrary to popular belief, the work that was consigned to slaves in the antebellum South was not confined to domestic service and field labor. There were some white (and free black) skilled workers, but most of the skilled craftsmen in the South were black slaves. Most of the blacksmiths and mechanics Olmsted encountered in his travels through all 11 Confederate states were slaves.

Olmsted cites numerous examples of this in his book. One very wealthy Georgia plantation owner, for example, had built a large mill for processing rice from his fields. The mill was powered by a steam engine, a bit of high-tech equipment that was pretty rare in the antebellum South. The planter's extensive operations required him to keep a staff of blacksmiths, wheelwrights, carpenters, and mechanics; all of whom were his slaves. The man responsible for maintaining and operating the steam engine was, like all the others, a slave.[100]

Even the Father of our Country had to depend on slaves for skilled labor on his plantation. Slaves did everything on George Washington's Mount Vernon estate. They ran his whiskey distillery, one of the largest in the nation, under the direction of a Scottish immigrant named James Anderson. They also ran the large waterwheel-powered grist mill on his Dogue Run property.

When Washington needed a bricklayer for a 1797 construction project, hiring a skilled and reliable white workman was not an option; the recently-retired ex-president had to buy himself a bricklayer. He negotiated with a neighboring planter who owned a slave with the necessary skills, but the planter refused to sell the craftsman's wife to Washington. Washington, who was less cruel than most Southern planters, was unwilling to break up a family to get the worker he needed, so he arranged to rent the bricklayer for a time, allowing him to return to the neighboring plantation to visit his spouse on a regular basis.[101]

Perversely, while depending on slaves to do most of the skilled labor in their society, Southerners forbad teaching slaves to read. The penalties for teaching a slave to read were severe, typically including prison time for whites and even worse things for any slave who might try to teach other slaves.[102] Planters tended to be so hostile to the idea of literacy among their slaves that they often imposed their own draconian punishments on any slave caught trying to learn, without bothering to consult with the police or other legal authorities.

The attitude of slave-holders is poignantly illustrated by a story Frederick Douglass relates in his autobiography. When Douglass was an eight-year-old slave, his owner sent him to live with relatives in Baltimore. His new masters had never been slave-holders before, and the lady of the house started teaching Frederick the alphabet. When her husband learned of it he ordered her to stop, "telling her, among other things, that it was unlawful, as well as unsafe, to teach a slave to read." A slave, the angry husband told his wife, "should know nothing but to obey his master." Learning to read would "forever unfit him to be a slave."

"These words," said Frederick Douglass, in recounting the tale years later, "sank deep into my heart."

> I now understood what had been to me a most perplexing difficulty – to wit, the white man's power to enslave the black man. It was a grand achievement, and I prized it highly. From that moment I understood the pathway from slavery to freedom.[103]

This was the revelation that changed his Douglass' life. He would rely upon his own exertions to free himself; literacy was the key. The youngster spent the next few years secretly teaching himself, with great difficulty and by unrelenting effort, to read and write. He proved how right his master's words were when he escaped to New York in September of 1838. In New York Douglass quickly made friends with Northern abolitionists, and became a powerful public speaker for the abolitionist cause.

The example of Frederick Douglass makes it easy to understand why Southern planters were so adamant about keeping their slaves illiterate. At the same time, the illiteracy of the region's highest-skilled workers makes it easy to understand why Dixie was so technologically and economically backward. Most of the people employed in operating and maintaining the most complex machinery in the South couldn't read a technical manual or a trade journal. They couldn't exchange ideas with their fellow journeymen by letter. They couldn't study math or physics to better understand the principles on which their machinery operated.

The chef in charge of the kitchen at George Washington's estate, like the cooks in virtually all the wealthiest households in the South, could not read a recipe.

Skill and effort are the twin keys to achievement, and Southern culture discouraged both. In addition to blocking their slaves from acquiring academic skills, the Southern slave-holders compounded the problem by robbing their slaves of any incentive to work hard. In the slavery system all the rewards of a slave's effort go to his owner. To make a slave work at all, the slave had to be "driven" by an overseer who would constantly threaten to punish those who were remiss in their efforts.

In the North the word "driven" had a very different meaning. Entrepreneurs like Benjamin Franklin, John Jacob Astor, Eli Whitney, and Cornelius Vanderbilt were driven by their own ambitions; driven by a characteristically "Yankee" belief that they would reap rewards from their efforts.

In the South, slaves responded quite rationally to their circumstances. Having had his very life stolen from him, a slave was not likely to do any more than he had to do to line the pockets of his oppressors. Slaves would often "obey the letter, but defeat the intention" of their orders.[104] A typical scene would look something like this:

> The overseer rode among them, on a horse, carrying in his hand a rawhide whip, constantly directing and encouraging them; but, as my companion and I, both, several times noticed, as often as he visited one end of the line of operations, the hands at the other end would discontinue their labour, until he turned to ride towards them again.[105]

Slaves also felt, quite understandably, no compunction whatsoever about stealing from slave-owning whites. Slaves stole pigs and poultry for their own consumption, and those who had access to buyers stole anything that wasn't nailed down and converted it to cash or bartered it for liquor or other products. Plantation owners complained constantly about their losses due to theft.

The theft issue put one more obstacle in the path of industrialization in the South. Those plantations large enough to have machinery for processing their crops were constantly having to replace expensive items. Plantations near waterways were particularly vulnerable; white traders traveled up and down the rivers on boats and bartered with slaves for stolen components. A piece of equipment worth 80 dollars might be stolen by a slave and bartered away for a glass of whiskey.[106]

Government Solutions

Southern political and business leaders were keenly aware of the economic and industrial shortcomings of their region. The obvious contrast between North and South was such a sore subject that some

Southern politicians scolded their own constituents in terms that no public official would dare use today.

In a public speech he gave in the 1840s, South Carolina Governor James Henry Hammond lamented that "of the 300,000 white inhabitants of South Carolina, there are not less than 50,000, whose industry, such as it is..." is not "adequate to procure them, honestly, such support as every white person is and feels himself entitled to. Some cannot be said to work at all," said the governor. "They obtain a precarious subsistence by occasional jobs, by hunting, by fishing, sometimes by plundering field or folds, and, too often, by what is, in its effects, far worse – trading with slaves, and seducing them to plunder for their benefit."[107]

In a similar speech given a few years later, Governor Henry A. Wise of Virginia described the dismal state of his state's economy to a group of constituents who must have been shocked at his candor: "You have no commerce, no mining, no manufactures," said the governor. "You have relied alone on the single power of agriculture..." yet "your inattention to your only source of wealth has scarred the very bosom of Mother Earth."[108]

Starting in 1837 political leaders from the various Southern states sent delegates to an annual Southern Commercial Convention to try to address the region's economic problems. The first few conventions focused narrowly on ideas that might actually have been helpful, like railroad construction and establishing direct shipping routes between Southern ports and European markets.[109]

Other ideas were not so constructive. Re-establishing the trans-Atlantic slave trade was a dominant theme of most of the conventions,[110] as most of the delegates persisted in the belief that slavery was a benefit, rather than a curse, to their region.

Other proposals demonstrated a tendency to blame the North's industrial and commercial superiority on unfair "exploitation" of the plantation owners by Northern business interests. Rich planters, addicted as they were to luxury and conspicuous consumption, tended to finance their spending via bank loans. It was not uncommon for a planter to borrow against expected crop revenues three or four years into the future.[111] Most of the nation's banks were headquartered in the Northeast, so planters who had saddled themselves with debt found it convenient to blame their problems on Yankee bankers. In the 1890s this resentment of bankers would find its expression in widespread support among Southern planters for the "Populist" movement headed by William Jennings Bryan. In the 1850s it often found voice in the deliberations of the Southern Commercial Conventions.

At the 1855 convention a delegate from Louisiana recorded the following resolution:

> Resolved, that this Convention strongly recommend the Chambers of Commerce and commission merchants of our Southern and Southwestern cities to adopt such a system of laws and regulations as will put a stop to the dangerous practice, heretofore existing, of making advances to planters in anticipation of their crops; a practice entirely at variance with everything like safety in business transactions, and tending directly to establish the relation of master and slave between the merchant and planter, by bringing the later into the most abject and servile bondage.[112]

Leaving aside the painfully ironic use of the terms "master" and "slave," this 1855 resolution shows how pointless the conventions were. The South's problems were not caused by Northern bankers granting loans to Southern planters who asked for them; the problems were in the South's dysfunctional culture, starting with the institution of slavery itself.

During all the years the conventions were held, no delegate ever offered a resolution that started with "free your slaves and teach them to read," nor did any delegate ever borrow from Tocqueville that every citizen should be "taught from his earliest infancy to rely upon his own exertions."

The Southern states would continue to be poor and backward long after the Thirteenth Amendment outlawed slavery in 1865. A culture of true freedom and self-reliance would not reach the South until roughly a hundred years after that, when the federal government, on constitutional grounds, forced the Southern states to abandon their "Jim Crow" policies of government-mandated racial segregation.

PROSPERITY COMES TO THE SOUTH

In 1964, some 99 years after the Thirteenth Amendment was ratified, a federal Civil Rights Act passed the Congress and was signed into law by the president. Within the next few years the Southern states were finally forced to give up all of the state, county, and municipal laws that had kept their society racially segregated. This marked the beginning of a long-overdue economic and technological awakening.

In 1970 only 29 companies with their headquarters in the 11 states of the old Confederacy were on the Fortune 500 list of America's largest companies. By 2014, 141 companies, a disproportionately large number, had their headquarters in Dixie[113]; including five of the top ten.[114] Number One on the list, the largest company in the United States and the world, was an Arkansas company that went into business with just a single small retail store in 1962, two years before the Civil Rights Act liberated the South from racial segregation.

When Sam Walton opened up his first Walmart store in 1962 he was living out the kind of rags-to-riches success story that used to be confined to the Northern states. Walton was born in Oklahoma in 1918 and grew up in a working class family that was hit hard by the Great Depression when Sam was 11 years old. He delivered papers and worked on his parents' small dairy from an early age.[115] His mother inculcated a love of learning in Sam early, and he excelled in his schoolwork. He worked his way through college without any financial support from his parents,[116] and went into retail when he graduated because it was the only job he could get.[117] In 1985 *Fortune Magazine* named him the richest man in the world.

As the Sam Walton story illustrates, freedom and self-reliance are the underpinnings of success in any region. Walton founded his company in Arkansas just as the South was finally being unshackled from the evil and idiocy of government-mandated segregation, and his company rapidly prospered and grew, like so many others in the South.

Walton was without a doubt the sort of person Alexis de Tocqueville was talking about when he described the typical American as a person who relies "on his own exertions" to achieve success. Walton's parents brought him up with the idea that he should expect to reap great results from great effort, as his autobiography makes abundantly clear. No one could be more different from the indolent, proudly-idle white slave-owners who made the antebellum South such a broken and backward place.

It's unfortunate that it took nearly 200 years for the principles of freedom and self-reliance to take hold in the South, but the results that Southern entrepreneurs have achieved over the last 50 years make it clear that these principles will work anywhere.

CHAPTER 6

Robert Fulton and His Steamboat

———

There are basically two types of people. People who
accomplish things, and people who claim to have
accomplished things. The first group is less crowded.

MARK TWAIN

IT'S NO COINCIDENCE THAT MOST of the great fortunes earned by self-made men in the United States over the last couple hundred years were earned in the fields of transportation and communication. Throughout human history, transportation and communication have always been central to the development of any society. No geographical region has a monopoly on good ideas; people in every part of the world have need of things that people in other areas can produce more efficiently. Even more important than the traffic in goods is the traffic in ideas; a society that doesn't have access to new ideas from other peoples will always be stagnant. Transportation of products, people, and ideas has always been a crucial engine of progress.

Illustrations of this principle are legion. Egypt has been the most powerful state in the Middle East for most of the last five thousand years largely because the Nile River is navigable year round for hundreds of miles and connects to the Mediterranean Sea. Easy transportation was as important in 3150 BC, when the first Egyptian Pharaoh came to power, as it is today. The earliest dynasties in China and India were established along the Yellow and Indus rivers, respectively, for similar reasons.

The Roman Empire dominated the world for centuries largely because Rome was located on the Mediterranean, and within a short distance of several good deep water ports. Roman society was built on trade, and the Romans dedicated significant resources to developing, protecting, and exploiting trade routes. Trade was not restricted to shipping on the Mediterranean; the Romans were pioneers in the science of road-building and their roads were engineering marvels by the standards of that era. The Roman army patrolled the highway system to keep the roads safe for trade, and the Roman navy protected Mediterranean shipping by its merciless treatment of seagoing pirates.[118]

Ancient Carthage, which like Rome was located on the Mediterranean and had excellent port facilities, was likewise a center of trade in the last few centuries before Christ. The two empires were rivals for control of the trade routes; the rivalry was so fierce that Roman Senator Cato ended every public speech with the words "and Carthage must be destroyed." In 146 BC Rome did in fact succeed in destroying Carthage, giving Rome a de facto monopoly on Mediterranean trade and making Rome the preeminent empire in the world.

More recently, England and Japan were able to establish powerful empires at least in part because they are island nations with substantial deep water ports.

Sub-Saharan Africa has been politically and economically weak for centuries, largely because of geographical barriers to overland travel and a terrible scarcity of decent ports and navigable rivers.[119] The same geographical liabilities have caused eastern Europe to lag behind the West in much the same way.[120]

In the United States, where "an unbounded desire of riches" was said to be a defining characteristic of the people,[121] it's not surprising that many of the most enterprising individuals chose careers in transportation and communication.

In the U.S. the telegraph, the telephone, and the shipping and railroad industries all offered terrific earning opportunities to those who made important contributions and managed their affairs wisely. (Telephone inventor Alexander Graham Bell made only a small fortune from his shares of the company that became AT&T because he sold most of his stock way too soon. The investors who bought those shares from Bell must have felt like geniuses.)

Andrew Carnegie, known to history as a steel mogul, built his whole career on transportation. He worked for a railroad, then went into bridge-building and other railroad-related businesses. When he finally went into the steel business full time the most lucrative product his company made was railroad rails.

John D. Rockefeller, who started the Standard Oil Company to market kerosene for lamps, saw his fortune multiply rapidly when petroleum started to be used as a fuel for motor vehicles.

Investment banker J.P. Morgan focused for most of his career on the financing of railroad companies and the companies that served them. It's easy to understand why; by the early 1870s 80 percent of the total value of the U.S. stock market was in railroad stocks.[122] Morgan was also an important early financial backer of new communication technologies.

Cornelius Vanderbilt, of course, focused on transportation from his start in business at the age of 16 until his death 66 years later. The same could be said of self-made millionaires Jay Gould, Daniel Drew, and Jim Fisk; as well as many others. Henry Wells and William Fargo, founders of Wells Fargo, both went from rags to riches in the freight business.

Virtually all of the great technological breakthroughs in these two key fields in the nineteenth century were made by Americans. Robert Fulton's steamboat was the first of these revolutionary inventions.

Fulton was certainly not the first man to recognize the potential of using the power of the steam engine to drive a vessel over the waves. Inventors in Europe and the U.S., and their financial backers, had been trying for decades to develop a functional steamboat by the time Fulton's *North River* took to the waters of the Hudson River in 1807. The first boat to move itself over the water using steam power was demonstrated by French nobleman Claude-Francis-Dorothee Jouffroy d'Abbans in 1775 on the River Saone in eastern France. The boat powered its way upstream for 15 minutes before the vibration of its engine started to tear the hull apart. The design was not practical, but it was a major technological milestone nonetheless.

In 1787 an American named John Fitch launched a boat that steamed around the Delaware River for a while at a speed of a couple miles per hour. The governments of New Jersey, Pennsylvania, Delaware, Virginia and New York, eager for the economic development that a functional steamship system would bring, all offered Fitch a substantial incentive to keep developing his boat design. The states offered Fitch a government-enforced monopoly on steamboat traffic on their waters if he could put a steamboat into commercial operation.[123]

Under this arrangement Fitch wouldn't have to worry about other boat companies copying his design and going into business in competition with him, so he and his financial backers expended the necessary resources to develop a better boat. Fitch spent the next three years experimenting on one design after another, and in 1790 he launched a boat that could travel up and down the Delaware River reliably. He operated the boat all summer on a commercial basis.

Fitch's boat was never efficient enough to make a profit; fuel and labor costs far outweighed revenues, forcing him to shut down the operation after a single summer, but it too was a significant milestone in transportation history.

Later in the 1790s two wealthy and influential power brokers in the New York City area formed a partnership and tried to develop a boat for the New York to Albany run on the Hudson River. Robert Livingston had been one of the five authors of the Declaration of Independence, and owned a large estate on a hill overlooking the Hudson between the two cities. John Stevens, Livingston's brother-in-law, came from a wealthy family and, like Livingston, had leisure time to spend experimenting on steamboat designs and various other inventions. In 1797 the partners hired an accomplished mechanic to build a boat they'd designed.

John Fitch had gone into an alcohol-fueled tailspin after the failure of his Delaware River venture, and by the time Livingston and Stevens had built their boat he was presumed dead. Livingston lobbied the New York state legislature to grant him the Hudson River monopoly that Fitch had had, and the state granted him a conditional monopoly in 1798. The legislation stipulated that Livingston would have exclusive rights to operate steamboats on the Hudson for 20 years if he could, within one year, demonstrate that his boat could reliably move upstream against the current at a rate of four miles per hour.[124]

In October of 1798 Livingston and Stevens launched their boat. It was able to make some progress over still water, but couldn't meet the requirements of the monopoly contract, and it vibrated so badly that the power train was damaged after just a short demonstration.[125] The two rich inventors discussed trying to build a new boat together, but ended up dissolving their partnership. Livingston took the precaution of renewing his agreement with the New York legislature from time to time, so that if he ever did come up with a viable steamboat he would have a monopoly on Hudson waters.

Livingston continued to experiment with boat designs, but President Jefferson distracted him from the project in 1801 by sending him to France to negotiate the Louisiana Purchase with Emperor Napoleon. While in Paris, Livingston somehow met Robert Fulton.

Fulton's Early Days

Robert Fulton was born in Pennsylvania in November of 1765, just a few weeks before Whitney's birth in Massachusetts. He was born on a small farm, but his father was apparently unable to make his mortgage payments, and when Robert was seven years old the farm was seized and sold at auction. The family moved to the nearby town of Lancaster, virtually penniless, where the elder Fulton went to work as a tailor. Two years later Robert's father died, leaving the family completely without resources.[126]

In his mid-teens Robert moved to Philadelphia to try to make a living. He worked for a jeweler for a short time, then supported himself by painting miniatures.[127] For several years he made a somewhat precarious living as a painter of miniatures and portraits. He moved to England in 1787 and continued his painting career for a few years, then tried to launch a new career as an inventor. Working entirely on his own initiative, he drew up new technologies for sawing stone, building bridges, and excavating ground for canals, but none of his ideas were ever put into commercially successful operation.

In 1797, 31-year-old Fulton moved from England to France. He tried to persuade the French government to fund his efforts to develop a military submarine and aquatic mines for use in its war with England; when the government refused, he found a private investor to fund his research.

In June of 1800 Fulton successfully demonstrated his submarine for the French Marine Minister and a crowd of onlookers. In November Napoleon's government granted him 10,000 francs to improve and arm his submarine, and promised to pay him a bounty on any British ship he managed to destroy with the craft. Fulton made several attempts, but his sub, which could stay underwater for hours at a time, proved to be all but useless as a weapon of war. His mines were effective enough when they could be brought into contact with a ship, but Fulton's attempts to deploy them by submarine or surface vessel were all failures.

By 1802, when he first met Livingston, Fulton had demonstrated a fertile mind and a knack for mechanics and engineering, but he hadn't produced anything that could be described as a successful invention. Yet Livingston somehow recognized that Fulton was the man who could do what Livingston and Stevens, with all their money and connections, had failed to do: produce a fast and reliable steamboat. It would be Livingston who first harnessed Fulton's talents for something practical. On October of that year the two of them signed the paperwork forming a partnership. Livingston provided 500 pounds for the initial research, with more to follow. Fulton was to provide his brain power and, when he could get it, some of the money for the project as well.

Fulton spent the next several months studying all the literature he could get on the boats d'Abbans, Fitch, and other inventors had put on the water over the last 27 years, and reading scientific papers about hydraulic resistance as it applied to boats.[128] In August of 1803 he demonstrated a 75 foot boat on the Seine. Powered by a French-made engine, his prototype was able to tow two other boats upstream at a speed estimated at three miles per hour. Fulton believed that he could achieve more power and speed with an engine made in England by Boulton, Watt; the company founded by Scottish inventor James Watt.

Shortly before he launched his first boat, Fulton was approached by an agent of the English government, who told him that the English wanted him to switch sides and use his talents to help the British navy against the French. Fulton, who doesn't seem to have had any scruples about selling his services to the highest bidder, snuck out of Paris under an assumed name in April of 1804. The fees he was able to negotiate with the British government allowed him to hire Boulton, Watt to build a steam engine, to his exact specifications, for eventual use on the Hudson River steamboat. His service to the English government helped him get permission to export the engine to New York.

In May of 1804 Livingston returned to the U.S., his diplomatic mission over.

In December of 1806 Fulton returned to the U.S. after an absence of nearly 20 years. His mines had not been much more effective for the English than for the French, but the fees the British government had paid him had alleviated his financial problems and allowed him to help pay for boat research and construction. Soon after his arrival in New York he examined the 12 U.S. patents that had been issued for steamboat designs by this time, none of which particularly impressed him. He paid the import taxes on his Watt steam engine and had it moved to the shipyard where the new boat he'd designed was to be built under his supervision.

The boat was finished in early August of 1807. Fulton named it the *North River*. He took it out for a preliminary run up the East River, then brought it back to the yard for some more tweaking in preparation for an official demonstration. On August 17 the boat left New York for Albany. It stopped overnight at Clermont, Livingston's plush estate on a hill overlooking the river, then continued up to Albany the next day. When traveling, the boat averaged five miles per hour against the current. When the *North River* docked in Albany, the world had changed. Steam powered navigation was now a reality. The North River immediately started making regular trips up and down the Hudson. Profits were high, and Fulton and Livingston had no trouble raising all the capital they needed for the construction of more steamboats.

Soon other engineers were copying Fulton's design and improving on it. The steamboat's rapid spread meant that people and goods could move rapidly, cheaply, and reliably over waterways that had been difficult or impossible to navigate in the past.

The year after the North River took its maiden voyage to Albany, the state of New York sent surveyors to lay out the course of a canal from Albany to Lake Erie. Construction on the Erie Canal started in 1817. When the canal was finished in 1825, passengers and cargo could travel by boat or ship from anywhere on the Great Lakes to Buffalo on the eastern shore of Lake Erie, then to Albany by canal, then down the Hudson to New York, the Atlantic, and the world. The Hudson River became a major arterial for U.S. and international trade.

The steam powered boat was soon followed by the steam powered ship. In 1807 sailing ships took from six to 15 weeks, depending on the ever-fickle winds, to travel from the U.S. to England or France. Ocean-going steamships cut the transit time down to just two or three weeks by 1840, then to 10 or 12 days by 1850.[129] By 1880 it was down to a week.[130]

As for Fulton, he got very rich, very fast. Within four years of that first voyage he had several more boats on the water and was earning an annual income of $20,000, a tremendous figure for that era.[131] His business and his fortune continued to grow until his death of pneumonia in 1815.

CHAPTER 7

Cornelius Vanderbilt

———

If they can depend on you, they'll deal with you.

CORNELIUS VANDERBILT

IN THE EARLY TWENTIETH CENTURY no fewer than 14 of the most expensive mansions on New York's swanky Fifth Avenue belonged to members of the Vanderbilt family.[132] Landscape architect Frederick Law Olmsted, who designed the Stanford University campus, the US Capitol grounds, and New York's central park, landscaped Vanderbilt properties.[133] In 1895 a Vanderbilt heiress became an English duchess when the Duke of Marlboro married her for her money.

The Vanderbilts' fortune, like the Astors' was founded by a man who started his career as a working class teenage boy.

Cornelius Vanderbilt was born on Staten Island in New York in 1794, the same year Eli Whitney patented his famous cotton gin in Georgia. Vanderbilt's father, also named Cornelius, farmed a few acres of land for sustenance and ferried people and freight back and forth across the Hudson River to earn what little spending money the family ever had. The older Cornelius was fond of alcohol, and not overly fond of hard work, so the Vanderbilts were never very prosperous.

One of Vanderbilt's biographers described the family estate and income this way:

> Along with the tiny house, the property included a few acres that Cornelius tilled rather unenthusiastically to produce vegetables and grains that were mostly consumed by his own family. Meanwhile, for cash money, he continued his Manhattan runs in the (small sailboat he owned) charging so-much per trip to transport other men's produce and goods.[134]

The Vanderbilt family "sat in wooden furniture hand-cut from hand hewn-lumber" and "wore clothes hand-sewn from hand-spun wool."[135]

When the younger Cornelius was around 11 years of age his father took him out of school for good and put him to work on the little boat.[136] The boy made the business more productive from the moment he entered it. When not working on the boat or helping the older Cornelius salvage the cargos of wrecked ships, he tended the crops on his parents' farm.[137]

In 1810, at the age of 16, Cornelius, who would eventually come to be known as "Commodore" Vanderbilt, bought a small boat of his own for a hundred dollars and went into business for himself.

There are differing stories about how he came up with the money. According to one version he borrowed it from his parents. Another account has it that he formed some sort of partnership with his father until he earned enough to go into business for himself. According to Vanderbilt's own account, related by him many years later, the Commodore's parents agreed to pay him the hundred dollars he needed if, in addition to his other chores, he would clear and fence a wooded and rock-strewn piece of property they owned, and get it to produce a corn crop for the first time.[138]

However he may have done it, all sources agree that Vanderbilt went into the boating business at age 16. Unlike his father, the younger

Vanderbilt was driven to succeed. He took business from other boat operators in the area by going out on the water in weather that kept his competitors at home. He kept his boat full and busy by charging lower prices and soliciting customers aggressively. He developed a reputation for dedication and reliability, qualities that customers found attractive in an industry where boozing and brawling were all too common.[139]

When the military started building fortifications in New York in anticipation of war with England, Vanderbilt took full advantage of the opportunity. He was able to keep his boat fully loaded and in continuous operation for several months hauling building materials, workers, and soldiers.

Like all good businessmen, young Vanderbilt was disciplined and thrifty. Early on he vowed to "spend less every week than he earned."[140] Amazingly, by the age of 19 the ambitious youngster had already saved up enough money to commission a shipyard to build him a 65-foot sloop to replace his little sailboat. When the sloop was ready to launch he hired a couple deck hands to help him sail it.[141]

Vanderbilt was still only 19 when he got married. From the beginning he was a gruff and thoughtless husband.[142] He and Sophia had 13 children, of whom only one died in childhood; a remarkable streak of luck by the standards of that era. But Vanderbilt was not much of a family man. By most accounts Vanderbilt was just as cold to his children as he was to his wife.[143]

In addition to being a poor husband and father, Vanderbilt was irreligious, profane, and for most of his life not very charitable, although he finally started making some significant donations to worthy causes when he was in his sixties and one of the wealthiest men in the world.

The subject of Vanderbilt's personal life invites comparison with the lives of some of the other great movers and shakers of the nineteenth century; John D. Rockefeller in particular. Rockefeller was a devout Baptist and a devoted husband. He always gave generously to charities, even when he was still young and poor.[144] He doted on his children and after a tough day at the office he liked nothing better than to crawl around the floor of his house on all fours with a son or daughter on his back.[145]

Even though the two men's personal lives couldn't have been more different, their business practices were remarkably similar. In contrast to the Commodore's neglectful and harsh treatment of his family, he was absolutely faithful in business deals. Anyone who shook hands with Vanderbilt could count on him to deliver. And as ruthless as he could be with his competition, he never betrayed the trust of a business partner, vendor, or customer. A deal was a deal with Vanderbilt.[146]

Rockefeller, just like Vanderbilt, always dealt honorably with his partners and customers. And just like Vanderbilt he was a ruthless competitor who always played to win. Both men understood the importance of hiring and retaining good people, although Rockefeller was more polite to his employees than the foul-mouthed Commodore.[147]

There were some differences in their styles, however. Rockefeller seems to have had good people skills from his youth. Vanderbilt, on the other hand, was a little slow in developing the communication skills that a person needs to succeed in business. Early in his career he preferred hauling cargo to carrying passengers, because the cargo didn't try to talk to him while he was piloting his boat.[148] Eventually Vanderbilt taught himself how to work with and for people without being rude.

While the teenage Vanderbilt took a while to learn the rules of business etiquette, he did at least offer many other virtues that customers appreciated. He worked long hours seven days a week and constantly looked for ways to increase the efficiency of his operations. He jealously guarded his reputation for dependability.

At the same time, he had a keen eye for opportunities and made strategic moves that almost always succeeded. He lived frugally and re-invested most of his considerable profits in his business. One long-time associate described him as "economical almost to extremes."[149] In 1814, when his sloop had only been in operation for about a year, he commissioned a shipyard to build him three more boats. He took personal command of a schooner that operated mostly on the Hudson River, and hired captains and crews for his original sloop and the two other vessels.[150]

In 1815 the 21-year-old Commodore bought a half interest in a fifth vessel, an ocean-going schooner named the *Charlotte.* This was a good strategic move on his part, because the *Charlotte* was built for the open ocean and the co-owner of the ship was an experienced sea captain. During a trip from New York to Savannah, Vanderbilt absorbed everything his new partner could teach him about commanding a ship on ocean waters.[151]

Vanderbilt excelled at the day-to-day details of running an efficient business, and he was equally adept at foreseeing the future and making good long term strategic decisions. For the first eight years of his career he learned everything he could about nautical transportation, focusing entirely on sail-powered sloops and schooners. Then, around 1818, he sold off his whole fleet, put the proceeds in a bank account, and accepted a job as captain of a steamboat owned by an entrepreneur named Thomas Gibbons.

Vanderbilt's initial salary was a fraction of what he'd been making running his own business, but in light of subsequent events it's easy to understand why he made the move. He was thinking of the future.

Great entrepreneurs tend to have much in common. There are certain characteristics that mark virtually all the great success stories in American history. All the great self-made men worked very hard and refused to be discouraged by failure. All were keen students who worked hard at developing their mental faculties. All were decisive. All of them understood that the most important resources are human resources.

It's also true that some of these men, those like Vanderbilt whose wealth would eventually reach absolutely fantastic levels, had an ability to see the future of an industry, and make appropriate strategic moves based on that vision. (Thomas Edison once said of Henry Ford "Ford's foresight is so long it sags in the middle.")[152] This kind of vision is what led Rockefeller to build tanker cars when the railroads were unwilling to build them. It's what led Carnegie to make each of his timely changes of focus. And it's what led Vanderbilt to walk away from his own successful business in 1818 to become one of Thomas Gibbons' employees.

(On a humorous note, it also seems to help to have a father whose first name is William. In the nineteenth century William Carnegie, William Rockefeller, and William Ford each had a son who started with nothing and eventually became the richest man in the world. In the twentieth century William Gates Jr. had a son who eventually achieved the same distinction, although Bill Gates III didn't have to overcome childhood poverty to achieve that status.)

When Vanderbilt accepted a job in Gibbons' company it was a good strategic move for several reasons. First, Vanderbilt could see that steamboats were the wave of the future and the sail-powered vessels he'd been operating were eventually going to become obsolete. Gibbons' fleet was all steam. Beyond that, Gibbons was a much older and more experienced businessman, who had achieved great success in several different businesses in three different states. Vanderbilt later described Gibbons as "one of the strongest-minded men I was ever acquainted with."[153] Even though Vanderbilt was already a successful businessman in his own right, he was apparently able to learn a good deal from the older man during the years he worked for him.

Gibbons was also an experienced lawyer, able to fight the legal and political battles that were a necessary part of the steamboat business in those early days. The heirs of Robert Fulton and Robert Livingston, who had both died by 1818, still held a government monopoly on most of the steamboat routes to, from, and around New York City; Gibbons was battling in court and on the water to establish himself as a player in the business. Vanderbilt could see that if he was to make a transition from sail to steam he would have to either leave the New York area or align himself with the Fulton heirs or someone like Thomas Gibbons.

Initially Gibbons paid Vanderbilt only 60 dollars a month to captain a single steamboat, but as the Commodore proved his merit his role in the company grew. Soon Mrs. Vanderbilt was running a Gibbons-owned hotel in New Jersey while the Commodore managed all of the day-to-day business of Gibbons' nautical operations.

In the fall of 1819 the Fulton heirs and their partners offered Vanderbilt a salary of $5,000 per year to bring his talents and his work ethic over to their side. While this was roughly a 25 percent increase over what Gibbons was paying him at that time, Vanderbilt remained loyal to Gibbons.

By 1824, according to a Vanderbilt biographer, "In addition to commanding the *Thistle*, (Vanderbilt) had the captains of the *Bellona* and *Mouse* reporting to him. It was Vanderbilt who set the schedules and fares for all the boats, administered the budgets, managed the food and drink service on the various boats, and made sure the craft were maintained properly. Vanderbilt also hired and fired crew members, negotiated the purchase of wood for fuel, and arranged advertising in New York and New Jersey newspapers."[154] Vanderbilt also helped design each new boat Gibbons commissioned, and oversaw the construction of each craft as it was being built.

That same year the U.S. Supreme Court ruled in favor of Gibbons and his company, ending the Livingston monopoly on steamboat routes between New York and New Jersey. This decision invited new competition to the field, but Vanderbilt and Gibbons kept a large share of the market by operating more efficiently than their competitors and cutting prices to attract passengers.

In May of 1826 Thomas Gibbons died, leaving everything to his son William, who lived in Georgia. With an absentee owner, Vanderbilt's management role in the company became even more important. Less than two years later William Gibbons made it known in New York that he would sell the steamboat business to any interested buyer for $400,000. Vanderbilt, who had apparently been interested in buying at least a part interest in the company himself, informed anyone who might be interested in buying that he would resign the minute the business was sold.

Vanderbilt was the most valuable resource the company had, so his ultimatum drove off any potential buyers. Vanderbilt then commissioned a shipyard to build him a steamboat of his own, and continued working for William Gibbons while the boat was being built. When it was nearly completed he resigned his position with Gibbons. When the new boat was launched in early 1829 Vanderbilt was 34 years old. The Commodore went into business for himself for the first time in 10 years. He would never work for a paycheck again.

Meanwhile the New York area steamboat business continued to be just as fiercely competitive as it had ever been. Without Vanderbilt's management skills, William Gibbons soon found himself unable to compete. His steamboat business started hemorrhaging money and he had to shut it down. Vanderbilt bought two of Gibbons' boats at fire sale prices and hired skippers for them, increasing his total fleet from one boat to three. He called his new company the Dispatch Line.

Vanderbilt put one of his three boats into service on the Delaware River, hauling passengers between Philadelphia, PA and Trenton, New Jersey. He formed partnerships with several stagecoach companies that could transport passengers from Trenton to New Brunswick, NJ, where his other boats would pick them up for transport to various New York area destinations. In offering through passage from Philadelphia to New York he put himself in the middle of a price war with the Union Line, a steamboat line owned by John Stevens, brother-in-law and onetime partner of the now-deceased Robert Livingston.

By the time Thomas Gibbons' lawsuit overturned the Livingston heirs' monopoly on Hudson River steamboating, several different shipyards were able to build viable steamboats, and Stevens and his family purchased several boats and went into business on a large scale. The Union Line had its own assets running stagecoaches between the Delaware River and the Hudson, and they were offering Philadelphia-to-New York tickets before Vanderbilt.

The competition between Vanderbilt's Dispatch Line and the Stevens family's Union Line created some great deals for their customers. Soon a passenger could take a steamboat upriver from Philadelphia, transfer to a stagecoach for the ride overland to the Hudson estuary, and then transfer to a second steamboat for the final trip to New York; all for a total cost of one dollar.[155]

By coincidence 1829 was also the year Englishman George Stephenson's steam powered locomotive the *Rocket* first demonstrated its ability to haul freight and passengers over the Manchester-to-Liverpool railroad Stephenson was building. The railroad went into full operation in 1830. Stephenson was not the first inventor to put together a steam-powered vehicle that could chug around a track in front of a few witnesses; that honor goes to Stephenson's fellow Englishman Richard Travithick, who demonstrated his locomotive way back in 1804. Other inventors experimented with locomotives, with limited success, throughout the early nineteenth century. The significance of Stephenson's *Rocket* is that it could, and did, operate profitably.

(A hundred years after the *Rocket* was first demonstrated, Stephenson's company built an exact replica of the historic vehicle for Henry Ford. It can be seen today at the Henry Ford Museum in Dearborn, MI.)

American John Stevens, the founder of the Union Line and Vanderbilt's bitter rival in the transportation business, was one of the inventors who were trying to make railroading a practical reality when George Stephenson beat them all to the punch. Stevens was investing his time and money in the railroad business long before Vanderbilt showed any interest in railroading. As early as 1815 he had obtained a charter from the State of New Jersey to put a line between Trenton and New Brunswick; the overland leg of that Philadelphia to New York route. By 1825 he had built a railroad around his large New Jersey estate, and was able to demonstrate an experimental locomotive of his own design.[156]

Vanderbilt, who would eventually become the most powerful figure in the American railroad industry, was still focusing all his attention on the steamboat business. His price war was so ruinous to John Stevens' business that in 1830 Stevens actually agreed to start paying Vanderbilt to keep his boats out of the Philadelphia to New York routes. Today it's illegal for anyone but the government to pay companies not to conduct their business (the federal government has been paying certain agricultural companies not to grow their crops since the 1930s), but in 1830 it was perfectly legal for businesses to bribe their rivals to leave them alone.

Vanderbilt used the money he was getting from Stevens to pay for a fourth boat for his fleet, and concentrated all his boats on Hudson River routes.

As a fleet owner, the Commodore always took care to hire and retain competent and reliable captains to operate his vessels. Many of his most dependable captains came from his own family. His brother Jacob, who had captained a sailing sloop for him during his pre-steam days, was a competitor in 1829 and 1830, but Cornelius bought a partnership with him in '31. Cousin John Vanderbilt operated a steamboat on the Hudson for Cornelius for years.

A steamboat captain named Noah Brooks gave Vanderbilt an opportunity to show how highly he valued his top human resources when the Commodore decided to violate convention by operating his boats on Sundays. Brooks, a devout Christian, felt bound by Exodus 20:10 to abstain from work on the Sabbath. Brooks knew the irreligious Vanderbilt would not be swayed by Bible-based arguments, so when the Commodore announced his new seven day workweek Brooks handed in his resignation.

Brooks was an extremely competent and responsible captain, and Vanderbilt soon decided that Brooks was too valuable to lose. He approached Brooks, agreed to allow the captain to honor the Sabbath, and offered him a pay raise. Brooks accepted the offer.[157]

This meritocratic attitude toward his workforce was something Vanderbilt shared with all very successful businessmen. Success in running an advertising agency, according to industry giant David Ogilvy, "depends on your ability to hire men and women of exceptional talent, to train them thoroughly, and to make the most of their talents." Whenever Ogilvy promoted someone to a management position, he gave the new manager a set of Russian nesting dolls with a message inside the smallest doll: "If each of us hires people who are smaller than we are, we shall become a company of dwarfs. But if each of us hires people who are bigger than we are, Ogilvy and Mather shall become a company of giants."[158]

Walmart founder Sam Walton, who like Carnegie and Rockefeller rose from childhood poverty to become the richest man in the world, sometimes went to great lengths to hire employees he coveted away from his competitors. When he identified someone as the kind of worker he wanted, he would apply all his legendary salesmanship, along with a package of performance-based financial incentives, to pull the human resource away from his competition. In his autobiography he describes one case where he courted a certain talented manager for nearly 20 years before finally persuading him to join the Walmart family.[159]

In the early 1830s Vanderbilt deployed his fleet of steamboats, and his roster of hand-picked captains, from New York City to points farther up the Hudson River. First he squeezed out the competition on the New York-to-Peekskill route, then he started competing with a trust called the Hudson River Steamboat Association that had controlled the Manhattan-to-Albany route. The association was made up of steamboat owners who cooperated with each other to divide up the market and keep fares artificially high. This was long before the Sherman Anti-Trust Act, and it was perfectly legal for a cabal of steamship owners to collude in this way. The association offered Vanderbilt a chance to join, but he chose to start a price war with the association members instead.

John Stevens' sons, who were still bribing Vanderbilt to stay out of the Philadelphia market, were members of the association. By December of 1834 the Stevens family and the other association members approached Vanderbilt and negotiated yet another bribe for noncompetition. They agreed to pay him $50,000 up front and $10,000 per year to stay out of the upper Hudson market for 10 years.

These cases of steamboat companies paying a competitor not to do business are something of an anomaly in the history of American business. Nothing like it happened in the careers of any of the other figures profiled in this book. And while Vanderbilt was sometimes willing to accept such payments, it's worth noting that he never offered to make the payments to anyone else. He was probably a good enough businessman to realize that it was a poor strategic move.

Vanderbilt was not one to sit around idle, even when someone was paying him to. While his competitors were bribing him not to do business in the Hudson and Delaware rivers he deployed his ever-growing fleet of steamboats in Long Island Sound and up and down the Atlantic Coast.

In 1833 Vanderbilt took his first ride on a railroad train, on the Camden and Amboy line owned and operated by John Stevens. An axle broke and the car in which Vanderbilt was riding overturned. Two men were killed and several were injured. Vanderbilt suffered three broken ribs and a punctured lung and spent the next several months convalescing, but the bad experience didn't dissuade him from entering the railroad business a few years later.

It seems incredible, in this era of safe and convenient travel, that nineteenth century travelers were willing to risk life and limb to reach their destinations, but it's certainly true. Vanderbilt was not the only famous person who suffered a traumatic incident involving train travel. In 1853, when newly elected U.S. President Franklin Pierce was traveling to the nation's capital to be inaugurated, the train carrying him and his family derailed and his 11-year-old son was killed right in front of him. In 1867 John D. Rockefeller arrived at a train station late and just missed his train. The train, which had Rockefeller's luggage on it, crashed, and several passengers were killed. Rockefeller wrote to his wife that he thought it was God's providence that made him miss the train.[160]

When Andrew Carnegie was a manager with the Pennsylvania Railroad in the 1860s, train wrecks were so common that organizing work parties to get the wreckage off the tracks was a major part of his regular duties. To clear the tracks and keep traffic flowing, Carnegie would often have his crews burn the wrecked trains where they lay.[161]

The dangers of nineteenth century travel were not confined to the railroads. Shipwrecks were common in the 1800s, as were lethal boiler explosions on steamboats. Stagecoaches were brutally uncomfortable, often overturned, and were attacked by armed robbers with frightening frequency.[162] That nineteenth century Americans endured what they did to get from one place to another shows how important travel has always been to the human race.

BOATS AND TRAINS

In 1835, the year Andrew Carnegie was born in Scotland, Vanderbilt started offering steamboat service up Long Island Sound from New

York City to Providence, Rhode Island, in anticipation of the completion of a railroad from Providence to Boston later that year. Passengers would be able to travel up to Providence on one of his boats and then transfer to a train to continue on to Boston. His competitor for this business was the Boston and New York Transportation Company (B&NY), which operated six small steamboats in the sound. This time, instead of launching into a price war, Vanderbilt decided to collude with the competition to keep prices high. He and the B&NY agreed on a price of eight dollars for one-way service between New York and Providence.

When the railroad was extended farther south, Vanderbilt and the B&NY shortened their boat routes accordingly, always with the intention of complimenting, rather than competing with, the railroad.

Over the next few years Vanderbilt kept a close eye on the railroad construction, deftly shifting his routes to avoid competing with the iron horse, and targeting incomplete railroad connections that could be completed by his boats. In 1844 he accepted a seat on the board of directors of the Long Island Railroad, his first official connection to a railroad company. Soon after that the Long Island bought two of Vanderbilt's boats for use as a connecting link between their own road and another railroad along that New York to Boston route.[163]

In 1845 Vanderbilt teamed up with investor Daniel Drew to buy a controlling interest in the Providence and Stonington Railroad, which connected with his steamboats from upper Long Island. Drew was the typical rags-to-riches story; he'd left his parents' farm in childhood to take a job as a circus "roustabout," feeding the animals and putting up and taking down the circus tents. At 14 he somehow joined the U.S. Army for a time, then, still a teenager, he went into business buying cattle in rural New York and driving them into the city for sale.[164] Drew, unlike Vanderbilt, was sometimes unscrupulous in his business practices, and the two of them would have a complex relationship over the years.

By the late 1840s the Commodore could see that trains would eventually replace steamboats on virtually all of his routes in the Northeast, and he began to sell off his boats to investors less far-sighted than himself. One exception was the Staten Island Ferry, which the Commodore continued to own and operate for several years, reasoning quite rightly that he wouldn't have to worry about competition from the railroads on that route.

When the Great California Gold Rush began in 1849, Vanderbilt quickly realized that there was a fortune to be made in transporting people, supplies, and gold bullion between New York and San Francisco. Railroads were not an option; the nation's east and west coasts would not be connected by rail for another 20 years. Vanderbilt commissioned the construction of several oceangoing steamships.

Competitors were bringing their passengers to eastern Panama, guiding them across the isthmus, then putting them on ships on the western shore for transport up to California. Vanderbilt identified a route about 500 sea miles shorter, crossing the isthmus in Nicaragua. He formed a publicly traded corporation called Accessory Transit and made plans to bring steam powered riverboats to eastern Nicaragua to travel 120 miles up the San Juan River, then 110 miles across stormy Lake Nicaragua to the western shore of the lake; a point just 12 miles from the shores of the Pacific Ocean.[165] A short 12-mile overland trip in horse-drawn wagons would then allow his customers to board a second steamship for the trip to San Francisco. Steamships that Vanderbilt owned under a separate company traveled between Nicaragua and San Francisco and between Nicaragua and New York. The steamboats that would operate on the river and in the lake were to be leased by Accessory Transit from Vanderbilt's private company.

Getting steamboats up the San Juan River was not going to be easy. The river was full of boulders and rapids that made navigation difficult and dangerous. In January of 1851 Vanderbilt arrived at the mouth of the river to explore the situation for himself. Seven days earlier a captain in his employ had started up the river in one of his steamboats, and it was unknown whether that captain had been able to reach the lake. Vanderbilt took command of the steamboat *Orus*, and headed up the river himself; only the second boat captain to attempt the journey. To power his way through particularly difficult stretches of rapids the Commodore built up the pressure in his engine by disabling the safety valve. After six days he reached the lake. Soon he would task a team of engineers with blasting the boulders out of the worst stretches of rapids, to make the trip less dangerous for his subordinates than it had been for himself.

Having seen the river for himself, he had two boats specially designed for the passage, with shallow draft and iron hulls. In July he brought one of them to the mouth of the river and, again, assigned himself the challenging task of getting the boat up the river. On the way upstream he steamed past the hulk of the *Orus*, which one of his captains had wrecked on the rocks after the Commodore's last visit.

By this time it had become apparent that Lake Nicaragua offered a whole different set of challenges. With over three thousand square miles of surface area, the lake was subject to violent storms that could capsize shallow draft riverboats. Vanderbilt resolved to get a deep draft lake boat up through the river's treacherous rapids and, again, he assigned himself the task. On November 2 the 57-year-old Commodore, one of the wealthiest men in the world, took the wheel of the 375-ton deep draft steamboat *Central America* and started up the river. He arrived at Lake Nicaragua 17 days later.[166]

Vanderbilt was not a timid man; he had a long track record of settling arguments with his fists, [167] and captaining his own vessels in all sorts of weather on all sorts of waters, so his macho approach to the problem of San Juan River navigation surprised no one who knew him.

The riverboats and horse-drawn wagons worked well enough for Vanderbilt to make a million-dollar-a-year-profit from his San

Francisco line in the short run, but his long range plan was to build a canal across Nicaragua. Meanwhile, doing business in any form in Nicaragua required the cooperation of the local government. Instead of offering a flat fee for access, Accessory Transit contracted to pay the Nicaraguan government a percentage of its profits each year, thus giving the government incentive to facilitate the company's profitable operation.

In 1853 Vanderbilt took his first real vacation. The ship he had built for the occasion was the largest steamship in the world at that time, and cost half a million dollars. He took his whole family and the families of several friends and toured Europe for several months.

When he returned to the U.S. he learned that two of the officers in Accessory Transit had staged a coup of sorts. Charles Morgan and Cornelius Garrison, both board members chosen by Vanderbilt himself, had conspired in his absence to take over the company and run it for their own personal benefit. They added several cronies to the board and arranged a vote to make Morgan the president of the company. Morgan then suspended the payments Accessory Transit was supposed to make to Vanderbilt's privately owned company for the use of his steamboats.

Cornelius Vanderbilt always regarded business deals as sacred. When Morgan and Garrison violated his trust he reacted with rage. According to some accounts he actually took out ads in New York newspapers to warn Morgan and Garrison that he intended to financially ruin them.[168]

Step one in the Commodore's war against Morgan and Garrison was to sell off all his shares in Accessory Transit in preparation for his assault on the company's business. He then put his considerable assets to work competing with his two enemies. Leaving Nicaragua and its unstable political climate to his rivals, he ran his gold rush steamships to and from Panama. Despite the greater distances involved, his faster ships allowed him to offer passengers a quicker trip between New

York and San Francisco than Garrison and Morgan could manage. The efficiency of his operations, combined with his deep pockets, allowed him to price tickets at levels ruinous to Morgan and Garrison.

In the summer of 1854 Morgan, as president of Accessory Transit, agreed to pay off all of Vanderbilt's financial claims against the company. Still not satisfied, Vanderbilt got a court order forbidding Accessory Transit to enter into any contracts with other companies owned by Morgan and Garrison. The resulting plunge in the value of Accessory Transit shares allowed Vanderbilt to buy up a large enough block to take back control of the company and force out Morgan and Garrison in December of 1855. Vanderbilt made himself president of the firm early in 1856.

While all this was going on the political situation in Nicaragua was becoming more and more complicated. In May of 1855 an American-born adventurer named William Walker went to Nicaragua with a small private army, formed an alliance with one of the warring local political parties, and seized control of the country. Garrison and Morgan made a financial arrangement with Nicaragua's new dictator while they were still in control of Accessory Transit.

When Vanderbilt got control of Accessory Transit later that year his enemies quickly formed a new company and persuaded the dictator to seize all the assets of Accessory Transit on land and in Nicaraguan waters and give them to the Garrison and Morgan company. They supplemented this property with a few steamships they legitimately owned and went back into the New York-to-San Francisco transportation business.

Vanderbilt asked the U.S. Government to help him recover his stolen property, but no meaningful help was to be had from that quarter. Left to his own devices, he quickly resumed his economic war. He deployed several Vanderbilt steamships in the Gulf of Mexico, where Morgan was operating a shipping company unrelated to Accessory Transit. Prior to this Vanderbilt had never had business interests in the gulf, but war is war, and he was determined not to allow any Morgan-owned business to operate profitably anywhere.

Costa Rica had declared war against Nicaragua shortly after William Walker took over the country. When Walker aligned himself with Vanderbilt's enemies, Vanderbilt aligned himself with Costa Rica, and his support would prove decisive. Armed and funded by Vanderbilt, Costa Rica was able to conquer Nicaragua and take Walker into custody by May 1 of 1857.

While the war was going on, the Commodore ran ads in American newspapers warning would-be travelers that Nicaragua was a dangerous war zone. New York-to-San Francisco travelers chose the much-safer isthmus crossing in Panama. Revisiting an old theme, Vanderbilt extorted payments from the companies doing business on the Panama route by threatening to compete with them. In the gulf Vanderbilt was cutting prices below his operating costs, which were lower than Morgan's. Morgan and Garrison were bleeding money in every direction. By December of 1857 Morgan and Garrison were, in fact, virtually ruined.[169]

ACROSS THE ATLANTIC

In April of 1855, in the middle of his feud with Garrison and Morgan, Vanderbilt announced the opening of a trans-Atlantic ship line which he called the European Line. His ongoing fight over Accessory Transit may have made the Commodore a little gun-shy about publicly traded companies; he created the European Line as a private company. Although the great majority of Atlantic traffic was still being carried by sailing ships at that time, the forward-looking Vanderbilt focused exclusively on steamships for this venture.[170]

Vanderbilt was not by any means a pioneer in the trans-Atlantic steamship business. The first ocean-going steamship in history was the *Savannah,* launched by a group of Southern investors in 1819.

Like all the steamships that would follow over the next few years the *Savannah* was a hybrid; it had a mast with a few sails to take advantage of favorable winds and supplement the power of the steam engine. The ship was a failure; it was converted to pure sail power right after its first round trip across the Atlantic.[171]

More practical steamships would take up the route starting in 1839. In 1840 Canadian Samuel Cunard launched his Cunard Line which is still in business today, having been purchase by Carnival Cruise Lines in 1998. After 1840 steam-powered vessels would gradually take market share away from the sailing lines, until steamships came to completely dominate after the Civil War.

The Cunard Line enjoyed a large financial subsidy from the English government, and Vanderbilt was initially reluctant to compete with it. In 1845 the U.S. Government offered an even larger subsidy to American steamship lines that would agree to carry U.S. Mail to and from Europe, and a couple of small one-ship lines were formed to take advantage of the offer. In 1850 American Edward Collins opened his Collins Line with three ships operating between New York and Liverpool, in direct competition with the Cunard Line.

The trans-Atlantic shipping business didn't look ripe to Vanderbilt until 1855. As in all his other ventures, the Commodore waited to enter the market until the commercial potential was proven, then used state of the art technology and astute management to squeeze out a profit at the expense of his competitors. In 1854, as he was preparing to enter the fray, he made it publicly known that he was willing to operate a trans-Atlantic steamship line on a government subsidy of less than half of what Collins was getting.[172]

Collins came to Vanderbilt's office for a meeting in November of 1854, and urged the Commodore to ask the government for at least as big a subsidy ($33,000 per trip) as he was getting. When Collins told him that it would be impossible to turn a profit without the large subsidies he was getting, Vanderbilt was characteristically rude in reply.

"Then you have got into a business that you don't understand," said the Commodore. The meeting ended on that note.[173]

Confident in the ability of his ships and captains to operate more efficiently than the Collins Line, Vanderbilt penned a letter to the U.S. Postmaster General in February of 1855, in which he offered to carry the mail for a subsidy of only $15,000 per voyage.

Government officials, then as now, made their decisions for political reasons. Collins' cronies in the U.S. Congress voted to ignore the good deal Vanderbilt was offering the taxpayers, and continue the much larger payout to Collins. President Pierce vetoed the cash-for-Collins bill, saying that it violated "the soundest principles of public policy." When the Congress maneuvered around the president's veto to maintain Collins' subsidy, Vanderbilt went into business without government support of any kind.[174]

To avoid direct competition with Britain's Cunard Line, the Commodore eschewed British ports and ran his ships between New York and Le Havre, a French port city just a few miles northeast of where the D-Day Invasion would land during World War II. Despite the lack of a subsidy, he undercut Collins' prices. His ships crossed the Atlantic faster than Collins'. Business was brisk from the beginning.

Many of the ships operated by Vanderbilt's British competitors had iron hulls.[175] It's a common misconception that the Monitor and the Merrimack, the two Civil War battleships that fought their famous naval battle in 1862, were the first two iron clad ships in maritime history. (In his *History of the English Speaking Peoples*, Winston Churchill said that as soon as news of the battle of the ironclads reached Europe "it was realized that all the war-fleets of the world were obsolete.")[176]

What really made the Monitor and Merrimack significant is that they were the first military vessels to utilize thick iron armor to protect them in battle. Iron-hulled commercial vessels had been steaming across the oceans for many years before the two ironclads fought their famous battle. In 1839, the same year John D. Rockefeller was born in a two room shack in a small town in New York, an iron-hulled commercial vessel crossed the Atlantic for the first time. By the time the Commodore entered the trans-Atlantic trade in the late 1850s iron-hulled steamships were starting to become fairly common. Unfortunately for Vanderbilt, his ocean-going ships had to make do with wooden hulls, because American iron foundries were not yet able to produce the very large sheets of iron needed for ship construction.

In August of 1856 the political winds finally started blowing against Edward Collins; Congress notified him that it would cancel his subsidy in six months. In February of the next year the government terminated Collins' subsidy and entered into a contract with Vanderbilt for delivery of the mail. The Collins Line stopped operating almost immediately. In 1858 all the assets of the Collins Line were sold at a sheriff's auction, the proceeds going to the company's creditors. With less competition, Vanderbilt's European Line really began to prosper.

From Ships to Trains

In 1857 Vanderbilt joined the board of directors of the New York and Harlem Railroad, in which he was already a major stockholder. By this time he held significant blocks of stock in several other railroads as well. For several more years he would divide his time between shipping and rail, but with an ever-growing emphasis on rail.

As he had done in all his other ventures he did his research, gave himself a clear understanding of the fundamental issues involved, and made wise strategic moves. Piece by piece he assembled a network of roads that gave him control over much of the rail traffic in the Northeast and Midwest. He put quality human resources in key positions on each of the routes he controlled and managed everything carefully.

He started right at home in New York. He bought a controlling interest in the New York and Harlem Railroad largely because it had a monopoly position in downtown Manhattan. The New York and Harlem Railroad (NY&H) also held a network of steam and horse powered trolleys that carried local traffic and connected with the railroad. He bought enough shares to make himself president of the Hudson River Railroad, which ran north from Manhattan to Albany. He gained control of the New York Central, which ran west from Albany to Buffalo, on the shores of Lake Erie. When connected to his other railroads the New York Central allowed direct rail access from Manhattan to Buffalo, establishing a rail connection between the Great Lakes and the city of New York.

Over the years he bought controlling interests in other railroads throughout several Northeastern and Great Lakes states, always with an eye for strategically important links. Eventually he made the New York Central a holding company for all his railroad interests.

As Vanderbilt increased his role in the railroad industry he continued to play a role in the shipping industry as well, although his shipping interests gradually declined. During the Civil War he donated a steamship worth nearly a million dollars to the Union navy in response to a personal appeal from President Lincoln. Vanderbilt had the ship refitted for wartime duty in his own shipyard in New York, and it performed admirably in protecting Union shipping from attacks by the Confederate navy over the next couple years.[177]

In 1863 Cornelius Vanderbilt promoted his son William to Vice President of the NY&H, with broad authority to control its day-to-day operations. William by all accounts proved a more than capable manager. As William proved his merit, Cornelius gradually gave him greater and greater responsibilities in his railroad ventures. Eventually, as the elder Vanderbilt eased into retirement, William would come to be the de facto head of the Vanderbilt empire.

Vanderbilt was not the only American who could see the importance of railroading to the nation's future. As the iron horse gradually made other modes of transportation obsolete, businessmen and politicians struggled for control of the lines. Frequently the methods used were less than honest.

Shortly after Vanderbilt started investing heavily in the New York and Harlem, he spotted an opportunity to increase his holdings and strike a blow for honest governance at the same time. Politicians of that era, like politicians of today, billed themselves as "public servants," but frequently used their power to line their own pockets. In 1863 most of the members of the New York City Council joined in a conspiracy to manipulate the price of the New York and Harlem for their own benefit. The cabal was led by William M. "Boss" Tweed, an utterly unscrupulous political power broker who would spend several years distributing bribes and stuffing ballot boxes for New York's Democratic Party machine before going to prison for larceny in 1873.

Tweed and his cronies quietly short-sold New York and Harlem stock when it was selling at around $100 a share, then voted to rescind the railroad's license to lay tracks and operate horse-drawn trolleys in the city. The trolley network was so important to the company's financial prospects that the councilmen expected their denial to send the stock price crashing down, thus allowing them to redeem their shorts for a quick profit. Vanderbilt, who had gotten wind of the scheme, started buying up every NY&H share that came on the market. With his considerable financial resources he was able to drive the share price up to any level he chose.

In 1863, as today, every short sale involved a time limit. When time runs out the short seller has to redeem the shares he shorted, no matter how much the redeeming shares might cost. Failing to redeem the shares was a crime and the punishment was prison. As the time limit for their shorted NY&H shares approached the corrupt politicians could only beg Vanderbilt to stop buying and sell them the shares they needed. After the council re-instated the trolley license, Vanderbilt finally agreed to sell the needed shares at $180, a loss to the councilmen of about 80 dollars a share. The Commodore made a five million dollar profit on the shares he sold the conspirators, and increased his holdings in a stock he wanted to own anyway.[178]

Amazingly, in 1864 a group of New York State legislators tried the same trick that had backfired so disastrously for the New York City Council members the previous year. They publicly committed to grant the New York and Harlem a license it needed, thus driving the price up to around $150 per share, then short sold the stock right before the vote on the license. They denied the license they'd been promising to grant, then waited for the shares to plummet. The legislators would pay a steep price for their hubris.

As before, Vanderbilt and a few rich friends bought NY&H shares en mass. One of the investors helping Vanderbilt bid up the shares was a businessman named Leonard Jerome, whose ten-year-old daughter Jennie would eventually grow up, marry an English Lord, and give birth to future Prime Minister Winston Churchill.

By the time the shorts were due the poorer-but-wiser politicians had agreed to grant the road its license, and the Commodore allowed them to buy their redeeming shares at $285. Many of them lost their homes. Vanderbilt made a two million dollar profit, to go with the five million he had taken from Boss Tweed and the city councilmen.[179]

In the middle of his battle with the state legislators the Commodore celebrated his seventieth birthday. He had been a major power broker in New York business for decades. The son of a poor Staten Island farmer had earned so much, and learned so much, that he could get the better of a business deal even when his rivals controlled the state government.

For many years Vanderbilt was the wealthiest man in the United States. When he died in 1877 at the age of 82, he left an estate valued at over one hundred million dollars. By this time his son William had been actively managing the Vanderbilt lines for some time, and the Vanderbilt name would continue to be a major factor in the railroad business for the rest of the century and beyond.

CHAPTER 8

A Brief History of Railroading in the United States

___

Nature and circumstance concurred to make the inhabitants of America bold men, as is sufficiently attested by the enterprising spirit with which they seek for fortune.

ALEXIS DE TOCQUEVILLE.

FROM THE 1830S THROUGH THE early years of the twentieth century the driving force in American business was the railroad, and almost all the most important figures in that industry, as in every other industry in America, were men who started out in life with nothing. Virtually all of the players named in this chapter were self-made men. Their biographies will be sketched out in brief at the end of the chapter.

EARLY TRANSPORTATION IN THE U.S.

Transportation has always been a central issue in the development of every society, and it was the central issue in American business long before the railroad train was developed. Before the American Revolution, transportation primarily meant ocean-going ships. After the colonies gained their independence, U.S.-flagged ships carried cotton and other raw materials to foreign ports and brought manufactured goods – and poor immigrants – back to America. Yankee "clipper ships," long and sleek and carrying multiple masts crowded with sails, were soon setting speed records carrying freight and passengers across the Atlantic and around the Horn to Asia. By the 1830s steam-powered ships, made in America and evolved from Robert Fulton's original design, were beginning to replace sailing ships on the world's oceans. Many men made their fortunes operating steam-powered boats and ships, and of course Vanderbilt was the most successful of them.

In those early years intra-U.S. travel happened almost exclusively along water routes. Small ships moved up and down the Atlantic coast from north to south, and people moved from east to west by paddling canoes or other small boats up the rivers and streams. The few dirt roads being built in the fledgling republic were generally poor; many were so muddy and soft as to be impassible during the winter months.

As late as 1844, overland transportation was so difficult that when a farmer near Cincinnati ordered a mechanical harvester from Cyrus McCormick's factory in Scottsville, Virginia, a mere 450 miles away by land, the machine had to be sent to McCormick's customer by a series of boats and an ocean-going ship, covering a total distance of over 2,500 miles. The harvester traveled by canal and riverboat to the Atlantic Ocean, then by ship down the Atlantic coast, through the passage between Florida and Cuba, and west through the Gulf of Mexico to New Orleans, then by steamboat up the Mississippi River to Illinois, then up the Ohio River to Cincinnati.[180]

The first serious threat to the nation's survival, the infamous "Whiskey Rebellion" of the early 1790s, was an indirect result of the transportation problems of that era. In 1791 President Washington signed a bill implementing a tax on distilled spirits. The tax was loathed in the area around Pittsburgh in western Pennsylvania, where virtually all of the farmers operated whiskey distilleries and depended on the whiskey business for most of their cash income.

The farmers organized a militia of sorts and renounced the authority of the federal government. In response, President Washington put on his military uniform and personally led an army of 13,000 men across Pennsylvania to put down the rebellion. After the rebellion was broken, and a couple of its leaders were convicted of treason, Washington pardoned the convicted men. In 1802 President Jefferson signed a bill repealing the federal whiskey tax.

The primitive state of transportation in the U.S. was the reason western Pennsylvania farmers depended so heavily on whiskey sales for their hard currency, and an indirect cause of the rebellion. There was no navigable river running eastward from Pittsburgh toward Philadelphia and the Atlantic, and transporting perishable food crops in horse-drawn wagons over 300 miles of muddy roads during the harvest season was not a viable option. Farm families ate their own crops at their own tables and converted their excess grain into whiskey, which could be stored for long periods and transported easily.

If the farmers of western Pennsylvania had had a viable way of getting their grain to market, they wouldn't have been so dependent on the liquor business for their cash income and the Whiskey Rebellion quite probably would never have happened.

Until the four corners of the nation were connected by a network of railroad tracks, overland transportation continued to be difficult, dangerous, and expensive. There were, however, a few intrepid entrepreneurs who made their fortunes running stage coach lines and freight services, particularly in the western states. Jesse Chisholm, after whom the famous Chisholm Trail was named, is one example. Chisholm ran freight wagons between various frontier trading posts from the early 1830s to the mid 1860s.[181] His freight wagons moved slowly and carried non-perishable items like tools, weapons, blankets, and animal pelts.

By the 1820s steamboats operating on the Ohio River allowed Pittsburgh area farmers to send their crops to the sparsely-populated areas to the west and south, but Philadelphia and the Atlantic sea-board were still out of reach. Without easy access to the eastern markets, many western Pennsylvania farmers continued to find it more economically viable to convert their crops to hard liquor.

THE CANAL ERA

Having harnessed the power of the steam engine to boats and ships, Americans spent the first half of the 1800s building canals to facilitate water transportation on routes where God hadn't seen fit to put navigable rivers. In four or five decades over three thousand miles of canals were dug, one shovel-full at a time, by an army of men who had never seen a diesel-powered bulldozer or excavator. The most important of these was the Erie Canal, which upon its completion in 1825 connected the Great Lakes to the Hudson River, and via the Hudson to the shipping ports of New York. Before the Erie Canal opened Philadelphia was the nation's leading seaport, with New York and Boston roughly tied for second place. By opening up the Great Lakes states to the European market the Erie Canal almost immediately made New York City the nation's leading seaport.[182] As new technologies like John Deere's steel plow and Cyrus McCormick's mechanical harvester increased the productivity of American farming, grain shipments through the Erie Canal multiplied rapidly.

Canals were constructed by private sector companies on rights of way granted by the state governments, or, in some cases, constructed by the states themselves (the Erie Canal was built by the State of New York). When private corporations built canals the business model was to borrow the large amount of money required for the construction, then repay the debt from revenues earned after the canal opened.

The beginning of the end of the era of canals came in 1830, when the railroad era began. The first two commercially successful railroads in world history were the Liverpool and Manchester Railway

(L&M) in England, and the Baltimore and Ohio Railroad (B&O) in the United States. (The English road is famous in history as the world's first working railroad because of a series of demonstrations that took place in 1829, before the owners of the B&O had come up with a viable locomotive design.) Rail transportation quickly became extremely important to the English and European economies, and even more important in the United States, where it was nothing less than transformative. The railroads gave American farmers fast, cheap, and relatively safe access to customers throughout the nation and across the Atlantic.

Establishing a pattern that would continue throughout the nineteenth century, these early railroads created business for themselves as soon as they opened. It was discovered that the mere availability of a railroad caused people in the vicinity to suddenly "need" a railroad. The English investors who hired George Stephenson to build the L&M had looked at the numbers and calculated that their passenger business should eventually reach 400 people per day. When the line opened for business, their initial passenger traffic was three times that figure, and it only increased over time.[183] American railroad builders had the same experience.

RAILS REPLACE CANALS

Prosperity continued to follow the canals for a time, but eventually railroads made most of America's canals obsolete. Milan, Ohio, the town where Thomas Edison was born, was an example of this. In the 1830s Milan was a sleepy little town of around 600 people, situated three miles from a navigable river that emptied into Lake Erie. In 1839 construction was completed on a canal connecting the town to the river. Milan became an important transportation center nearly overnight. By 1847, the year of Edison's birth, over a million bushels of wheat and corn were shipped annually from the port of Milan.[184]

Unfortunately for the people of Milan, a railroad that ran from east to west across northern Ohio, bypassing Milan, opened for business that same year. As was happening all across the nation, the canal's usefulness declined sharply as soon as a railroad started serving the same area. Within two years grain shipments through Milan declined by 69 percent. The canal was soon abandoned and eventually filled in. Today Milan is a tiny town of only around 1,400 residents, famous only for being the great inventor's birthplace. Arial views provided by Google Earth show no trace of the canal.

Canals and railroads were both being built in the U.S. through the 1830s and 40s, but by the middle of the century canal construction came to a halt as it became apparent that railroads were the superior technology. While the railroad was bad for towns like Milan it was certainly good for farmers, who took advantage of the iron horse to send their crops to market faster and at lower cost. The farmers of western Pennsylvania finally enjoyed that privilege in 1854, when the Pennsylvania Railroad completed construction of a line that connected Pittsburgh to Philadelphia.

Through the last two thirds of the nineteenth century the evolution and spread of railroads was so crucial to the nation's development that it's probably no exaggeration to say that U.S. history *was* railroad history, and vice versa. By 1840, just ten years after the first railroad opened in the United States, the U.S. already had some 3,000 miles of track.[185] Ten years later there were 9,000 miles.[186] Between the 1830s and the 1850s the volume of shares traded on the New York Stock Exchange multiplied a thousand fold, driven by the explosive growth of railroad stocks.[187]

To encourage railroad construction, the states offered the railroad companies rights of way and sweetened the deal with land grants along them. When a group of investors formed a railroad company to take advantage of one of these opportunities they would spend a great deal of money, most of it borrowed, to construct the road. When the line opened it would earn revenues both from the road itself and from the sale or leasing of the acreage adjacent to the road that had been granted by the state. The land, of course, would be worth far more after the road was built than before, so the land grants cost the states little and yet were a significant part of the railroads' revenue streams.

Cornelius Vanderbilt first took an active role in the railroad business in 1844 when he became a member of the board of directors of the Long Island Railroad.[188] The following year he and Daniel Drew bought a controlling interest in the Providence and Stonington Railroad. For the next several years Vanderbilt would continue to devote more time to his boats and ships than to his railroad interests, but during the Civil War years he divested himself of all his ships and focused entirely on rail. During the post-war years Vanderbilt would be recognized as the most powerful figure in the railroad industry, and, as such, the most powerful figure in American business.

THE MID-1800's: AMERICA GROWS UP

By the middle of the nineteenth century Americans were starting to produce and transport more than just raw materials like grain and timber. Manufacturers all around the Northeast, constantly improving on Eli Whitney's methods, learned to economically mass-produce products of every kind.

In 1844 Samuel Morse first demonstrated his telegraph, launching the new field of electronic communications. Within 10 short years the U.S. already had 10,000 miles of telegraph cable.[189] Rail and telegraph companies began to operate jointly, with telegraph wires strung beside the tracks along railroad rights of way.

In 1850 the American Express company went into business transporting money and messages between businesses. In its early days American Express operated primarily by sending horse-drawn coaches along overland routes, using the nation's still-primitive roads, but they adapted their business models as the railroads spread. Abandoning the long-haul service, they put their stagecoaches and freight wagons into service on feeder lines, bringing people and products to and from the railheads.

In 1851 the famous Chrystal Palace Exhibition in London featured several American inventions including the Colt revolver and a McCormick grain harvester, showing the world for the first time that the U.S. was becoming a center of technological innovation. Around this time the U.S. began to export manufactured products as well as raw materials, but cotton and foodstuffs would continue to be the nation's primary exports for many more years.

The New York Central and the Pennsy

In the early 1850s America's two great railroad companies came into existence. In 1853 the New York Central Railroad was born when several short roads were consolidated into one company, with tracks running from the Lake Erie port of Buffalo to the City of Albany on the Hudson River. In 1854 J. Edgar Thompson's Pennsylvania Railroad completed a continuous single-track railroad from Philadelphia to Pittsburgh. The Pennsylvania (or "Pennsy," as it was universally called) grew so rapidly that by the end of the Civil War it was the world's largest corporation. Under Vanderbilt's post-war leadership the NY Central soon rivaled the Pennsy in size and economic power.

In 1857 only 65 companies were listed on the New York Stock Exchange, and 40 of them were railroads.[190] Railroad stocks would continue to dominate the U.S. stock market for the rest of the century and beyond.

In 1858 inventor Theodore Woodruff demonstrated a railroad car with seats that could be converted to sleeping berths at night - a "sleeper car." Seeing the commercial potential of this invention in a nation where train routes were constantly growing longer, Andrew

Carnegie and Thomas Scott quickly entered into a partnership with Woodruff, providing him with the capital he needed to start producing and selling his sleeper cars on a large scale. Later the partners engineered a merger with their largest competitor, a man named George Pullman, to form a company that dominated the sleeper car business.

In 1859 "Colonel" Edwin Drake was able to pump oil out of the ground on a patch of farmland near Titusville, Pennsylvania. Within a couple years oil derricks and refineries were everywhere in northwestern Pennsylvania, and crude oil and refined kerosene shipments were becoming a major cash cow for the Pennsylvania Railroad. As a side benefit, whale oil became obsolete virtually overnight and several whale species were probably saved from extinction.

Refineries began popping up in nearby Cleveland in the early 1860s, and the Erie and New York Central railroads, both of which served Cleveland, began to compete with the Pennsy for the refiners' business. Grain shipments continued to be the most important single source of revenue for the railroads, but petroleum, which unlike agricultural products had to be shipped year round, quickly became an important revenue source as well.

Railroads and the Civil War

By the start of the Civil War in 1861 America had over 31,000 miles of railroad track,[191] most of it in the Northern states. The seven largest corporations in America were all railroad companies.[192] During the war years the Union's advantages in building and operating railroads and telegraph lines was a decisive factor.

With its severe shortage of literate and skilled engineers, the Confederacy had a hard time just operating the railroad system it had during the Civil War, and building new lines was all but impossible. The Union had the human resources to keep its roads operating, to rapidly re-build the roads damaged by Confederate forces, and to build new roads as needed. Having personnel with superior technical skills ultimately meant that the Union army was able to transport troops and materiel more rapidly and coordinate its efforts more efficiently than its enemy. Union forces in the field were kept well supplied with weapons and equipment from Northern factories, and food from Northern farms, most of which were shipped by rail. Ultimately these advantages allowed the Union to win the war and put a forcible end to the institution of slavery.

Thomas Scott, vice president of the Pennsylvania Railroad, took a leave of absence for the duration of the war and accepted a position as Assistant Secretary of War in the Lincoln administration. Andrew Carnegie, Scott's right hand man, was brought in to reconstruct roads damaged by Confederate sympathizers and manage telegraphic communications.[193]

Northern railroad construction continued at a rapid pace all through the war years. Despite the destruction of Union roads by Confederate forces and vice versa, the total number of rail miles in the nation continued to climb. There were over 200 separate railroad companies operating in the U.S. during these years (although many of them had overlapping ownership structures and were managed cooperatively), and most of them managed to keep building track despite wartime shortages of manpower and materials. By 1865 the Pennsylvania Railroad was the largest corporation in the world, with 30,000 employees and a capitalization of 61 million dollars.[194] Cornelius Vanderbilt's New York Central was not far behind.

When the war ended the pace of railroad construction only accelerated. Virtually every large-scale business in the nation depended on the railroads for transportation, or depended on sales of products and services to the railroads, or both. Telegraph companies carried huge volumes of messages from railroad managers to their far-flung stations and crews. Iron and steel mills made most of their revenue from sales to the railroads, and delivered their products by train.

European investors lent millions of dollars for railroad, bridge, and tunnel construction as the railroad companies raced to build tracks in new areas, with Junius and J.P. Morgan handling much of the financial traffic. Transportation moguls like Vanderbilt, Edgar Thompson and Jay Gould saw the continent as a chessboard, where the right strategic move could increase their power. Each tried to gain monopoly positions by controlling all the roads to and from a given territory.

In the race to get tracks laid first, transportation companies had to rely heavily on borrowed money. By the time a road was open it would already be burdened with a heavy debt load. Bond payments to investment bankers were a fixed cost that had to be paid each month. The only way to pay all the fixed costs and come away with a profit was to keep the trains loaded and running all the time. Any interruption in the stream of revenue could be disastrous, as demonstrated by the dozens of railroad bankruptcies suffered when the market crashes of 1873 and 1893 caused temporary reductions in the volume of traffic on the roads.

THE TRANS-CONTINENTAL RAILROAD

It was during the war years that construction started on the transcontinental railroad, which ended the isolation of California and the West Coast from the rest of the Union. The road was chartered by the federal government, a new thing in American railroad development. For the first three decades of the railroad era the states provided rights of way and land grants for railroads. Interstate networks like the Pennsylvania and the New York Central were formed when the companies that owned small intra-state lines merged to form larger, interstate corporations. The two companies that built the trans-continental took advantage of a federal charter and built on land provided by the federal government stretching in an east-west line over several different states and territories.

The support of President Lincoln was crucial to the trans-continental railroad. Fortunately for the backers of the project, Lincoln was well aware of the importance of efficient transportation to the nation's development. Before coming to the White House Lincoln had made his living as an Illinois lawyer, which in the 1830s involved following circuit court judges from one town to another on horseback, representing clients in one town after another. As railroads began to be built in the state his law circuit travels became easier and the number of cases he could take (and fees he could collect) grew. From the 1850s he began to represent railroad companies in court, and some of them were among his most lucrative clients.

By the time Lincoln ran for president he was a prosperous man, and much of his wealth had come from the work he did for various railroads. Many of the cases he won established legal precedents that would be cited by other attorneys in subsequent railroad related cases through the years.[195]

In 1862 President Lincoln signed the Pacific Railroad Bill into law. Under the terms of the bill, construction of a line stretching eastward from a point near Sacramento would be the responsibility of the Central Pacific Railroad, a company that had been incorporated under the laws of California the previous year. West-bound construction, starting at the Iowa-Nebraska border, would be the job of a new corporation called the Union Pacific Railroad, charted by the federal government as part of the bill. The primary stockholders of the Central Pacific were the so-called "Big Four," four wealthy California businessmen.

Back on the East Coast the Union Pacific boasted a much larger pool of stockholders, most of whom took only small stakes in the project. The dominant figure was Thomas C. "Doc" Durant. The bill that created the corporation established a board of commissioners and left it up to the commissioners to sell shares of the company's stock to private investors. Union Pacific shares were hard to sell, despite the government's offer of generous land grants along the road and cash loans to be doled out to the builders for each mile of track built. Potential investors were frightened away by the technological challenges involved and by the construction costs. Everyone knew the actual cost of building the roads would be much larger than the government loans, which would eventually have to be repaid with interest.[196] Durant liquidated nearly everything he had to buy shares, then borrowed money to buy more shares. He played a leading role in persuading other East Coast businessmen to invest, and ended up leading a bloc of investors that controlled nearly half of the Union Pacific shares.[197]

The chief engineer of the Union Pacific from the end of the Civil War until the road was completed in 1869 was Grenville Dodge, who had achieved the rank of general and spent most of the war years building and repairing railroads for the Union Army. Thomas Durant tried to lure him away from the army to take the position of chief engineer with the Union Pacific Railroad while the war was still going on, but Dodge refused to resign his army commission until the war was won.[198]

Limited as it was, the federal government's financial support for the Union Pacific was still a new thing in American history. Before the Civil War, total annual federal spending was only $78 million.[199] That's about $2 billion in today's dollars, which is roughly what our current federal government spends every five hours. For the federal government to lend millions of dollars in support of a civilian infrastructure project was unheard of at that time. The only reason the railroad project got as much support as it did, in that era of limited government, was that the president and others viewed it as part of the Union war effort.[200]

THE POST-WAR YEARS: CONNECTING A NATION BY RAIL

The Central Pacific met up with the Union Pacific at Promontory Point, Utah on May 10 of 1869, giving the nation a rail route from

East Coast to West. Within a few years competing lines connected the two coasts along other routes. At the same time connecting roads were laid in every direction, often entering fertile but unpopulated areas where farms and towns would suddenly spring up as soon as the railroad was constructed. Land that was considered worthless would become valuable as soon as the rails reached it. In the eight years after the end of the war the number of track miles in the United States doubled again, from 35,000 to 70,000.[201] And where the rails went people and prosperity followed.

While the war was going on, Grenville Dodge was not the only businessman who put the Union war effort ahead of his own career. Andrew Carnegie continued in his management role with the Pennsylvania Railroad all through the war years even though his duties were a distraction from far more lucrative business interests. By 1863 his salary from the railroad represented only about one twentieth of his total income and he was eager to spend more time on his other businesses, but he considered his railroad work a civic duty. He stayed with it until a few days before General Lee's surrender at Appomattox Courthouse.[202]

In 1865, just as the war was ending, Cornelius Vanderbilt constructed a bridge over the Hudson River at Albany, connecting his New York Central network with the port city of Boston and the New England states. At this point Vanderbilt was fully committed to his railroad interests, having sold off the last of his boats and ships during the war. Soon his network of roads would reach Cleveland and Chicago and spread throughout the upper Midwest. He quickly established the New York Central as the Pennsylvania Railroad's primary rival, but Jay Gould's Erie Railroad would soon rival them both. By 1868 Vanderbilt would recognize the threat and try unsuccessfully to wrest control of the Erie from Gould and Gould's partners Jim Fisk and Daniel Drew.

By 1867 railroads had reached much of Kansas, but hadn't yet reached the Southwest. Texas ranchers started organizing cattle drives up the Chisholm Trail through Texas and Oklahoma to put their steers on east-bound trains in Kansas towns like Dodge City and Abilene, where crime rates were driven skyward by drunken cowboys celebrating reaching the end of the trail. This in turn created a need for tough lawmen like Wyatt Earp and Bat Masterson, who eventually became famous in books and movies. Eighteen years later, when Texas was connected to the rest of the nation by rail, the Chisholm Trail became obsolete and the cattle drives came to an end.

Andrew Carnegie had diverse business interests at this stage of his career, and all of them were railroad related. The year after he merged his sleeper car company with Pullman's, his Keystone Bridge Company was hired as a subcontractor by architect and builder James Buchanan Eads, who was building a history-making iron and steel railroad bridge across the Mississippi at St. Louis. Carnegie's bridge company bought most of the materials it used for the project from the Freedom Ironworks, yet another Carnegie company. The bridge opened for business in 1874.

In 1868 John D. Rockefeller, who already controlled one of the largest oil refining companies in the nation, negotiated a deal with one of the subsidiaries of Vanderbilt's New York Central that gave his company the lowest freight rates in the industry. One key element in Rockefeller's favor was that he was building most of his refineries in Cleveland, a city that was served by all three of the nation's dominant railroad networks. By playing Jay Gould's Erie Railroad and J. Edgar Thompson's Pennsylvania Railroad against Vanderbilt's company he was able to increase his negotiating power. Having lower transportation costs than his competitors allowed Rockefeller to rapidly increase his market share and his power. His Standard Oil Company came to dominate the oil industry so completely that it was broken up by the federal government in 1911.

Railroad technologies continued to evolve, with most of the important innovations engineered by self-educated self-made men. In 1869, the same year the trans-continental railroad was completed, George Westinghouse took the railroad industry by storm with his automatic air brake. Up until that time stopping a train had involved sending strong men onto the roofs of all the cars to hand-crank mechanical brakes. Westinghouse' brake was faster, safer, and more reliable, and was universally adopted virtually overnight. In 1872 Elijah McCoy introduced an equally revolutionary innovation; an automatic oiler for the running gear on trains. Until McCoy's oiler came along, a train would have to come to a complete stop every few miles to have its moving parts manually lubricated. McCoy's invention allowed the trains to run continuously. Both men would go on to patent other useful inventions that contributed to the nation's growth.

THE CRASH OF 1873

In 1873 80 percent of the value of the U.S. stock market was in railroad stocks.[203] That year a financial panic rocked the nation. It was caused by the very business model that had allowed the railroads to spread so rapidly. The 35,000 miles of railroad track that had been built since the end of the war was mostly financed with borrowed money, and bankers and investors on both sides of the Atlantic carried millions of dollars in railroad loans on their books. Most of the railroads were so deeply in debt that any reduction in revenue threatened their ability to make their payments to the banks on time. In the summer of 1873 the Northern Pacific Railroad declared bankruptcy and defaulted on its debts to the banking firm of Jay Cook and Company. In September Jay Cook and Company also declared bankruptcy. The problem cascaded throughout the economy as bank failures caused a slowdown in business which reduced railroad revenues, leading to more railroad defaults and more bank failures.

As with every economic downturn, there were those who benefited from the panic of 1873. Depressed labor and material costs during the mid-1870s depression allowed Andrew Carnegie to build his first steel mill for less than it would have cost him a few years earlier or later, and by the time the mill was completed the economy was coming back to life and railroad rails were Carnegie Steel's most lucrative product. Like the three earlier financial depressions of the nineteenth century, the 1873 depression ended within a few years. By the late 1870s railroad track was again being laid at a manic pace. By 1880 the nation had 93,000 miles of track, and by 1890 there were 163,000 miles.[204] Thousands of miles of those new railroad rails had been manufactured in Carnegie's mills.

Carnegie and his partners had built their mills in an area served by two different railroads in an attempt to keep the kind of bargaining power that Rockefeller exploited so skillfully in his freight rate negotiations. Unfortunately for Carnegie, as his steel business increased it became apparent that the Baltimore and Ohio Railroad didn't have the routes and capacity to be a viable option, and the Pennsy came to enjoy a near-monopoly on his business, particularly in regard to delivering raw materials to his mills. This would be an ongoing problem that Carnegie and his partners would have to struggle with until they finally built their own railroad in 1896-97.

A Power Struggle in Pennsylvania – Rockefeller Wins

In 1877 Thomas Scott, who had succeeded J. Edgar Thompson as president of the Pennsy, made an ill-advised decision to try to seize control of the oil business. He set up a subsidiary company that operated refineries in the state of Pennsylvania in competition with Rockefeller's Standard Oil Company, and jacked up the freight rates he charged Rockefeller's refineries, particularly those in the state of Pennsylvania, where the Pennsy had a monopoly.

Rockefeller retaliated by boycotting the Pennsy. He gave all his Cleveland business to the N.Y. Central and the Erie, and he simply shut down all his refineries in Pennsylvania. The loss of Standard Oil's business was so damaging to the Pennsy that Scott had to lay off workers, and cut the pay and increase the hours of the employees he was able to retain. On July 14 of that year laid-off workers started a riot in which they killed several people and destroyed so much Pennsylvania Railroad property that the railroad could not resume normal operations, even after Scott capitulated in his war with Rockefeller and Rockefeller re-opened his Pennsylvania refineries. During the rampage the Pennsy's ex-employees burned down 27 buildings and destroyed 2000 freight cars, 500 tanker cars, and 120 locomotives. Pennsy stock plummeted as the company suspended its dividend, sold off assets, and approached J.P. Morgan's Drexel, Morgan and Company for an emergency loan.[205]

The New York Central, controlled by Cornelius Vanderbilt's son William since the Commodore's death earlier that year, was a beneficiary of the Pennsy's troubles. The loss of so much infrastructure made it difficult for the Pennsy to rebuild its business for a time, and Vanderbilt snapped up business that the Pennsy couldn't handle in its weakened condition.

In 1883 the railroads collaborated to divide the U.S. into four time zones: Atlantic, Central, Mountain, and Pacific. The time zones were accepted by businesspeople immediately, but the U.S. Government didn't formally recognize them until 1918. In 1884 the Dow Jones Company started publishing a stock market index representative of the broader stock market. The index was based on 11 stocks, nine of which were railroad companies.[206]

ANOTHER POWER STRUGGLE IN PENNSYLVANIA – CARNEGIE LOSES

In that same year, 1883, Andrew Carnegie and several other Pittsburgh area manufacturers bought a minority interest in a railroad company that owned a charter and right-of-way for an as yet unbuilt railroad from Pittsburgh to Harrisburg. A majority stake belonged to William Vanderbilt's New York Central network. Vanderbilt was eager to take away the Pennsy's monopoly on Pittsburgh businesses for two reasons. One, obviously, was the revenues that could be earned hauling freight to and from the manufacturers in that area. The other reason was that the Pennsylvania was doing the same thing to him. The Pennsy was building a line from New York City to Albany up the west side of the Hudson River, in direct competition with the New York Central's most important arterial. Vanderbilt was eager for revenge, and welcomed the opportunity to take advantage of the financial support of the Pittsburgh manufacturers in building a line that would hurt his rival. Construction on the Pittsburgh to Harrisburg line continued for two years at cost of several million dollars.

J.P. Morgan, who by this time was the nation's most influential investment banker, viewed the Pennsylvania and New York projects with horror. Competition between two lines over the same route could only do what Carnegie was counting on: force freight rates down. American railroad companies, burdened as they always were with debt, could ill afford to be giving up their monopolies to compete with one another on parallel routes. As Morgan and his investors well knew, the financial panic and depression of the previous decade had been caused by a failure of railroads to earn enough money to service their debts. In the mid-1880s Morgan and his father were already having a hard time persuading English investors to send their money to the United States precisely because increasing completion was putting a crimp on railroad profitability.

On July 10, 1885, Morgan welcomed the presidents of the Pennsy and the New York Central onto his yacht, the aptly-named *Corsair*. As the boat cruised up and down the Hudson River Morgan made his case for cooperation. A gourmet lunch was served at mid-day. The cruise lasted nine hours, because Morgan wouldn't let the skipper return to port until the heads of the two rival lines agreed to put their differences aside and come to an agreement. When the boat landed an agreement had been hammered and the two presidents had shaken hands on it. The details were complicated, but effectively the two railroad companies traded their respective new lines. The New York Central took over ownership of the New York to Albany line and promptly shut down construction; the Pennsy became the majority owner of the line Carnegie was counting on and shut it down just as promptly.

Carnegie was understandably furious when he learned that he had been sold out. Soon after the *Corsair* meeting, the Pennsy informed him that it was raising his freight rates.[207]

THE CRASH OF 1893

Despite the best efforts of J.P. Morgan to reduce competition in the railroad industry, it continued to be a highly volatile business. The roads continued to carry heavy debt burdens, and any misstep could cause bankruptcy. In May of 1893 another financial panic rocked the nation. The panic was caused, at least in part, by the failure of the Philadelphia and Reading Railroad. Once it started, the crash tore through the business world much as the 1873 crash had; railroads failed and defaulted on their debts, then the railroad defaults caused banks to fail. One year after the initial crash nearly 200 railroads, controlling 40,000 miles of track, were in receivership.[208] Railroad shares still represented the greater part of the stock market, and at any rate the general panic caused profits of virtually every industry to plummet, so investors lost fortunes. Railroad construction came to a complete stop for three or four years, then resumed.

In 1896 Andrew Carnegie and his partners purchased a bankrupt railroad based in the Lake Erie port of Conneaut, Ohio and started extending it toward their properties in and around Pittsburgh. In addition to being a port city, Conneaut offered easy connection to the New York Central and Erie Railroad networks. In May of that year, while Carnegie's new road was still under construction, the Pennsy agreed to drastically reduce his rates on all the products they carried to and from his plants. Two years later they gave Carnegie another round of rate cuts, to roughly half of what he'd been paying before he started building his railroad. The improved freight rates greatly enhanced the profitability of the company, helping Carnegie Steel to dominate the steel industry the way Rockefeller dominated the oil business.[209]

The Growth Finally Stops

In the early 1900s the railroads were still the nation's most important business. Early in 1901 railroad shares were still such a dominant part of the New York Stock Exchange that a battle for control of the Northern Pacific Railroad drove volume up to 3.3 million shares on a single day, shattering the old record of two million shares.[210]

The explosive growth in track miles finally came to a halt around the start of the First World War when the rails had finally reached virtually every city and town in the nation. During the 1930s the number of track miles actually started to decline as unproductive lines were taken out of service.[211] Today railroads are just one of several technologies that make up the nation's transportation infrastructure.

Rags-to-Riches Railroad Men

During the 80 year period when railroading was the nation's most important industry, virtually all of the dominant characters were self-made men. Vanderbilt's rags-to-riches story is the subject of a chapter in this book. Daniel Drew ran away from home as a child and earned a living as a circus "roustabout," feeding the animals and doing other chores. Drew joined the army at the age of 14 and later started a business buying cattle in upstate New York and driving them down to the big city for sale.[212] J. Edgar Thompson was the son of an engineer, and started his career as a surveyor's assistant at the age of 19.

Thomas Scott had to start earning his own living at age 10 when his father died and his widowed mother was unable to support her 11 children.[213] Andrew Carnegie has his own chapter in this book. Theodore Woodruff left his family's farm at 16 to make his living as an apprentice to a wagon builder.[214]

J.P. Morgan, the banking mogul who thwarted Carnegie's effort to get a second railroad connection in 1885, was an unusual case; he grew up in a wealthy family and his father sent him to exclusive schools before helping him get started in the banking business.

Virtually all the important players in the story of the transcontinental railroad fit the rags-to-riches pattern. Abraham Lincoln was born in a log cabin with a dirt floor, to illiterate parents; he started taking unskilled jobs as a teenager and worked his way through law school in his mid-twenties by splitting rails and working as a farmhand.[215]

The "Big Four" stockholders in the Central Pacific Railroad were Leland Stanford, founder of Stanford University; Collis Huntington; Mark Hopkins; and Charles Crocker. The road's chief engineer, also a significant stockholder, was Theodore Judah. Stanford was the son of an innkeeper whose hotel was put out of business by a decline in stagecoach traffic caused by the advent of a railroad in the area.[216] Huntington left home at age 14 to earn his living as a farmhand, then got a job assisting a storekeeper.[217] Hopkins started out as a storekeeper, then got a job as a bookkeeper.[218] Crocker started out in business at age 12, peddling newspapers. After that he tried his hand unsuccessfully at farming, before taking a job as a blacksmith.[219] Theodore Judah was the son of an Episcopal clergyman.[220]

Thomas Durant, the driving force behind the Union Pacific, was the one significant player in the trans-continental railroad story who didn't grow up poor; his family owned a successful grain exporting business.[221] Chief engineer Grenville Dodge was the son of a common laborer. Grenville had to go to work at the age of 14, assisting a surveyor who was laying out the path of a new railroad.[222]

Jay Gould, who controlled the Erie Railroad and was Vanderbilt's bitter rival, grew up on a small farm, then left home at the age of 15 to take a job as a surveyor's assistant.[223] Jim Fisk was the son of a debt-ridden peddler. Like Daniel Drew, Fisk left home as a teenager and made his living for a while as a circus roustabout.[224]

George Pullman's father was a carpenter. George dropped out of school after the fourth grade and went to work in a cabinet shop to help support his family.[225] James Buchanan Eads had to go to work full time at the age of 13 to help support his impoverished family.[226] George Westinghouse had an easier start than most great American entrepreneurs; his father owned a machine shop and allowed young George to work with the tools in the shop at an early age. Elijah McCoy's parents had a much tougher life than Westinghouse's; both of McCoy's parents were runaway slaves who made their way to Canada with the help of the Underground Railroad.[227]

The development of American railroads was dominated by self-confident and self-reliant individualists, most of whom started out in life with little more than the clothes on their backs. In that respect, the railroads were like every other important American industry of the nineteenth century.

CHAPTER 9

The Mellons

-----

*It was from the struggles necessary to remove the
obstacles in my way…that I derived the most
enjoyment; and in my case the opportunities for
pleasure in overcoming difficulties were abundant.*

THOMAS MELLON

IN THE EARLY 1920S THE three Americans who paid the highest federal income taxes were John D. Rockefeller, Henry Ford, and Andrew
Mellon.[228] In 1926 future U.S. President Franklin Roosevelt, already
angling for the political support of lower-income voters, singled out
Mellon as "the master mind among the malefactors of great wealth,"
blaming Mellon and his fellow millionaires for all the suffering of the
poor in America. In the 1930s President Roosevelt's administration
very publicly accused Mellon of tax evasion and fraud; after a long
and expensive trial Mellon was cleared of all charges.[229]

Roosevelt's public flogging of Mellon may have been smart politics, but it was not entirely just. Mellon had always scrupulously
complied with the tax laws. (The IRS team that audited him during
Roosevelt's first year in office found that Mellon had over-paid his
taxes, and recommended a $7,507 refund.)[230] Roosevelt's over-heated

rhetoric about rich men oppressing the poor might also have been a bit hypocritical. Roosevelt himself was very rich, as were his ancestors going back at least five generations.

The Mellons, unlike the Roosevelts, were not an "old money" family. Andrew started out in business with a relatively modest inheritance from his father and turned it into a great fortune during his lifetime. His father, Thomas Mellon, started with nothing.

Thomas A. Mellon was born in February of 1813 on his father's tiny 23 acre farm in Northern Ireland. [231] It must have been very difficult for the family to grow enough food for their own survival on 23 acres. By comparison, the standard plot size the U.S. government allowed homesteaders to claim under the various Homestead Acts of the nineteenth century was 160 acres; seven times as much farmland as the Mellon family had at their disposal before they fled Ireland for the United States.

In 1818 Thomas' father sold the family farm for the equivalent of a thousand dollars, and the family immigrated to the United States, following Thomas' grandparents and several other relatives who had already made the crossing. [232] In early October of 1818, five-year-old Thomas arrived with his parents at the port of Baltimore. [233] It was just the three of them; none of Thomas' younger siblings had yet been born. After a brief stay in a quarantine facility they bought a covered wagon and team of horses, then spent three weeks traveling by wagon over the primitive roads of that era to settle near their relatives in the farmlands near Pittsburgh.

In the spring of 1819 Thomas' father bought 160 acres of mediocre farmland in an area called Poverty Point, roughly 20 miles east of Pittsburgh. [234] The land was only partially cleared and the two-room cabin on the property had been abandoned for so long that it was "in a dilapidated condition." [235] The Mellons didn't have enough money to pay for the land along with the farm equipment and seeds they needed, so they gave the owner of the property the last of their money as a down payment and signed a mortgage contract for the rest.

Thomas' father managed to plow part of the land and get a crop of oats planted before the spring planting season was over. Both his parents worked hard to tend their oat crop while clearing more of the land and attempting such repairs to their broken-down cabin as could be affected without money.

Before their first small crop was ready for harvest, disaster struck. The Financial Panic of 1819, which started in the summer of that year, tore through the American economy with a vengeance. The value of farmers' crops plummeted. Lenders repossessed so many farms and other properties that real estate prices also crashed. After living on their new home for only a few months, the Mellons were in grave danger of losing it, and their life's savings with it. The money they'd gotten for their Irish farm was all gone, and the value of their new farm was suddenly much less than the debt they still owed on it.[236] In modern parlance they were "underwater on their mortgage." Compounding their debt problem, the oat crop in their field was worth much less than they'd expected to get for it when they planted it.

The three Mellons focused day and night on keeping their home. Writing about it decades later, Thomas showed obvious pride in his parents' "industry and perseverance." "They had put their money," he recalled, "into the land which, though small in amount, was their all, and looked on the place as their home. No matter how great the difficulties or discouraging the prospect, they entertained no thought of giving up the struggle."

The terms of their mortgage stated that payments could be made "in money and bags and oats at market prices." The word "bags" in that sentence literally means empty cloth bags, which were a commodity that had some financial value in those more-primitive times. Even during the depression, sturdy three-bushel bags were worth 50 cents apiece. The Mellons began growing flax and weaving and sewing it into bags in their broken-down shack; a true "cottage industry" if ever there was one. Six-year-old Thomas worked alongside his parents to produce the precious sacks. Home improvements were put on hold. The family made due without new clothing or furniture or much of anything else for the next four years. Nearly every waking hour was spent growing food for their own consumption and manufacturing three-bushel bags for use as mortgage payments.[237]

After four years the debt was paid off and the nation's economy was showing signs of recovering. By this time Thomas had two younger sisters. (A brother, the last of the Mellon children, was born in 1825). With the mortgage paid off and crop prices recovering the Mellons could get back to their original plan of saving up a little money for a rainy day while making some much-needed improvements to their house, barn, and property. Thomas still had to work long hours on the farm, but he was able to attend school during the winter months when his parents could spare him in the fields.[238]

One of the improvements Thomas' father installed in the late 1820s was a small brandy distillery. This was several decades after the infamous Whiskey Rebellion of the early 1790s, but western Pennsylvania was still geographically isolated, and many of the farmers in the area still converted much of their grain to whiskey. The Mellons' property had a sizable orchard of peach and apple trees, but most of the fruit just rotted on the ground every autumn until the distillery was built. Once the facility was built the Mellons were able to sell their annual brandy production for some much needed hard cash.

The schools Thomas attended in his youth were typical of nineteenth century American elementary schools. Textbooks included the Bible and other religious works, along with something called *The United States Spelling Book and Western Calculator*. Classes were held six days a week, Monday through Saturday. Teachers were paid a quarterly fee by the parents of the students.

In 1823 Thomas was able to persuade his parents to let him visit the big city of Pittsburgh. There was no question of the 10-year-old being too young to make the three day trip alone; in that era children grew up fast and their parents expected them to be self-reliant. The only reason his parents were reluctant to give their permission is that they needed him on the farm. Finally it was decided that they could spare him for three days "between the first and second corn hoeings" when the press of farm chores was less urgent than at other times. Better still, in preparation for his trip his father allowed him to load a pack horse with rye, haul the rye to a nearby town, and keep the 99 cents he got for it.

When the appointed day came Thomas put his traveling money in his pocket, said goodbye to his parents, and walked the 21 miles to Pittsburgh alone. Along the way he walked for a time beside a wagon being driving by a farmer on his way to market. The farmer, upon hearing that Thomas was on his way to the big city, told the boy that he would "see more there in a day than at Poverty Point in a lifetime." The comment rankled the youngster, who didn't like to think the neighborhood where he was growing up was a backward place, but eventually he admitted that "the truth very nearly justified" the unpleasant remark.[239]

In Pittsburgh Thomas saw wonders that left an indelible mark on his mind. He visited not one but two factories that were powered by steam engines. He saw the homes and estates of wealthy businessmen, some of whom had started out as poor immigrants like himself. He even walked by the home of a rich merchant named Malcolm Leech who had come from the same neighborhood in Northern Ireland as the Mellons.

Thomas ended up returning to Poverty Point with his 99 cents still in his pocket. Room and board in Pittsburgh for the two nights he spent there were courtesy of a relative who lived in the city, and his sightseeing hadn't cost him anything.[240]

Thomas had an uncle who was kind enough to send him the works of Shakespeare and other great writers, and the youngster quickly became an avid reader. During meal breaks or while resting his plow horses he would pull out a book or pamphlet and catch a few more minutes of reading.[241] Sundays were a day of rest, so he was able to spend more time in his books before and after church.

When Thomas Mellon was around 14 years old he stumbled upon a copy of Benjamin Franklin's autobiography, a moment he would later describe as "the turning point of my life."

> It was about my fourteenth year, at a neighbor's house, when plowing, that I happened upon a dilapidated copy of Dr. Franklin's autobiography. It delighted me with a wider view of life and inspired me with new ambition - turned my thoughts into new channels. I had not before imagined any other course of life superior to farming, but the reading of Franklin's life led me to question this view. For so poor and friendless a boy to be able to become a merchant or a professional man had before seemed an impossibility; but here was Franklin, poorer than myself, who by industry, thrift and frugality had become learned and wise, and elevated to wealth and fame. The maxims of "poor Richard" exactly suited my sentiments. I read the book again and again, and wondered if I might not do something in the same line by similar means. I had will and energy equal to the occasion, and could exercise the same degree of industry and perseverance, and felt no misgiving except on the score of talent. But a want in this respect I supposed might only limit my field of operations, and I might well spare a vast amount of Franklin's success and still be fully compensated for the effort. I soon had an electric machine constructed of big-bellied bottles and glass fruit jars, which in its effects astonished the neighbors. But I never carried my researches in that direction any further, concluding that other and more useful practical branches of knowledge

would suit my purposes better. After that I was more industrious when at school, and more constant than ever in reading and study during leisure hours. I regard the reading of Franklin's Autobiography as the turning point of my life.[242]

In light of the direction Thomas' life took after he reached that "turning point," it might be worth the reader's while to look at the specific lessons young Mellon gleaned from Franklin's story.

First, "read more Franklin": Mellon obviously got his hands on more of Franklin's writings after reading the autobiography. He speaks approvingly of "the maxims of 'poor Richard'," none of which are in the autobiography; he must have read them somewhere else. It's not surprising, of course, that he would go out of his way to find and read more of his role model's words of wisdom.

Second, and crucially, "guys like me can succeed": The message in Franklin's autobiography that so inspired Mellon is that in America any ordinary kid without money, connections, or status; and without any particularly special in-born talent; can achieve success in life if he makes wise choices and works very hard. This is the message that changed his life.

Third, self-educate; become "learned and wise": Thomas Mellon apparently didn't think of himself as exceptionally intelligent or talented when he was introduced to the principles of Benjamin Franklin, yet he believed that if he used the methods Franklin used he could make himself "learned and wise." He also made the very sensible observation that even if he did have less God-given talent than Franklin had, if Franklin's methods allowed him to achieve even a fraction of Franklin's success, the rewards would be worth the effort.

Fourth, be "diligent and thrifty": The autobiography inspired Mellon to apply himself diligently both to his studies and to his work. It also reinforced the importance of thrift, a value he had already been learning from the good example of his Scots-Irish parents.

Inspired by Franklin's example, Thomas began to dream of a career doing something "superior to farming." As he considered his options he faced one obstacle that Benjamin Franklin hadn't had to contend with. Thomas' father vehemently opposed the idea of his son leaving the farm. The elder Mellon expected his sons to follow in his footsteps, as small farmers. He also depended heavily on Thomas' labor for his own success. By the time Thomas was in his late teens his father had bought two neighboring farms in addition to their original 160 acre plot, and he and Thomas did virtually all of the strenuous outdoor work on all three properties. Early nineteenth century farm labor required a lot of male muscle, and Thomas' brother Samuel, the only other boy in the family, was 12 years younger than Thomas and still too small to contribute much work.

When Thomas finally confessed to his father that he wanted to go to college to prepare for a non-agricultural career, the elder Mellon threatened to not contribute a penny to Thomas' college expenses. He also made it clear that he would always react with sorrow and anger to any discussion of his son leaving the farm to take his chances in any other profession. He even offered to buy even more farmland for the family to work together, with the understanding that he would eventually give the new fields to Thomas.[243]

Reluctant to break his father's heart, and with an obvious financial incentive to stay on the farm, Thomas agonized over his decision. The breaking point came when Thomas was around 17 years old. His father was about to sign the paperwork on the purchase of 200 acres of new land. Forced to make a final decision, Thomas ran 10 miles to town to keep the papers from being signed.[244] He would be his own man.

Faced with the loss of his work force, Thomas' father began to make appropriate preparations. One of the new farms he'd bought already had buildings on it, so he rented it out to another family. The other recently-acquired property had no house or barn, so Thomas spent one whole winter building them so that his father could rent out this property too.[245]

Thomas spent the next seven years working his way through preparatory school and college, earning his way by teaching school and doing farm work for his father, who apparently was willing to give Thomas some cash for his tuition in payment for his labor. Work on the farm caused him to be frequently absent from class, and he was forced to make up for the lack of classroom time by studying all the harder on his own. In his autobiography he recalled the difficulty of his college days, and his own tenacity and diligence, with obvious pride:

> This was pursuing a course of classical studies under difficulties, it is true; but in all my experience, whether of study or business, I succeeded the best when hardest pushed to overcome difficulties. The greater the obstacle the stronger my desire to overcome it; and my power to succeed seemed to rise with the occasion for it. Energy, persistence and the contrivance of ways and means inspired by a strong will would always overcome the difficulty.[246]

Thomas was never idle. While plowing on his father's farm he rehearsed Latin grammar exercises in his head, referring to the book while the horses were turning around at the end of a furrow. When he was seriously ill for two months in 1833 he read the complete works of Virgil, in the original Latin, in his sick bed.

In 1837, at the age of 24, Thomas finally graduated from Western University (which is known today as the University of Pittsburgh). A college graduate at last, he agonized over what his next move would be. He was attracted to law as a profession but concerns about his own perceived lack of speaking skills made him afraid to pursue a legal career.

Whenever he visited the courtroom as an observer he heard attorneys speak with impressive eloquence and obvious self-confidence, and he couldn't help but compare his own verbal skills, which he thought were poor, with the skills he saw on display in court. He was "nervous and diffident" whenever he had to speak to strangers, and couldn't imagine himself giving the kind of flowery speeches he heard lawyers make in front of juries. He'd grown up in Poverty Point and until he went to college he'd had very little practice conversing with educated people. The books he'd spent every spare minute reading had developed his mind, but reading doesn't teach a poor boy how to speak eloquently in public.

While he was struggling to make a decision, the university offered him a temporary job filling in for the regular Latin professor, who was unavailable due to illness. Thomas accepted the job and served as a professor of Latin at his alma mater for several months. During this time he was finally able to overcome his fears and commit himself to a career in law.

Early In 1838, at the age of 25, he left the university and began the study of law under the mentorship of an attorney named Charles Shaler. (In the nineteenth century a degree from a formal law school was not necessary; candidates for the bar simply studied independently or with a mentor until they could pass the bar exams.) During this period Thomas supported himself by working full time as a law clerk at the Allegheny County Courthouse. The salary was 20 dollars per month, later raised to 25, which thanks to his frugal lifestyle was enough to cover all his expenses with something left over. With money he'd saved from his teaching job, plus what he was able to save from his meager courthouse salary, he was able to make some small but prudent investments.

Mellon had read in Franklin's autobiography how Franklin lent drinking money to his London coworkers, who would spend the money on their immediate gratification and then repay Franklin with interest at payday. During his time as a courthouse clerk Mellon was able to profit from other people's impatience in similar fashion. When someone had been awarded a judgment from the court that didn't mature right away, Mellon would pay cash up front, at a discount, to buy the award from its recipient. When the money came due Mellon would collect the full amount.[247]

Thomas passed the bar exams and was sworn in as a member of the Pennsylvania bar in mid-December of 1838.

By June of 1839 he had accumulated 700 dollars in savings; enough to pay for a fairly complete library of law books. He gave up his clerking job and opened his own law office Pittsburgh, in a small room he rented for six dollars a month.[248] He was pleasantly surprised at how soon his business began to attract clients. According to his autobiography, the amount of work he was able to get in his first year in business "entirely exceeded my highest expectations." He quickly earned a reputation for winning his cases, and as his reputation grew his income grew with it.

Mellon attributed his early success as a lawyer to a number of factors. One was that he always did his homework and was "of an earnest, cautious, and painstaking disposition." He charged relatively modest fees, which his clients appreciated. He was passionate about his work. He would only accept a client if he believed the client was in the right, and once he made the commitment to represent someone he invested himself emotionally in the case, and fought hard to win it.[249]

And, to his surprise, Mellon soon discovered that his ability to stand up in court and address a jury was one of his greatest strengths. The young man who had compared himself to other public speakers and felt that he came up short soon learned that speaking beautifully and speaking persuasively are two different things. He soon numbered among his own advantages "not so much eloquence as the faculty of persuasion on jury trials."[250] He would show up in the courtroom very well informed on all the facts and legal principles of the case, after his usual rigorous pre-trial preparation, and fired with a passion to get what he regarded as justice for a deserving client. More often than not he would win his case.

For salesmen as well as for lawyers, great eloquence is an overrated asset. The same is true in almost any field of endeavor; the speaker who impresses people with his verbal skills is not necessarily the one who gets results.

Advertising pioneer David Ogilvy illustrated this point beautifully on the first page of his 1983 textbook *Ogilvy on Advertising,* by citing a story from ancient history. In the fourth century BC, King Philip of Macedon was threatening to conquer Athens. An Athenian statesman named Aeschines urged the leaders of the city to make peace with Philip. Aeschines' rival, Demosthenes, argued that Athens should go to war with Philip to protect its independence. When Aeschines spoke, the people said "How beautifully he speaks." When Demosthenes spoke, they said "let us march against Philip," which of course is exactly the response Demosthenes was trying to get, and far more gratifying than any personal compliments he might have gotten for his speaking style.[251] To use Thomas Mellon's words, Demosthenes had "not so much eloquence as the faculty of persuasion."

Using his plain-spoken approach, Mellon achieved a record of success that soon started to attract wealthier clients and more lucrative jobs. His role model had once described America as the place where people ask "not 'what is he?' but 'what can he do?'." Mellon proved the truth of that in his own career.

After a couple of years in the profession, Mellon began to see that success in the practice of law is not determined primarily by whom you know, but by what you know. "Caste or class," he learned, "have little influence." As the son of a common farmer, Thomas soon had many wealthy and prominent clients, some of whom had nephews or other relatives who practiced law but preferred to hire Mellon because of his track record.[252]

After four years in the legal profession Mellon felt prosperous enough to marry and start a family. Having read many times the praise Benjamin Franklin heaped on his wife Deborah in his autobiography,[253] Mellon resolved on finding a wife of the same character; a "helpmate...who could bear up and help me in adversity should it overtake us, or share with me the satisfaction of success, as the case might be."[254] In this he succeeded, although it took some time.

Sarah Jane Negley, whom Mellon met through some mutual friends, appeared to him to have all the character qualities he was looking for. He visited her home several times, and the more he got to know her the more he believed she was the woman he wanted as a wife. The only obstacle to his plan was "her manifest indifference, which wounded my self esteem." Mellon was used to overcoming difficulties in life, so he persisted in his pursuit of Sarah until he managed to win her over to his way of thinking. They were married in August of 1843. Thomas and Sarah had eight children over the next 15 years, of whom four survived to adulthood in good health: sons Thomas Alexander, James, Andrew, and Dick.

Thomas Sr. continued to work very hard at his law practice while simultaneously managing an ever-growing portfolio of investments. He primarily bought bonds and real estate. He bought coal-bearing properties and tried to find reliable partners to mine and market the coal and pay him his share of the profits. After a major fire destroyed most of Pittsburgh in 1845, he built several single-family houses on small plots of land and rented them out. By the late 1850s the demands of his law practice combined with the time he was spending managing his various investments were consuming all his time and threatening to wreck his health.

Mellon's integrity and diligence apparently impressed his colleagues as much as it impressed prospective clients. In 1859 three of his fellow attorneys came to his office to persuade him to run for election as a county judge. Their visit was timely; Mellon had already been looking for a way to escape the demands of his law practice so he could spend more time on his investments and his family. A government job seemed like just the thing. In 1859 he ran for and won a ten-year term as a judge in the Allegheny County Court. The job provided a steady paycheck, and the schedule was light enough that Mellon could manage his business affairs and have time left over for his family and his other interests. For the first time since opening his law practice, he had time for recreational reading.[255] He would retire from the bench after a single term, but he would be known to his business associates as "the Judge" for the rest of his life.

When Thomas Mellon, Sr. began his ten-year career as a county judge his son Thomas Alexander was 15 years old, and his son James was nearly 14. It would not be long before the Judge began to rely on Thomas Alexander and James in much the same way his own father had relied on him.

Occupied as he was with his legal career, Mellon frequently tried to establish himself as a "silent partner" in various financial ventures. He would provide the initial financing for a project and try to find a competent and honest business partner to run his various ventures for a share of the profits. After a few bad experiences as a silent partner he started looking at his own children as prospective human resources. One partner in particular turned out to be such a skillful liar and cheat that Mellon lost a great deal of money on their joint venture before resorting to a lawsuit to recoup some of his losses, leaving him to conclude that "If I had known then what I discovered soon afterwards regarding the capacity of my son Thomas for such business," he would have entrusted the whole affair to young Thomas from the start.[256]

Unlike their father when he was a child, the Mellon children had no farm chores to call them away from the classroom, so they were able to attend school full time until old enough to start their careers. Raised as they were on the homilies of Ben Franklin, they were all avid readers and diligent students. And, being raised in that environment, they reached adulthood believing in the power of their own efforts, and expecting to create success for themselves. While it's true that some wealthy parents spoil their children, Thomas and Sarah Mellon certainly did not. Discipline was strict and expectations were high in the Mellon household.

There were times, of course, when Mellon's wealth did allow him to provide his children with resources that poorer children don't get. When he became unsatisfied with their school he found a teacher more to his liking and started his own school. On another occasion Thomas Alexander and James became fascinated with the work of a blacksmith who had his shop in their neighborhood. The boys asked for permission to sign on with the blacksmith as apprentices and spend their days working in his shop, promising their parents that they would hit the books in the evenings after work.

The Judge made a counter-proposal. The boys would continue their daytime studies at the school and he would provide them with the materials and tools they would need to put together a blacksmith shop of their own in a shack on their parents' property. The boys embraced the deal and soon had a shop where they spent many happy hours teaching themselves to melt iron and hammer it into useful shapes.

But Mellon was always careful not to pamper his children. He focused on teaching them to "in self-reliance travel the rugged road of experience, and learn to surmount the natural difficulties on the way to success." Instead of giving them an allowance he gave them opportunities to earn their pocket money working at odd jobs and small-scale business ventures.

One of the early ventures of his two older boys was a nursery. On a corner of their parents' property they planted fruit trees and shrubs, which they tended during their after-school hours (after, apparently, they had lost interest in hammering pig iron into horseshoes in their little blacksmith shop). The boys worked hard and had the satisfaction of selling their plants profitably.

When Thomas Alexander was eighteen years old and finished with his school work he asked his father to lend him three thousand dollars so he could buy the much larger nursery of a man who wanted to sell all his property and leave the area. Junior was able to repay Senior with interest within a couple years, and ended up with a substantial profit from the venture. After that the elder Mellon lent the two enterprising youngsters enough money to buy a lumberyard, which turned out to be even more successful for all involved.

In his autobiography Mellon claims that by the time his two older boys were both 21 years of age they had accumulated a net worth of over $100,000 between the two of them. If the figure is accurate it is quite remarkable; $100,000 in 1867 is roughly $1,700,000 in 2015 dollars.

Mellon attributes the remarkable success of his boys in their early business ventures not to "talent or extraordinary abilities," but to "good judgement and persevering industry," and to a post-war economic boom that was creating prosperity all over the nation. Their success, as he saw it, was something anyone of ordinary ability could achieve in a strong economy by following the maxims of Benjamin Franklin.

At the end of 1869 Mellon's 10 year judicial term was finished. He resigned from the bench and was able to spend all his time managing and enlarging his investment portfolio. In 1869 he opened a bank, which he called Mellon and Sons, with an initial capital of $10,000 taken from his other holdings.[257] The bank was a great success, and in 1871 he built a four-story building to house the bank and his private office. He rented parts of the building to other businessmen until the Mellon interests became large enough to occupy the entire building.

As an homage to his role model he installed a large statue of Benjamin Franklin over the entrance to the building.[258]

In 1872 younger sons Andrew and Dick were finished with their schooling and ready to start their careers. Andrew had already been helping his father at the bank for a couple of years, but now that the 17-year-old was ready for a full time career his father offered to set up him and Dick with a lumberyard of their own. He would be a silent partner, collecting a share of the profits as his reward for putting up the front money, and letting the two teenagers run the business without supervision. Like their older brothers, Andrew and Dick achieved remarkable success from the start, although the economic crash of 1873 hurt all the Mellon businesses severely.

During the post-crash depression years the Mellons managed their properties and collected the meager profits available. Lumber had no value when no one in the area was building anything, so the boys wound down their lumber operations as quickly as they could. The value of their real estate holdings plummeted, at least on paper, but rents and mortgage payments continued to come in, at least where the tenant or borrower had not been forced to declare bankruptcy. Similarly their coal operations continued to generate revenue, though at a much-reduced rate. Andrew went to work at the Mellon and Sons bank on a full time basis. Dick went back to school and graduated from Western University in 1876.[259]

By 1877 the economy was recovering, and the boys asked the Judge to join with them to fund the completion of a railroad spur line connecting the fertile but isolated Ligonier Valley to the Pennsylvania Railroad. Construction of the railroad had been started before the economic crash and then been abandoned, and the citizens of the valley, eager to have access to rail transportation, offered to give the Mellons 80 percent of the railroad company they had created if the family would front enough money to complete the road.

The senior Mellon did his research and learned that horse-drawn traffic in and out of the valley amounted to only a handful of passengers and three or four freight wagons per day on average; too little traffic to make the proposed railroad venture profitable. The younger Mellons told their father that the mere presence of a railroad into the valley would stimulate business and create more traffic. Thomas allowed himself to be persuaded, and the family financed the venture. As soon as the road was operational the younger generation was vindicated; traffic exploded and the spur line was a great financial success.

Over the next several years the family continued to invest in various businesses, generally with great success. Sometimes, as in the spur line project, all five Mellons participated. At times Thomas Alexander and James would enter a venture as partners without their two younger brothers, or vice versa. As the Judge grew older he began to take a less active role. Eventually he simply entrusted his funds to Andrew and Dick and let them invest the money for him.

By in the mid-1880s the two older Mellon sons, who were both around 40 years of age, had largely retired from active business to enjoy their wealth and spend time with their families. Andrew and Dick continued to pursue every opportunity to increase their fortunes. In addition to managing their bank with great success, Andrew and Dick provided venture capital for many up-and-coming young businessmen with good ideas.

Over time Andrew developed a reputation for near-genius in the art of funding risky-looking projects that almost always turned out to be winners. One was a small company called the Pittsburgh Reduction Company that had developed a way to produce aluminum from bauxite. This was at a time when no one really had any practical use for aluminum; it was a rare and expensive metal that people like Thomas Edison would use for laboratory experiments.[260] When the founders of the company came to ask Andrew for a $4,000 loan, he did some research before telling them that the amount they were asking for was too small. He lent them $25,000, and soon after that was able to start buying shares in the company, which soon justified his faith by developing and dominating the aluminum market in the

United States.[261] The company is known today as Alcoa, and is still the largest aluminum producer in the U.S.

The Gulf Oil Company started out the same way, with Andrew finding and funding a small company with excellent human resources and good ideas, and reaping millions of dollars of profits over the ensuing years.[262]

One reason for Andrew's success is that he always put a premium on the value of human resources over any other kind. His decision to fund the Standard Steel Car Company is illustrative. In 1901 J.P. Morgan, the nation's premier investment banker, pulled together the United States Steel company, the world's first billion-dollar corporation. The major stakeholders included financial giants like Charles Schwab, John "Bet a Million" Gates, and Morgan himself. The company had a near-monopoly on the production of raw steel and steel products in the United States, and was viewed by many as impervious to competition. Carnegie biographer Joseph Wall, for example, claims that after 1901 it would be all but impossible for a start-up company to "enter the field at this late date and effectively compete with the vertical power of United States Steel."[263]

One division of the U.S. Steel conglomerate was the Pressed Steel Car Company, a manufacturer of railroad cars. Capitalized at 25 million dollars before the merger and now backed by the parent company, Pressed Steel was the dominant railroad car manufacturer in the nation. Legendary salesman James Buchanan "Diamond Jim" Brady worked for Pressed Steel before the merger, but he disliked U.S. Steel management and turned in his resignation, taking the company's chief engineer, John M. Hansen, with him.

Brady and his new partner were able to convince Mellon that with a mere three million dollar investment from him and his brother they could start up a car company that could successfully compete with the United States Steel division they had just left. Andrew and Dick judged that a company with nearly unlimited non-human resources, but without Brady and Hansen, would be no match for a small startup company with Brady and Hansen, so they put up the money. The Standard Steel Car Company went into business early in 1902. By the end of that year Brady had sent in a flood of purchase orders from some of the nation's biggest railroads, and the new factory was up and running filling the orders. The company was a tremendous financial success for all involved. Brady's skill as a salesman and his partner's skill as an engineer trumped all the advantages possessed by the nation's biggest conglomerate, just as the Mellon brothers had expected.[264]

Eventually the bank that the Judge had founded under the name Mellon and Sons was re-named the Mellon National Bank. When Andrew and Dick put up a new building for the bank in 1924 it was the largest bank building in the United States. To honor the role model who had contributed so much to their family's success, they removed the statue of Benjamin Franklin their father had commissioned for the original four story building and installed it in a prominent place in the new structure.

CHAPTER 10

Andrew Carnegie

———

The real tragedy of the poor is the poverty of their aspirations.

ADAM SMITH

WHEN J.P. MORGAN ENGINEERED THE merger of America's biggest manufacturers of steel and steel products to create the United States Steel conglomerate in 1901, the Carnegie Steel company was the indispensable centerpiece. It was by far the largest and most profitable steel company on the planet. When Andrew Carnegie agreed to sell Carnegie Steel to the U.S. Steel group, Morgan said to him "Mr. Carnegie, I want to congratulate you on being the richest man in the world."[265]

When Carnegie was born in a small town in Scotland 65 years earlier he had a long way to go to make himself the richest man in the world. His father William was a skilled craftsman, a weaver, whose craft had been made obsolete by new technologies. The family was poor. Andrew's parents didn't put him in school until he was eight years old, and when they did the cheapest school in town was all they could afford.[266] There was only one teacher, and the class size varied between 150 and 180 students.[267]

In 1848 Andrew's father, William Carnegie, decided to take his family to the United States to join some relatives in the Pittsburgh area. When the family left Scotland, Andrew's school days ended; from then on he would have to self-educate in what little spare time was available to a child who worked 60 hours a week. Reading quickly became a passion for the 12-year-old.

The Carnegie family bought the cheapest tickets to America they could find, on an old sailing ship that had once been a whaler.[268] The passengers were all poverty-stricken Scots like the Carnegies. The accommodations were dirty and crowded and the food was poor. Most of the passengers were miserable, but Andrew chose to see the voyage as an opportunity to make new friends and learn new skills. He charmed the sailors by showing interest in their work and volunteering to carry messages. They taught him the ropes of sailing a ship, and even shared their special Sunday dessert rations with him.[269]

They arrived in the U.S. in July of 1848. Things didn't get better right away. William Carnegie had heard about America being the "land of opportunity," but didn't fully understand what the expression meant. Sadly, the senior Carnegie continued to try to make a living as a hand weaver in the new world, where his skills were just as obsolete as they were in Scotland. Clinging to his old ways, he made tablecloths and sold them for pennies.[270]

Andrew, who started his career before his thirteenth birthday, understood what "land of opportunity" really means. He would spend the next 50-odd years seeking out and seizing opportunities. For him America was a land where the sky was the limit. His first job was as a "bobbin boy" changing bobbins in a textile factory. The pay was $1.20 per week, the equivalent of about $35 per week in today's money. Looking back on that first job as an adult, he would say "I have made millions since, but none of those millions gave me such happiness as my first week's earnings. I was now a helper of the family, a breadwinner, and no longer a total charge upon my parents."[271]

Soon he was able to secure a job at another factory, at a wage of $2.00 per week, a 67 percent increase in pay. Here the 13-year-old spent his days all alone in the basement of the factory, shoveling coal into the steam engine that ran the plant. Andrew was not content with his sweatshop job, but he never doubted that he could improve his situation through hard work and good decision making. In his autobiography he said of that time "my hopes were high, and I looked every day for some change to take place. What it was to be, I knew not, but that it would come I felt certain if I kept on."[272]

Andrew could see that if he made himself more valuable to employers, he could get better pay and working conditions. He understood while he was still in his early teens that people were resources and some human resources were more valuable than others. For his own benefit, he set out to make himself a more valuable human resource.

He was able to demonstrate his penmanship and math skills to the owner of the factory, who started pulling him out of the basement on an intermittent basis and putting him to work as a clerk. Andrew liked office work much better than his basement duties, so he continued to look for ways to make himself more valuable upstairs. As a step in that direction, he talked several young friends into pooling their money with him to hire an accountant named Mr. Williams to teach them double-entry bookkeeping at night.[273]

Before Andrew could complete his training as a bookkeeper another opportunity presented itself. A family friend mentioned that one of the telegraph offices in town had an opening for a telegram delivery boy. The job, if he could get it, would be a definite upgrade from what he was doing at the factory. The pay was 50 cents a week higher, and instead of spending half his time alone in a basement shoveling coal into a steam engine he would be out in the fresh air delivering telegrams to wealthy businessmen.

Andrew's father, by now a defeated and bitter man, told Andrew that applying for the job would be pointless. Andrew rejected that poisonous message and went to the telegraph office for an interview. He sold himself to the boss, and when asked when he would be able to start he told his new employer that he was ready to start immediately. He spent the rest of the day in training.

Andrew launched himself into his career with characteristic enthusiasm. "There was scarcely a minute," he says in his autobiography, "in which I could not learn something or find out how much there was to learn and how little I knew. I felt that my foot was upon the ladder and that I was bound to climb."[274] Andrew loved his father, but he somehow managed to protect himself from the "can't win; don't try" attitude William was always expressing. The younger Carnegie raced through his workday duties enthusiastically, then did self-assigned homework at night.

At home in the evenings he would drill himself on the names and addresses of the businesses he'd passed that day, until he could close his eyes and recite the names of the businesses on each street in the city in geographical order. Next he memorized the names and faces of all the businessmen who regularly sent or received telegraphs, so that if he passed the intended recipient of a telegraph on the street he could immediately deliver the message to the person and save a trip to the recipient's office.[275] Telegram recipients he approached in this way would often give him a tip for quick service, and, more important to the boy, they would remember his name and think highly of him.[276]

Andrew Carnegie's enthusiasm for jobs that some people would describe as "menial labor" was one of the key elements in his success. When he was a messenger boy his life was "in every respect a happy one,"[277] and from that time until his retirement many years later he would apply the same cheerfully aggressive attitude to everything his hand found to do. The same passion for excellence that would make him a millionaire in future years made him the best telegram boy in Pittsburgh in 1850.

While he was honing his messenger boy skills, Carnegie made time to improve his mind in other ways as well. At 14 he learned that an entrepreneur and philanthropist named Colonel James Anderson had just established a free lending library for the use of "working boys," but that the definition of "working" used by the librarian in charge didn't include clerks or messengers. Andrew wrote a letter to the editor of a local newspaper, arguing that kids like himself could benefit from education just as much as boys who worked with their hands.

The colonel directed his librarian to change the policy to include all categories of young workers. Carnegie immediately started taking full advantage of Anderson's generosity. "The treasures of the world which books contain," he would later say, "were opened to me at the right moment." He would spend every spare moment reading, even bringing a book with him to the telegraph office so he could read whenever he had an idle minute between delivery assignments. Years later Carnegie would erect a monument to Colonel Anderson in Pittsburgh. When he wrote his autobiography, he was not shy about the gratitude he felt. "I bless his name" said Carnegie of Anderson.[278]

Young Andrew Carnegie continued to distinguish himself among the other telegram boys with his work habits and his ever increasing skills. The office manager gave him a raise and put him in charge of distributing the messages between the other boys.[279] More promotions and raises would follow.

Books from Colonel Anderson's library were not the only educational resource the youngster used to improve his mind. Around the time he gained access to the library he and five friends formed a study group much like Benjamin Franklin's "Junto." The boys would study some issue of the day, then get together to debate the issue in conformance with a set of rules.[280] Carnegie may well have gotten the idea from reading Franklin's autobiography, although he doesn't mention Franklin's book in his own autobiography.

At work, Andrew started experimenting with the telegraph equipment before the office opened each morning. Soon he was able to exchange messages with similarly ambitious message boys in other offices around the state. One morning when he was doing this an emergency message started to come through. Andrew tapped out a response, warning the operator at the other end that the Pittsburgh office was not opened, but offering to take down the message if it was sent slowly. Impressed, his boss soon started letting him relieve the regular telegraph operators for short periods. Soon he was made a telegraph operator on a full time basis, with a salary of $20 per month. At the age of 15 he was his family's primary breadwinner.[281]

Andrew made it a matter of pride to be faster and more accurate than other operators. When he heard a rumor that there were telegraph operators who could take down an incoming message just by listening to the clattering of the key, without recourse to the long paper tape that recorded the dots and dashes, he challenged himself to master this new skill. After a period of time his mastery was so complete that his employer would sometimes invite clients into the office to watch Andrew perform.

Businessmen started asking for Andrew by name when they had important messages to send.[282] Young Carnegie was "diligent in his calling," and although he had not yet stood before kings, he was on his way to fulfilling Benjamin Franklin's favorite proverb. Ten years later, at the age of 25, he would be running a telegraph office frequented by President Lincoln. In later years he would meet several other U.S. presidents as well as an English Prime Minister and a German Kaiser.

At 17 Andrew was promoted to telegraph operator on a full time basis. He now regarded himself as "performing a man's part, not a boy's; earning a dollar every working day."[283] Because of Andrew's earning power his younger brother Tom was able to stay in school until he had completed two years of high school.

Andrew continued to work on improving his speed with the telegraph key. When the telegraph company needed an operator to man a temporary remote office, the company dispatched Andrew to the office, confident that he could send and receive more messages in a day than any other operator they had.

One of the customers on whom Andrew made a positive impression was a railroad superintendent named Thomas Scott, a self-made man like Andrew whose father had died, leaving the family in poverty, when he was 10 years old.[284] Now 29, Scott was in charge of the western region of the Pennsylvania Railroad. In 1853 Scott was able to persuade his superiors to open a private telegraph office for the railroad's exclusive use. There was only one telegraph operator in the city Scott wanted for his office. He offered 17-year-old Andrew Carnegie the job, and won a brief bidding war with Andrew's old employer by offering 35 dollars per month.

The Pennsylvania offered terrific growth opportunities to an ambitious teenager in 1853. Transportation and communications have always been the two golden geese of American business, and running a telegraph office for a railroad put Carnegie at the intersection of the two. The "Pennsy" was still a very small railroad at this time, but it was about to start growing at a tremendous rate. By the end of the Civil War J. Edgar Thompson's Pennsylvania Railroad and Cornelius Vanderbilt's New York Central would be the two dominant railroad companies in a nation where railroading was the dominant industry. During that time of rapid growth, from 1853 to 1865, Andrew Carnegie worked for the Pennsy and reported directly to Thomas Scott.

At first there weren't enough messages to send to keep an operator busy full time, so Carnegie worked as Scott's clerk and secretary when he wasn't at the telegraph key. Carnegie was eager to do any kind of work that came to hand, to show his capabilities to his new boss. He explained his philosophy years later: "(T)he great aim of every boy should be to do something beyond the sphere of his duties – something which attracts the attention of those over him." Carnegie's compensation grew with his responsibilities. While he was still in his teens he bought the house his family had been renting. He was 19 when his father died, and by that time Andrew had already been the family's primary breadwinner for years. Andrew and his family continued to live frugally, despite the healthy salary that Andrew was earning. By living without luxuries they were able to pay off the mortgage on their small house in just two years.[285]

Shortly after his father's death Carnegie became a stockholder for the first time. Thomas Scott told him of some shares in a company called Adams Express that had become available because the woman who owned them had a sudden need for cash. Scott, who already owned some Adams Express stock, encouraged Carnegie to buy the shares, and even offered to lend his protégé the money for the purchase. This would be the first of many timely and profitable investments. Like the other people profiled in this book, Andrew resisted the temptation to spend his money on indulgences, and invested in his future instead.

Soon Scott was entrusting Carnegie with management duties. In 1856 Scott left Pittsburgh for two weeks and left Carnegie to run the entire district in his absence. The 21-year-old kept things running smoothly, and his bosses continued to increase his responsibilities.

Late in 1856 Thomas Scott was promoted to General Superintendent of the Pennsylvania Railroad, reporting directly to company president J. Edgar Thompson. The new job required him to move to Altoona, and of course he brought his right hand man with him. Carnegie's salary was now $50 per month, and he was able to bring his mother and brother to Altoona to live with him. They kept the house in Pittsburgh and used it as a rental property. At 21 years of age, and with only four and a half years of formal schooling, Carnegie was only two steps below the president of a company that would be the largest corporation in the world within a few years.

In Altoona, Carnegie's position as Thomas Scott's go-to guy continued to open up opportunities both inside and outside the railroad. In 1858 an inventor named Theodore Woodruff persuaded Thompson and Scott to order two of the sleeper cars he had developed (some accounts say it was four cars). It would be an important milestone in Andrew Carnegie's career. Woodruff was a typical American rags-to-riches success story. He'd left his parents' farm at age 16 to become a wagon maker's apprentice, then worked in a foundry for a while before going back into the transportation business as a metalworker. He was in his twenties when railroads first came to the U.S. and he went to work for one of the first companies building railroad cars.[286]

Carnegie, showing the foresight that he would demonstrate time and again throughout his career, bought a one-eighth interest in Woodruff's company. Before long the Pennsylvania and other railroads were buying Woodruff's sleeper cars like hotcakes. By 1860 those sleeper car shares were earning Carnegie $5,000 per year, far more than his salary at the railroad.

In 1859 Scott was promoted to vice president of the railroad. The promotion required him to move to the company's head office in Philadelphia. Carnegie didn't move with him; he moved back to Pittsburgh to take over his mentor's old job as superintendent of the western district. Scott was still his boss, but the two would no longer be working together on a daily basis. Andrew's brother Tom, now 16 years old, had already been trained as a telegraph operator by this time. He went to work as Andrew's secretary in the Pittsburgh office.

Carnegie had always been a hard worker, and being entrusted with the sole responsibility for a long section of the road drove him to even greater exertions. He would sometimes stay out on the road for several days and nights tending to wrecks and breakdowns, grabbing the occasional catnap on the floor of a railroad car. Despite the rigors of his job, Carnegie attended night classes whenever possible, to help supplement the four or five years of formal schooling he'd had in his childhood.

The responsibilities that drove 24-year-old Carnegie were more than financial. Decisions he made could literally mean life or death for the company's employees and passengers. The trains of the 1850s were nowhere near as safe or reliable as the ones we have today. Breakdowns and accidents were common. The rails themselves were made of brittle iron, rather than steel, and would often break under the weight of the locomotives, causing trains to derail and crash. Axles broke at high speeds, couplings failed, brakes were primitive; any number of factors could cause a serious accident.

As a superintendent, young Carnegie spent much of his time reading and writing telegrams. Any mistake in organization or communication could send two trains crashing into each other, or allow a moving train to hit one disabled and stationary on the tracks.

Railroad cars before 1888 were made almost entirely of wood, and if an accident happened in a remote spot where clearing the tracks was difficult Carnegie would give orders to have the train cars burned in place. His reasoning was that the time saved was worth more than the property destroyed. The idea raised eyebrows at first, but eventually it became standard operating procedure for the railroad. While the cars were still burning he would often have a crew build a temporary railroad around the crash site, so traffic could keep flowing.

Carnegie had only held his job as Western Superintendent for a couple years when the Civil War broke out. Although he would describe himself as a pacifist in later years, he was passionate in his support for the Union war effort. Soon after coming to the United States he had become an ardent abolitionist. In letters to his cousin Dodd back in Scotland he often described slavery as a violation of everything America stood for, and predicted that it would come to an end soon. A letter he wrote in 1852 is typical of his statements on the subject:

Allow me to say that I am an enthusiastic & ultra abolitionist, admit and deplore the great evils that necessarily flow in the wake of slavery feel as keenly the great wrong perpetrated upon the African as you can do. It is the greatest evil in the world and I promise you that whatever influence I may acquire shall be used to overthrow it. In short I am a Republican and believe in our noble declaration that "all men are born free and equal."[287]

Dodd was not the only one who heard about his political sentiments. Andrew wrote several anti-slavery letters to the editor while he was still a teenager, and at least one of them was published in a New York newspaper. He even formed a literary society among railroad employees to debate the political issues of the day, most of which involved the expansion or curtailment of slavery. In November of 1860 Carnegie was old enough to vote in a presidential election for the first time, and he proudly cast his vote for Abraham Lincoln.

The Civil War started just 39 days after President Lincoln's inauguration, and the Union nearly lost the war in the first few days. Washington, DC was located on the border between Virginia and Maryland, two slave states. Virginia joined the Confederate side right away, and the governor of Maryland at first showed a similar inclination. Lincoln had not had the foresight to bring large numbers of troops into the capital before hostilities began. As his government attempted to correct this oversight, pro-Confederate mobs in Maryland tore up railroads and bridges to prevent the transport of Northern troops to Washington from the port cities of Baltimore and Annapolis on Chesapeake Bay. As soon as war broke out, Lincoln's Secretary of War wisely persuaded Thomas Scott to take a leave of absence from his job with the Pennsylvania Railroad and come to DC to take charge of the rapidly deteriorating transportation situation. Scott immediately persuaded Carnegie to come and help him.

Carnegie's first task was to re-establish rail service and telegraphic communications between Chesapeake Bay and Washington. He tackled the challenge with his usual tireless energy and ruthless efficiency. Crews worked around the clock to repair the roads and bridges. On

April 25 Carnegie personally supervised the first trainload of troops from Annapolis to the capital, riding in the locomotive with the engineer and fireman to watch for obstructions on the rails.

Spotting a place where anti-Union vandals had grounded the telegraph wires, Carnegie jumped off the train to release them. One of the wires sprang up and cut his face. He would ever after boast that he was the first man to be wounded in the defense of the capital.[288]

Carnegie, who always had a positive attitude about everything, expected the Union to win the war and end slavery very soon. "You shall at no distant time," he wrote to a friend, "be able to proclaim in New Orleans that God has made all men free and equal and that slavery is the sum of all villanies." [289]

Carnegie's Scottish constitution was not made for the heat in Virginia in July and August, and shortly after the First Battle of Bull Run he suffered sun stroke while supervising road construction in the area. While he was convalescing, Scott, now Assistant Secretary of War, asked Carnegie to take a desk job in Washington. The two of them would once again be working in adjacent offices in the same building. Scott was responsible for all Union railroad and telegraph operations, and he put Carnegie in charge of the Washington telegraph office.

President Lincoln would frequently visit Carnegie's office to get the latest information from his generals in the field. Lincoln found an admirer in Carnegie, who called him "the most perfect democrat, revealing in every word and act the equality of men." The president, said Carnegie, "had a kind word for everybody, even the youngest boy in the office."[290]

In September Carnegie, still in fragile health, returned to Pittsburgh to resume his old job with the Pennsy. The railroad was taxed to the limit hauling war materiel from Pittsburgh's factories and provisions for the soldiers from Pennsylvania farms, along with all the usual civilian traffic.

Carnegie's business interests continued to expand during the remainder of the war years. He made very successful investments in the oil industry, the Western Union telegraph company, an iron foundry, and a bridge-building company. By 1863, according to his income tax return, he was only getting about five percent of his income from his full time job with the railroad. The other 95 percent came from his other interests, most of which could have benefited from his more-direct involvement. His patriotism and anti-slavery passions were the only things that kept him on the railroad payroll. He quite rightly saw his efforts to keep the trains running on time as a significant contribution to the war effort.[291] In late March of 1865, with Union forces closing in on the Confederate capital, Carnegie collected his last paycheck and resigned. Confederate General Robert E. Lee surrendered 12 days later.

The late 1860s were a busy time for Andrew Carnegie. When he resigned from the railroad he was able to focus his energies on his own businesses. One was the Keystone Bridge Company, a bridge building concern he had co-founded with a couple of fellow rail-road employees in 1862. Another was the Central Transportation Company, the sleeper car company founded by inventor Theodore Woodruff. Another important company, a portent of the direction his career would eventually take, was a manufacturing concern called the Freedom Iron and Steel Company that made components and equip-ment for the railroads.

Always a skillful deal-maker, Carnegie functioned as the primary salesman for all three companies.[292] His activities during this period increasingly brought him into contact with wealthy and powerful fig-ures, and he moved in those circles with ease. Although his formal education had ended at age 12, Carnegie had always focused on self-education in whatever time he could spare from his work, and by the time he was in his twenties he was able to converse comfortably with well educated "old money" businessmen like Junius Morgan.

In 1867 Carnegie's Central Transportation Company was competing with several other sleeper car companies for the contract to provide sleeper cars to the Union Pacific, the longer half of the soon-to-be-completed trans-continental railroad. One competitor was George Pullman's Pullman Palace Car Company. Another was the Wagner Palace Car Company, owned in part by Cornelius Vanderbilt.

Carnegie recognized George Pullman as a highly capable businessman, and wanted him as a partner. Pullman had grown up poor and dropped out of school to earn a living early,[293] just like Carnegie. He impressed Carnegie with his work ethic, his management and marketing skills, and his aggressiveness. Pullman was also extremely vain, and Carnegie knew it.

Carnegie approached Pullman on a hotel staircase and suggested that they merge their two companies and pursue the Union Pacific contract together. Pullman asked what the proposed new company would be called, and Carnegie, knowing what kind of man he was talking to, gave the right answer: they would call it the Pullman Palace Car Company. "This suited him exactly," according to Carnegie, "and it suited me equally well." Carnegie and his original partners would hold a majority of the stock in the new company, but Pullman would have the pleasure of seeing his name on the masthead. Their new company immediately became the dominant player in the sleeper car business. Eventually even Vanderbilt's New York Central was using Pullman cars.[294]

In 1862 Carnegie had founded the Keystone Bridge Company to build railroad bridges out of iron, rather than wood, a radical idea at the time. All through his career Carnegie was able to see the future more clearly than most of his rivals, and his early embrace of iron bridge-making is just one example of a career-long pattern. He formed the bridge company with a mechanic and an engineer from the Pennsylvania Railroad. Carnegie's salesmanship allowed them to broaden their customer base quickly. In 1865, shortly after resigning his own position with the railroad, he persuaded Thomas Scott to invest $40,000 in the re-organized Keystone Bridge Company. Carnegie used the extra capital to expand the company's production facilities. He gave himself the job of drumming up enough business to keep the factory busy.

In 1864 Carnegie learned of the existence of the Illinois & St. Louis Bridge Company, a construction company formed specifically to build a bridge across the Mississippi River at St. Louis. He made it his goal to get a contract for part of the bridge construction once it started. Carnegie coveted the trans-Mississippi bridge project for many reasons. First, of course, was the money. This was to be the largest and most expensive bridge that had ever been built in the United States, and by far the biggest order Keystone had ever had. No less important was the marketing value. The railroad industry was writing the nation's story in the nineteenth century, and a bridge that would allow trains to cross the Mississippi carried an extremely high profile.

The engineer hired by the Illinois and St. Louis was James Buchanan Eads, another self-made man. Eads was born in Indiana in 1820 and named after then-Congressman James Buchanan. He grew up in a poor home and had to drop out of school at an early age and get a job to help put food on the family table. Like Carnegie, he educated himself in what little leisure time he could find. In Eads' case the self-educational efforts focused on math, science, and engineering.[295]

Construction on the trans-Mississippi bridge began in 1868. Carnegie's Keystone Company sub-contracted with the Illinois and St. Louis Bridge Company to build the superstructure. Not surprisingly, Keystone bought virtually all of the structural iron for the project from Carnegie's Freedom Iron and Steel Company. Not satisfied with double-dipping, Carnegie found a third way to make money from the nation's most high-profile construction project.

The Eads Bridge project needed some $6,000,000 in financing before it could get started. American companies depended heavily on loans and investments from Europe in that era, so the bridge company needed someone who could cross the Atlantic to borrow the money. Carnegie persuaded the executives of the Illinois and St. Louis to hire him to sell the bonds that financed the project. Carnegie traveled to London, and with the help of Junius Morgan managed to negotiate the sale of all the bonds, earning himself a quick $50,000 commission. The mutually profitable collaborations between Carnegie and the House of Morgan would continue for 17 years before coming to a sudden and acrimonious end in 1885, when, as related in chapter 8, Junius' son J.P. Morgan engineered the deal that cost Carnegie a needed railroad option and made Carnegie's multi-million dollar investment in the project worthless.

In 1872 Carnegie made the decision to focus his energies on the steel business. His Freedom Iron Company had deployed its first Bessemer process steel mill (and changed the company's name) in 1868, but the cost of steel-making in '68 was still high enough that the output of that first furnace was only used for specialty products. Freedom's core product was railroad rails which were still made of iron, not steel. The original purpose of Freedom's one steel furnace was to forge steel caps to go on iron rails to increase their strength and durability. The steel-capped rails turned out to be a failure, but the Bessemer furnace continued to be used for special orders of high strength products for various customers.

The Bessemer process was patented in England in 1855, and made it possible to make large enough quantities of relatively affordable steel for use in products larger than knife blades and plowshares. Initially the Bessemer process required high grade iron ore with a very low phosphorus content, and was too expensive for large scale commodity products like railroad rails, but the allure of the money to be made motivated entrepreneurs to solve these problems over time. By 1872 a good source of low-phosphorous ore had been developed in northern Michigan, and a transportation infrastructure put in place to bring the ore to market. Meanwhile engineers like Alexander Holley had been improving the efficiency of the Bessemer process with various innovations.

Carnegie decided that the time had come for steel to replace iron in American industry. As in so many other cases, his judgment was right and his timing was excellent. He made his commitment to steel at exactly the right time in history, and almost every strategic move he made proved to be sound. As in all his other ventures, he focused first on getting the best human resources. As his plans for a large scale steel mill took place he approached his partners in Freedom Iron and Steel – his brother Tom, an efficiency expert named Henry Phipps, and a brilliant engineer named Andrew Kloman – and asked them to help him found and run the new company. The three partners lacked Andrew's foresight. All three of them refused to take active roles in the company, although they did make small financial investments in it. Additional investment funds came from various businessmen, mostly in the Pittsburgh area.

Denied the managerial talents of his Freedom partners, Carnegie focused on assembling a management team that would have the skills and habits he valued. First he hired Alexander Holley, America's foremost expert on Bessemer steel-making, to be his plant manager. Holley had learned his trade directly from Henry Bessemer in England. Holley's chief assistant would be Captain William Jones, a typical self-made man of that era. Jones' father was a poor minister in an unpopular denomination, who suffered from health problems. William Jones had had to go to work full time at age 10 to put food on the table.[296] His first job had been in an iron foundry, and with the exception of his service in the Union Army during the war he made his career in iron and steel. He came to Carnegie's company after distinguishing himself as Holley's number two man at a new Bessemer plant Holley had just started up in Johnstown, PA.

William P. Shinn was another business manager Carnegie targeted for his team. In 1872 Shinn was vice president of the Allegheny

Valley Railroad. Carnegie was so impressed with Shinn that he went to great lengths to lure him away. He flattered and cajoled Shinn while offering him ever increasing financial compensation. Shinn finally joined the team as general manager. Carnegie compensated all his key employees with shares of stock in the company, a very unusual move at the time but something that many companies do today. Carnegie wanted his key players to care as much about making the company a success as he did.[297]

Charles Schwab, who would rise through the ranks at Carnegie Steel and become the first president of United States Steel when Carnegie retired, started his career as a teenage store clerk, then went to work for Captain Jones for a dollar a day at age 17.[298] Jones brought him along when he went to work for Carnegie in 1872.

The site Carnegie choose was just south of Pittsburgh, on the banks of the Monongahela River. Trying to keep his transportation options open, he picked a site that had access to two railroads, the Pennsylvania and the Baltimore and Ohio (B&O), although time would show that the B&O was not really a viable option. The new company was incorporated in November of 1872.

Steel railroad rails were to be the new mill's chief product, and in choosing a name for the plant Carnegie offered some flattery to his largest prospective customer, President J. Edgar Thompson of the Pennsy. He named it the J. Edgar Thompson Works. In letters between Carnegie and his partners everyone called the plant "the E.T."

Construction on the E.T. had barely begun when the banking house of Jay Cooke and Company started defaulting on its debts, initiating the great financial panic and depression of 1873. Carnegie's partners balked at the idea of funding a two to three year construction project in the depths of a depression, but Carnegie never lost faith. With his usual clear foresight, he predicted that the depression would soon be over, and that construction costs would be lower during a depression than during a boom. Fortunately for Carnegie, his shares in Western Union and the Pullman Palace Car Company held their value fairly well during the crash. He sold some of them to help fund plant construction.

Carnegie's experience as a bond salesman was invaluable during the depression. American banks had little money to lend after the crash, but Carnegie was able to go back to London to renew his acquaintance with Junius Morgan, this time selling bonds not on a commission basis, but for his own company. His reputation stood him in good stead there, and Morgan was able to help him find buyers for the bonds in short order.

The plant opened in 1875. Carnegie and his partners had built "the most modern and most efficient Bessemer steel plant in America," and the depression allowed them to build it at a cost that was only "three-fourths as much as the same plant would have cost two or three years earlier or later."[299] Steel rails quickly made the old iron rails obsolete, and the E.T. operated around the clock to fill customers' orders.

Carnegie and his partners paid themselves only relatively small dividends, and re-invested the profits from the E.T. to expand their operations. Over time they opened additional steel mills. To reduce costs Carnegie started looking for opportunities to buy sources of the two main raw materials of steel production: coke, or processed coal; and iron ore. Carnegie purchased iron-rich land in northern Michigan, then leased even richer iron-bearing properties in Minnesota. He acquired Pennsylvania's richest coal-bearing properties, and the facilities for processing raw coal into coke, via a merger with another Pennsylvania businessman.

The nation's leading coke producer at that time was Henry Clay Frick, yet another self-made man of that era. Frick's father, John Frick, was poor and shiftless, but his mother Elizabeth came from a prosperous family. After Elizabeth married John her father allowed the couple to live rent-free in a small house on his farm; this was where

Henry Clay Frick grew up. The boy went to work as a store clerk at 17, proved himself as a salesman, and soon got a 12-dollar-a-week job in a large department store.[300] He started investing in the coke business when demand for the product was still low, and his foresight paid off when steel mills started to be built in the United States in the 1870s. To finance the expansion of his operations he borrowed money from Judge Thomas Mellon and his sons; he and Andrew Mellon took a liking to each other and soon became lifelong friends. Carnegie and Frick negotiated a merger of their two companies in 1881.

By 1895, 20 years after the E.T. mill opened, Carnegie's company was the largest steel producer in the world, and by far the most profitable.[301] Three years later Carnegie had completed his railroad from Pittsburgh to the shores of Lake Erie, which reduced his freight rates by half and made his company still more profitable.[302]

Three years after that J.P. Morgan came calling. When Morgan proposed buying Carnegie out, Carnegie demanded highly liquid gold-backed bonds, rather than stock, so he could easily make donations of any size to worthy charities. He spent the rest of his life carefully identifying, vetting, and supporting worthy causes. By the time he died he'd given away virtually all of his wealth; leaving his heirs only a few million dollars and a castle in Scotland.[303]

Carnegie's success is best explained in his own words. When he was still poor he told a cousin that he expected to make a success of himself in America. "If I don't," said the-15 year-old messenger boy, "it will be my own fault, for anyone can get along in this country."[304]

CHAPTER 11

John D. Rockefeller

——

In America most of the rich men were formally poor.

ALEXIS DE TOCQUEVILLE

JOHN DAVISON ROCKEFELLER WAS THE wealthiest man in the world for the last quarter-century of his life.

He was born poor on July 8 of 1839 in Richford, NY. At the time of his birth, railroad trains had been operating in the U.S. for about eight years. J.P. Morgan was two years old, Andrew Carnegie was not yet four, and 45-year-old Cornelius Vanderbilt was operating a fleet of steamboats in and around Long Island Sound.

Rockefeller's father was a handsome, charming, and utterly unscrupulous criminal named William A. "Devil Bill" Rockefeller. John's mother was a God-fearing Baptist named Eliza (formally Eliza Davison) who had fallen for Devil Bill's charm and married him against her father's wishes[305] at age 17. John D. was the second of Eliza's five children; and one of at least seven children William is known to have fathered.

John D. and his siblings had a tough childhood. Often there was not enough money to pay the bills. The financial difficulties the Rockefeller family suffered during John's childhood were not caused by any lack of earning power on William's part; the elder Rockefeller had a knack for separating honest and trusting people from their money, and he always lived well. The family's problem was that their provider was selfish and unreliable.

Devil Bill would disappear for weeks or months at a time, leaving his wife without a dime and instructing her to buy the things her children needed on credit. He would travel far, peddling fake cancer cures to gullible farmers and small town folk. When he returned from his wanderings he would pull out a fat role of bills and pay off his family's account at the local store. During his absences Eliza would live as frugally as possible, not wishing to over-tax the trust of storekeepers who could never really know when or whether Devil Bill was going to return.[306]

A Rockefeller neighbor quoted in one biography of John D. said that John and the other children were "pitiably neglected." "Their clothing was old and tattered," said the neighbor, "and they looked dirty and hungry."[307] On at least one occasion a charitable neighbor donated money to pay for the children's school books.[308]

In school John D. was a dedicated, though not particularly gifted, student. "I was not an easy student," he said, "and I had to apply myself diligently to prepare my lessons.[309] His diligence in school in his childhood would pay big dividends later in life.

In 1852 John D. and his younger brother were enrolled in a school called the Owego Academy, where most of the students came from more prosperous families. During the year the school hired a photographer to take a class picture, but excluded the Rockefeller boys from the picture because they were too poorly dressed. John, always positive in his attitude, chose not to be angry or resentful. "In Eliza Rockefeller's household," according to a Rockefeller biographer, "one didn't morbidly dwell on slights but kept one's sights fixed on the practical goals ahead."[310]

Transportation and communications in the 1840s and 50s were primitive, and by traveling from town to town Devil Bill could always find gullible people who knew nothing about him. These simple honest country folk would be the customers for his patent medicines. For much the same reason he tended to move his home and family from one community to another on a regular basis. Whenever the Rockefellers moved to a new town John's father would be respected and popular for a while, until the locals got to know him too well and he wore out his welcome.

There were accusations that William was involved with a gang of horse thieves in one town, and on another occasion he was actually indicted (but not tried, for some reason) for rape.[311] When the locals learned to see through Devil Bill's act it would be time to move on again. All of this made for a turbulent childhood. John D. Rockefeller had lived in nine different houses by the time he dropped out of high school at age 15.

The family usually lived on a small farm that Devil Bill purchased or rented near a town. Whenever the family had farmland to cultivate the children and their mother did all the chores; William considered manual labor beneath his dignity. Young John would have to get up at dawn to milk cows before going to school. In the evenings farm chores and schoolwork left little time for recreation.

The elder Rockefeller would frequently use an assumed name while traveling around peddling his quack medicines, and in 1855 he signed the name "William Levingston" on the marriage license he used when he married a teenage girl named Margaret Allen. The new Mrs. Levingston had no idea that her groom was already married, nor that his real name was Rockefeller. Eliza and the children were living in Cleveland by this time and Margaret's home was in Ontario. Devil Bill managed to keep his wives ignorant of each other's existence for many years, although Eliza's feelings became a moot point for Devil Bill when he abandoned her for good a couple years after he married Margaret.

The sources of stability in John D's childhood were his mother and his Christian faith. Eliza was tireless in protecting and caring for her children. She'd made the great mistake of her life at 17, and she endured her dysfunctional marriage without wasting much time on self-pity. She stretched her meager financial resources during William's absences, made the best of it while he was around, and did everything in her power to prepare her children for a better life. Eliza's love was tough love. She made sure her children grew up with the self-discipline her husband so notoriously lacked. John D's rare misdeeds were swiftly corrected with a hickory switch. As the eldest boy he quickly earned his mother's confidence and began to serve as a father figure for the younger children. As he grew he learned to cherish principles like honesty, loyalty, and promise-keeping; things that were clearly of no consequence to Devil Bill.[312]

In some sense John D. and his father had reversed roles in the family.[313] When William was home he acted more like a big brother than a father. He left the whole issue of discipline to his wife and taught the kids how to ride and shoot, took them fishing, and regaled them with stories of his travels. John D., as the oldest boy, took responsibility for helping to raise his younger siblings. Still, both parents played important roles in John D. Rockefeller's early education. Eliza taught him good values and principles, and Devil Bill taught him all about shrewd business dealings. Aristotle tells us that "It is the mark of an educated mind to be able to entertain a thought without accepting it," and young Rockefeller seems to have been able to follow that principle with his father's dishonest ways. He made the best of the time he was able to spend with William, enjoying the fun and games without ever starting to emulate the bad behavior.

The things Devil Bill said and did provided good training for John's career in the cutthroat business world of the late nineteenth century. John never cheated in his business deals, but it's interesting to note that no one was ever able to cheat him either. Brilliant businessmen like Cornelius Vanderbilt and Andrew Carnegie were taken in by unscrupulous partners or rivals on occasion, but John D. Rockefeller never was.

The other great influence in young Rockefeller's life was the Church. His commitment to Christian charity started with his mother giving him pennies to put in the offering jar during Sunday services.[314] While the family was living in Moravia, New York, a Presbyterian neighbor would often drop Eliza and the children off at their Baptist church on the way to his own church on a Sunday morning,[315] illustrating Tocqueville's observation that Americans belonged to many different Christian sects but all "agree(d) in respect to the duties which are due from man to man."[316]

When John D. was around 15 years old he fell in love with a girl named Melinda Miller. Melinda's parents quickly broke up the relationship. Biographer Ron Chernow expressed the irony of her parents' decision in his Rockefeller bio: "In one of the less prophetic judgements in parental history, they argued that they didn't want their daughter to throw herself away on a young man with such poor prospects."[317] After the break-up with Melinda, Rockefeller's love life would remain on the back burner for several years as he finished his education and focused all his energies on building a career.

In May of 1855, at the age of 15, John D. dropped out of high school to take a three-month vocational course in bookkeeping. When he finished the course he went looking for a job. By training, talent, and inclination he was a bookkeeper, but few businessmen in 1855 Cleveland were willing to entrust their books to a 16-year-old. Times were tough, and older and more experienced applicants were available.

Every morning for six weeks the youth dressed up in his best suit and walked from one office to the next asking for work. He made a list of the larger companies in town and visited each one in turn. When all of them had rejected him he started at the top of the list and visited them again. "I was working every day at my business," said Rockefeller, "the business of looking for work. I put in my full time at this every day."[318] He walked from one office to the next, trying to sell himself to every businessman who would listen, every business day for six weeks. The tenacity Rockefeller demonstrated at 16 is one of the common threads that run through all great American success stories. "The real genius," as Thomas Edison once said, "is sticking to it." In addition to hard work, decisiveness, vision, and an eye for the best human resources; all great American entrepreneurs had the tenacity to overcome rejection and failure, and Rockefeller was no exception.

On September 26 of 1855 Rockefeller's persistence finally paid off. The partners of a smaller company called Hewitt and Tuttle agreed to let him help with their books on an un-paid, probationary basis, with the understanding that if his work was good enough he'd eventually start drawing a paycheck. Rockefeller was thrilled. For the rest of his life he would always celebrate September 26 as "Job Day." To him this was the day he started on the path of self-sufficiency.[319]

After three months Hewitt and Tuttle agreed to start paying him for his labors, and even paid him retroactively for the time he had already put in, at a rate of 50 cents a day (less than one dollar per hour in today's money). Going forward, his salary was to be $25 per month.[320] The partners certainly got their money's worth out of their young clerk; his workday started at 6:30 AM and he often stayed at the office long after it closed. On one occasion he made a promise to himself to go at least 30 days without working past 10:00 PM, presumably because that had been a regular occurrence.[321]

His new employer was a brokerage house that mostly handled shipments of foodstuffs like grains and fresh vegetables. While he was still working for Hewitt and Tuttle, the teenager started making a few small transactions with money he had saved from his meager wages, buying and selling commodities in parallel with what his bosses were doing.

Before he'd even gotten his first paycheck Rockefeller invested 10 cents in a small red notebook that he used to record, in meticulous detail, all his expenditures and income. He was familiar with

Benjamin Franklin's observation that "industry and thrift are a means to distinction," and he made a point of being both industrious and thrifty. After three years with Hewitt and Tuttle, Rockefeller's wages had been raised to $50 a month, and he had already saved up an $800 nest egg, after paying all his living expenses and giving generously to his church and other worthy causes.

Rockefeller left Hewitt and Tuttle after less than three years, and he would never work for a paycheck again. In 1858, a few months before his nineteenth birthday, he made an agreement with a 28-year-old produce broker named Maurice Clark. Each man would invest $2,000 in cash, and the two of them would go into the food brokering business as partners.

Clark was the usual rags-to-riches story. Born in Britain, he'd had little education, and had worked as a gardener until his boss pushed him too far and he responded with a punch to the face. He fled to the U.S. penniless, to avoid arrest, and got work as a teamster for a while before finding his place in the world trading commodities.[322]

Rockefeller didn't have the full two thousand dollars on hand, so he had to borrow the balance at 10 percent interest to buy his share of the partnership. The new company opened for business on April 1. Despite his youth, Rockefeller turned out to be an effective salesman for the new company. His earnestness, sobriety, and obvious dedication to details appealed to older businessmen. Soon he was traveling around two states modestly but confidently asking prospective new clients to give his company a try. "I found that old men had confidence in me right away," said Rockefeller, "and after I stayed a few weeks in the country, I returned home and the consignments came in and our business was increased and it opened up a new world for me."[323]

It shouldn't surprise anyone that a reserved youth like Rockefeller, who always valued his privacy and kept his personal and business interests strictly separate, could succeed as a salesman. The stereotype of salesmen as extroverts who slap backs and tell jokes in a loud voice is not very accurate, at least where *successful* selling is concerned. Glibness and extroversion are highly over-rated as sales skills, and thorough product knowledge and direct, plain talking are grossly under-rated; many highly successful salespeople are, as Rockefeller was, soft-spoken and modest in their approach.

When the Civil War started in 1861 it increased demand for the foodstuffs and other commodities Clark and Rockefeller were buying, transporting, and re-selling. The company steadily re-invested its profits, and the client list, revenues, and profits all grew steadily.

Rockefeller, like Carnegie and virtually every other great entrepreneur of that era, was a passionate opponent of slavery and a strong supporter of President Lincoln and the Union cause. From childhood Rockefeller had always been a vocal abolitionist. At 14 he wrote an essay for school in which he said it was "a violation of the laws of our country and the laws of our God that man should hold his fellow man in bondage…How under such circumstances can America call herself free?"[324] His little red notebook of personal expenditures, which survives today, shows that while still a teenager he donated money to various black charities and churches, and in 1859 even gave money to help a black man buy his wife out of slavery.[325] The woman Rockefeller would eventually marry was an even more passionate abolitionist. Laura Celestia Spelman grew up in a home that was part of the Underground Railroad; during her childhood escaping slaves often slept in her parents' home.[326]

Rockefeller, again like Carnegie, was old enough to vote for a presidential candidate for the first time in 1860, and proudly cast his vote for Lincoln. Before the war broke out he attended meetings with fellow abolitionists who railed against the evils of slavery. When the war started Rockefeller, despite his Union sympathies, did not volunteer for military service. In explaining his reasoning later, he pointed out that he'd been the sole support for his mother and siblings at this time and that abandoning his business at this stage would have left them without financial resources. Like many other wealthy men of that era he hired a soldier to fight in his place for the standard sum of $300, and in addition he gave generously to various war-related charities.[327]

By 1862 Rockefeller and his partner were already making an annual profit of $17,000 from a company they had founded with only $4,000 in capital four years earlier. Both partners were willing to live frugally and re-invest most of their profits in the business, although Clark was never as thrifty as Rockefeller.

Developments in nearby Pennsylvania soon presented the partners with an opportunity to invest in something even more lucrative than foodstuffs. In 1859 "Colonel" Edwin Drake had drilled the first successful oil well in history, near a town called Titusville, Pennsylvania, about a 150 miles southeast of Cleveland. Soon oil wells were sprouting up all around Titusville. In 1863 24-year-old John D. Rockefeller entered the industry that would define his life. A chemist named Samuel Andrews persuaded Rockefeller and Clark to put up $4,000 in capital to found an oil refinery. Soon Clark's two brothers invested additional funds and became partners as well. Rockefeller put a great deal of thought into the location for the refinery, and chose a site on a river that ran into Lake Erie, right next to the right-of-way on which a new railroad was soon to be built. With two transportation options available, the site gave the partners bargaining power for their negotiations with shippers. For the rest of his career Rockefeller would choose the sites for his facilities based on the available transportation options.

Rockefeller soon abandoned his other business interests to focus on oil. He often showed up at the refinery at 6:30 AM to help with manual labor, helping to build barrels or hauling out refuse.[328] Always eager to operate efficiently, Rockefeller figured out a way to recycle waste chemicals for sale as fertilizer. He always maintained a razor-sharp focus on eliminating waste, streamlining operations, and making the business grow. He was blessed with exceptional foresight, and he predicted several crucial things about the oil business with such confidence that he was able to bet his career on all of them coming true. In each case he was right.

First, at a time when all the world's known oil reserves were located within a couple hundred feet of ground level in one small part of Pennsylvania, Rockefeller was confident that the supply would continue to grow.

This was far from a universal belief at the time. Many of the drillers and refiners in those early days of the industry threw together shoestring operations and tried to put as much cash in the bank as possible before the oil ran out and the rigs had to be abandoned. And it wasn't just wildcat drillers who expected the petroleum industry to be a temporary phenomenon. Even Andrew Carnegie, whose foresight in business matters was generally very good, expected the oil supply to dry up quickly.[329]

Rockefeller, on the other hand, quickly became convinced that God had provided petroleum for mankind to use, and that the blessing would be large and lasting.[330] "(T)hese vast stores of wealth," he said, "were the gifts of the great Creator."[331]

Second, Rockefeller saw from the first that refining was the part of the business where the greatest opportunities lay. Rockefeller made up his mind early that drilling for oil was not for him. There was too much risk involved, and success depended entirely too much on luck. By running a refinery, he could concentrate on efficiency and growth while counting on other people to hunt around for the raw material. He had no reason to worry about which drillers succeeded and which ones failed; all that mattered to him was that some of them were going to succeed.

Third, he could see that the oil business was eventually going to become a classic commodity market, where efficiency and volume determined the winners.

Armed with these three assumptions, he laid out a plan to dominate the refinery business. It was an audacious goal for a 25-year-old, but his actions at that time indicate that he planned on nothing less than the kind of success he ended up achieving.

When selling a mass market commodity like oil, the largest producer quite often has the best profit margin. Large volumes of business not only allow for economies of scale, they also provide the producer with bargaining leverage. Rockefeller focused obsessively on growth during his early years in the refining business, knowing that becoming the largest refiner would give him key advantages over his competitors. Starting out with very little ready cash, Rockefeller was determined to live frugally and plow the company's profits back into the business, while borrowing every dollar he could persuade the banks to lend him to fund still faster expansion. The future mogul spent every dime wisely. Always the careful accountant, he looked at every expense as an opportunity for increased efficiency.

Wooden barrels at $2.50 apiece were a major expense, so he started his own barrel factory and managed to get his unit cost down to less than a dollar. Plumbing contractors were expensive, so he hired his own plumbers, paid them by the hour, and supplied them with piping and other materials that he bought in bulk directly from the manufacturers. Where other refiners focused on kerosene and burned or dumped waste products, Rockefeller reduced waste (and environmental pollution) by aggressively marketing by-products like benzene, paraffin, and petroleum jelly. There was no market for gasoline in this pre-automotive era, but Rockefeller burned it to power his operations. Most of his competitors burned off the gasoline they produced in open pits, or simply dumped it out and let it soak into the ground.

Soon he had a falling out with most of his partners over the debts he was racking up. He arranged for financing and bought the Clark brothers out. Andrews, the chemist, stayed with Rockefeller's new company, which they called Rockefeller and Andrews, and focused on the day-to-day management of the refinery. Soon the two of them took on a third partner, a man named Henry Flagler.

Flagler was another rags-to-riches story like so many in America's history. His father was a poor Baptist minister who once stirred up a controversy by marrying a black man to a white woman. Henry struck out on his own at age 14, first working in a general store and then making a small fortune trading in wheat and corn.[332]

Rockefeller's use of credit to expand his business makes an interesting study. In later years, when Standard Oil was established as the dominant company in the refining business, Rockefeller was content to fund the company's continued growth with re-invested profits. But during the company's early years he was so eager to borrow that it caused a breach with the Clark brothers. The borrowing was not reckless or irresponsible, it was something the future mogul had thought out carefully. Those of us who are over a certain age can remember the profligate spending of young executives during the "Dot-Com" boom and bust that took place around the end of the twentieth century. Several unprofitable companies that paid over a million dollars per half-minute to advertise during the Year 2000 Super Bowl were out of business by the time the 2002 Super Bowl was played.[333]

This kind of recklessness with money would have appalled John D. Rockefeller. He avoided waste both in his business and in his personal life. His cost-cutting and operational efficiencies allowed his company to earn healthy profits that grew rapidly month by month. Personally he was so frugal that he continued to live with his mother and siblings while his company was one of the most profitable in the state. Even after his 1864 marriage he and his wife shared a house with his mother for several years. Only in 1868, when he was the biggest stockholder in the world's largest refinery business,[334] did he finally buy a new house for his own family and provide a separate home for his mother.

Rockefeller was willing to borrow money in the early days because he was desperate to become the largest refiner in the area, and eventually in the nation. He understood the advantages that size would bring in selling a high volume commodity like petroleum products, and he was willing to rack up big debts to win the race for growth. Cleveland area bankers saw Rockefeller and his partners as nearly ideal customers. Every loan was repaid as promptly as clockwork, and the company's profits and assets were always growing. By the time Rockefeller repaid one loan and applied for another his company would already be able to boast greater profits and collateral, to justify a larger loan.

By December of 1865 he and his partners were using all the space available at their original campus, and they opened a second refinery site, which they called the Standard Works. John D. put his younger brother William Rockefeller II in charge of the new campus. This was not just nepotism; William had already distinguished himself working for another company, earning raises and promotions at a rapid rate, before coming to work for his big brother.

To reduce the cost of his primary raw material, Rockefeller opened a purchasing office near Titusville where his agent bought crude oil directly from the drillers, eliminating the middleman. Marketing was not neglected either. By the end of the Civil War most of the kerosene produced in the United States was sold in Europe, with the ports of New York being the most direct route. In 1866 John D. sent William to New York to open an export company under the name "Rockefeller and Company."

Transportation costs were a hugely important issue in the petroleum business, and Rockefeller made it his business to secure the lowest freight rates in the industry. In 1868 Rockefeller made a crucial deal with the president of the Lake Shore Railroad, a subsidiary of Cornelius Vanderbilt's New York Central. Rockefeller committed to ship 60 carloads of oil per day, regardless of market conditions, and further sweetened the deal by building infrastructure like holding tanks and terminals that would have been difficult for the debt-laden railroad to afford. In exchange he got the lowest freight rate in the oil industry; a cost savings that gave him a tremendous advantage over all the other refiners in the nation. Most observers, both critics and admirers of Rockefeller, have pointed to this cost-saving 1868 freight deal as the launching point of Rockefeller's dominance of the oil industry.

With his faith in the future of the oil business, Rockefeller continued to make critical investments in transportation infrastructure that the railroads were unwilling to make. These investments included, most critically, his decision to build hundreds of tanker cars that the railroads would be able to use to transport his products. His foresight in this area would pay huge dividends over time.

In the early 1870s Rockefeller and his partners started buying out many of their larger competitors, starting in their own back yard, in Cleveland. The first man they approached about a merger was Oliver Payne, the managing partner of the city's second biggest refinery company. To persuade Payne to agree to the merger, Rockefeller allowed him to see the Standard Oil Company books. Payne was "thunderstruck" at Standard's low costs and high profit margin, and agreed to the deal in December of 1871.[335] Over the next few months Standard bought out 22 of the remaining 26 refiners in Cleveland.[336]

When Rockefeller offered a buy-out deal to a rival refiner he always offered two options: cash, or Standard Oil shares. He always recommended that the seller take the shares, but most ignored his advice and took the quick cash.[337] Those who took the cash always ended up regretting it, as the value of Standard Oil shares continued to grow rapidly for decades. By 1873 Standard Oil was the largest oil refining company in the world.[338]

When the 1873 financial panic and depression struck, Rockefeller, like Carnegie, took advantage of the crisis. Rockefeller and his management team had the most efficient operation in the refining business, and the lowest freight rates. Standard continued to operate profitably even as kerosene prices plummeted. Rockefeller redoubled his efforts to buy out his rivals, many of whom were hemorrhaging money and near bankruptcy. He slashed the Standard Oil dividend and borrowed heavily from several banks to come up with cash for the refiners who refused to accept Standard Oil stock for their properties. Refiners who were reluctant to sell out were allowed to look at Standard's books, a tactic that virtually never failed.

Standard took advantage of the low wages and low raw material costs of the depression years to build a large fleet of tanker cars, a luxury the railroad companies could not afford during an economic depression that was driving many of them into receivership. For many years after this the railroads would have to pay Standard a fee for every load of oil they hauled in a Standard Oil car, even when the oil was being shipped by a Standard Oil competitor. Also, during this period of low wages and prices, Standard started putting together a network of pipelines to transport crude oil from the wellheads to the refining facilities and, eventually, to transport finished kerosene as well.

In 1877 Thomas Scott of the Pennsylvania Railroad started his ill-advised feud with Rockefeller (which was described in more detail Chapter 9), and the end result was to make Standard Oil even more powerful. By 1890 Standard Oil controlled 90 percent of America's oil refining capacity.[339] As the company continued to increase its dominance of the refining business, Standard branched out into other lucrative areas. Standard Oil subsidiaries began to produce and market natural gas. Other subsidiaries began buying up huge tracts of oil-producing land in several states to ensure that Standard would always have access to an ample supply of their primary raw material.

Standard's core product in the nineteenth century was kerosene, which was used as lamp oil, but the company successfully marketed many other petroleum-based products. The increasing mechanization of the country throughout the late nineteenth century steadily drove up the demand for grease and lubricating oil. Oil-based paints and varnishes were a money maker. The electric light eventually began to threaten the kerosene business, but by the time it did a new market for petroleum was making Standard Oil more profitable than ever.

Nationwide adoption of the electric light took decades. Thomas Edison first demonstrated a handful of low-powered, direct current (DC) lamps for a group of journalists in his New Jersey home in 1879, and by the late 1880s Edison's DC generating system had spread to only 200 small areas,[340] most of them in high-rent districts in America's larger cities. The overwhelming majority of people, in America and around the world, still depended on Standard Oil kerosene to light their homes and businesses. In the 1890s, faced with competition from George Westinghouse and Nicola Tesla, Edison abandoned his DC system for the alternating current (AC) power that we all use in our homes and offices today.[341] By the early twentieth century AC electrical systems were beginning to be a serious threat to Standard's worldwide market for kerosene, but skyrocketing demand for gasoline and diesel soon drove the company's profits to new heights.

It is one of those ironic footnotes to history that the man most responsible for making gasoline a cash cow for Rockefeller's company, just as Edison's electric light was making kerosene obsolete, was Henry Ford, a man who worshipped the ground Edison walked on. Ford was an extremely independent thinker who generally cared very little about what other people thought, and Edison was his only role model. Ford launched the Ford Motor Company in 1903, using principles he had learned from his hero, and by 1908 Ford's company was turning out 11,000 automobiles per year. By 1925 Ford was producing 9,000 cars per *day,* and they all burned gasoline.[342]

By the time the U.S. government broke up the Standard Oil monopoly in 1911, Rockefeller's fortune had surpassed that of Andrew Carnegie, and Rockefeller was widely acknowledged to be the wealthiest man in the world. At the time of his death, 26 years later, he still held that title.

CHAPTER 12

Thomas Edison

———

The American spirit of endeavor as
represented in its fullness by Thomas Alva
Edison is the real wealth of the nation.

Henry Ford

When Thomas Edison died, President Herbert Hoover asked the American people to honor the inventor by turning out the lights in their homes and businesses for 60 seconds at a prearranged time, symbolically returning the nation, just for a minute, to the darkness from which Edison's brilliance had liberated it.[343] It was a fitting tribute to the man who literally brought light to the world; a man whose ideas earned 1,093 U.S. patents and radically raised living standards all around the planet. Edison was so universally admired that when the appointed moment came, at 10:00 PM Eastern Time on October 21 of 1931, the entire nation went pitch dark as virtually every household and business in America participated in the tribute.

It was an ending no one would have predicted when Edison was struggling to make a living as an itinerant teenage telegraph operator.

Thomas Alva Edison was born in February of 1847 in Milan, Ohio, the last of seven children. Three of his siblings died of various illnesses before reaching adulthood; a tragic situation that was quite common all around the world before twentieth century technologies started reducing child mortality rates. Everyone called the youngster "Alva" or "Al"; no one who know him well would address him as "Thomas" until he met his second wife in 1886.

Milan's prosperity was dependent on a canal that became obsolete when a railroad reached the area the same year Edison was born. In 1854 the Edison family left Milan and moved to Port Huron, Michigan, where Al's father, Samuel Edison, struggled to make a living trading in commodities and working as a storekeeper.

Al had recurring health problems and didn't start to attend school until he was eight years old. Frequent ear infections made him hard of hearing, and he was easily distracted. He was physically small and sickly, with a scrawny body and a large head, and the other children teased and bullied him.[344] When his teacher described him as "addled," meaning insane or weak-minded,[345] he told his mother about it and she pulled him out of school and started teaching him at home. Despite the schoolteacher's disparaging remarks, Nancy Edison had high expectations for her son. She him read Dickens and Shakespeare, and heavy nonfiction tomes like Edward Gibbons' *The Rise and Fall of the Roman Empire*. He embraced his lessons and progressed rapidly.

In 1857, when Al was 10 years old, Samuel Edison was indicted for "selling real estate not his own." A credit report issued a few months later stated that the elder Edison's business had "totally failed."[346] With the family in difficult financial straits, Al had to help support the family by farming a ten-acre parcel of land and selling the produce in town.[347] His mother continued to home school him when he wasn't cultivating his garden.

In 1859 Al's parents enrolled him in an institution called the Union School, where he acquired a lifelong love of science. He applied himself to his lessons, and there is no record of any of the teachers at the Union School ever questioning his intelligence or sanity. It was during this time that he read his first book about telegraphy and constructed a telegraph line between his home and that of friend who lived nearby. Unfortunately the Edison family's precarious financial situation forced Al to leave school for good the following year.

At age 13 Al went to work full time peddling newspapers and sandwiches on the train that ran between Port Huron and Detroit. The train left Port Huron six days a week at 7:15 AM, stopped at several towns along the way, and arrived in Detroit four hours later. It left Detroit at four and arrived back in Port Huron at eight PM. Al had to get up at 6:00 each morning and typically didn't get to bed until around 11:00 PM.[348]

During the daily five hour layover in Detroit the train's baggage car would be empty, and Al used it as his private office. He would nap, read, and experiment with the chemistry set he'd assembled. Unfortunately his midday chemistry research came to an abrupt end one day when his supply of phosphorous came into contact with air, burst into flames, and caught the baggage car on fire. The baggage master put out the flames, boxed Al's hears hard enough to aggravate his hearing problems, and threw all his chemicals and instruments off the train. From then on Al had to content himself with reading about science during his midday layovers; his chemistry experiments were restricted to Sundays in his parent's home.[349]

Even as a boy Edison had a knack for unconventional and opportunistic thinking. When he arrived in Detroit the morning of April 6, 1862, there was a large crowd of people around the bulletin board outside the telegraph office at the station. Al immediately smelled opportunity. The news that was creating such a buzz was about the Battle of Shiloh, by far the bloodiest battle of the Civil War up to that time. The young entrepreneur quickly realized that similar crowds would gather in any railroad station where news of the battle was made public. He bribed the telegraph operator in Detroit to send the news to all the stations between there and Port Huron, with a request that the other operators all make reference to the battle on their blackboards.

Having stimulated the public's interest, he calculated that he could sell a thousand newspapers; 10 times his usual number. He had to pay for his papers in advance, and he only had enough money for 300 copies, so he talked his way in to the office of the Editor of the *Detroit Free Press* and persuaded him to hand over the other 700 copies on credit. The retail price of a paper was five cents, but the crowds he found waiting for him on the return trip that afternoon were so hungry for news that he took it upon himself to start charging a dime, then more. He sold the last of his thousand papers for 25 cents apiece.

Later that year, Al saved the life of a three-year-old boy who was playing on a railroad siding in the path of a runaway boxcar. In gratitude the boy's father, a telegraph operator named James MacKenzie, offered to teach young Edison telegraphy. The rapid growth of telegraph networks was creating an ever-expanding job market for operators, and after spending the summer of 1863 working 18-hour days studying with MacKenzie and practicing alone, 16-year-old Al got a job at the small Port Huron telegraph office.

The field of telegraphy was a meritocracy; inexperienced telegraph operators like Al were known as "plug" operators, and could only get jobs in out-of-the-way places like Port Huron. The high-traffic offices, where wages were higher, would only hire "first class" operators who could demonstrate higher levels of speed and accuracy. The elite of the fraternity were the "press wire operators"; those who rapidly transmitted and transcribed large amounts of text for the newspapers. The situation was clear to young Edison: he could become more valuable to himself by becoming more valuable to his employers, and the way to do that was by sharpening his skills.

For the next five years Edison traveled around from one town to another working for the telegraph offices, always striving to make himself a more valuable operator. Often he would work his shift at the telegraph key and then remain in the office for several more hours, practicing his skills by trying to transcribe the messages a first class operator was taking. When he found that he couldn't keep up with the pace, he invented a device to slow down the messages to a speed he could handle. As his skills improved he gradually ramped up the speed of his practice machine.[350]

Another practice tactic involved the buddy system. Edison and another plug operator set up a pair of telegraph keys on a table and sent messages back and forth between them. The pair even turned their practice into a money making venture; they would make multiple copies of the script of a play by sending it back and forth across their practice wire, then sell the copies to the theater company that was putting on the play.[351]

When he wasn't honing his telegraphy skills Edison was educating himself in other areas. He was a frequent visitor to the free libraries in all the towns and cities where he worked. He read good literature; for a time his friends called him "Hugo" because of his fondness for the novels of Victor Hugo. He made some effort to teach himself Latin and Spanish[352] and read books on science and technology at a rapid rate.

He also continued his childhood habit of experimenting with chemistry and electricity, a habit that helped prepare him for his later career as an inventor, but sometimes interfered with his career as an operator. The telegraph office in Port Huron, where he got his first job as an operator, fired him after a few months when he mixed something with the acid in the system's batteries and caused an explosion that damaged the building.[353] While working in Louisville a couple years later he was fired again when he borrowed some acid from the system batteries for an experiment, but accidentally dropped the jar on the floor, and the acid leaked through the floorboards of the second story office and ate its way through the carpeting and furniture of the bank offices on the ground floor below.

When he was working as a telegrapher Edison spent most of his money on books,[354] and never managed to save anything. His life could quite literally be described as a rags-to-riches story; for a while he only owned one suit of clothes, and wore them every day until they were so ragged he had no choice but to buy a new suit.[355] When he was between jobs he sometimes had to sleep on the floor of a vacant building.[356] When the war ended the civilian job market was flooded with experienced telegraph operators who'd been working for the military, and Al had a harder time finding employers willing to overlook his odd habits and give him work. Stranded in Memphis late in 1865, the scrawny teenager had to take a job as a common laborer on a crew laying track for a railroad.[357]

Later that year, when he had made his way to Louisville, he was able to demonstrate the skills of a first class operator to the station chief, who hired him on at a rate of $125 per month. Making a stable living for a while, he began to lose interest in chemistry and spend more time tinkering with telegraph-related inventions. While working near his hometown in 1867 he built a working model of a "duplex telegraph" apparatus; a machine capable of using a telegraph wire for two messages at the same time. An article he wrote about the machine was published in the trade journal *The Telegrapher* in April of 1868.

By the time the article was published he was working in Boston as a press wire operator. Having brought his skills with the telegraph key to that elite level, he no longer needed to spend his off hours practicing telegraphy, and he could devote more time to reading and research. It was in Boston in 1868 and '69 that he began to take his experimentation with telegraph technology beyond the tinkering stage and began to work seriously toward the goal of making a living from his inventions.

He was granted his first U.S. patent, for an electric vote recording machine, in June of 1869. He had come up with the idea after visiting a session of the Massachusetts State Legislature and observing how slow and cumbersome the vote counting process was. His invention was small and reliable, and would have allowed all the legislators to vote simultaneously, right from their seats, in a matter of seconds. His invention worked perfectly when he demonstrated it, but he couldn't sell it. The politicians had no interest in a more efficient voting system; they actually preferred the time-consuming process of roll call voting because it allowed time for the legislators to negotiate with each other, trading votes in a process known to professional politicians as "log rolling." Edison then tried to sell his new technology to the United States Congress and got the same answer, for the same reason.

The commercial failure of his first patented invention taught Edison an important lesson. For the rest of his career he made a point of always trying to gauge the marketability of an idea before expending any effort trying to turn the idea into an invention. Predicting the future is difficult, and Edison sometimes misjudged an invention's commercial potential, but he always tried.

He continued to refine his duplex telegraph design, hoping to make it robust enough to be commercially viable. He also started working on a "telegraphic printer," a device that could print telegraphic messages in letters of the alphabet. When the investor who was backing his duplex project refused to provide any more funding Edison spent the last of his own meager funds on the research before leaving Boston for greener pastures in New York.

Twenty-two-year-old Edison arrived in New York City in the summer of 1869 hungry and without a dime. He managed to talk a tea salesman into giving him a packet of samples, which he then traded to a restaurant owner for apple dumplings and a cup of coffee.[358] He went to the home of a friend who he hoped would give him a place to sleep, but the friend was out of town. Literally homeless, Edison spent his first night in New York walking the streets to stay awake.[359]

He then called on an engineer named Franklin Pope at the Laws Reporting Telegraph Company, a company that transmitted commodity prices for banks and other clients. Pope had no jobs to offer, but he lent the penniless inventor a few dollars and allowed him to sleep in the company's battery room. After a time Edison did get a job at Laws Reporting Telegraph, where he perfected one of his first really successful inventions: a "unison stop" device that kept mechanical problems in a single stock-ticker from damaging all the other tickers the company was operating. Over the next few months he proved his value to Laws by developing several other significant improvements in telegraph technology, including a printing telegraph that was far superior to what the company had been using.

Late in 1869 Edison lost this job, after only a few months, when the Laws company was bought out by a competitor, the Gold and Stock Telegraph Company. The management of Gold and Stock recognized Edison's talents, but had no immediate need for the project the young inventor was working on at that moment because Gold and Stock already had the rights to a similar device from another source.

Firing Edison was a mistake. Excellent businessmen like John D. Rockefeller have always "hired talented people as found, not as needed,"[360] because they understand how valuable and rare human resources of that caliber are. It's much easier for a business owner to find something useful for a talented employee to do than to find and recruit a talented employee when one is needed. By the time the owners of Gold and Stock realized their mistake, the price for Edison's services had gone up dramatically from the salary he'd been earning as a Laws employee.

Edison, of course, was initially unhappy about being dismissed. After eight years of living hand to mouth he'd finally gotten a steady job with a good paycheck, and now he was unemployed yet again. In a letter to a friend he admitted that losing this job just as his career was beginning to go somewhere "has upset all my calculations."[361] He wasted no time on self-pity; his next move was to form a partnership with Franklin Pope, under the name Pope, Edison and Company.

Pope, Edison quickly developed several new devices that allowed them to go into business providing stock quote services to various clients in direct competition with Gold and Stock. The management of Gold and Stock belatedly realized that Edison was either going to be a valuable ally or a dangerous rival, and in 1870 they bought out Pope, Edison and Company for cash, and signed two separate contracts with Edison. Under the terms of the new contracts Gold and Stock provided Edison with a fully-equipped laboratory and machine shop, paid him $7,000 to design a new printer, and paid him a retainer to function as the company's consulting engineer for the next five years. The terms of the agreements were non-exclusive, so Edison was able to contract out his services to other companies while still collecting his fees as a consulting engineer for Gold and Stock.

In October of 1870 Edison signed an agreement that made him a partner, along with an investor named George Harrington, in a new company called American Telegraph Works. Harrington's capital allowed Edison to operate a laboratory and machine shop separate from the ones Gold and Stock had provided for him. Edison hired technicians and machinists to staff both labs, and oversaw all operations, dividing his time between the two.

In 1871 the Western Union conglomerate purchased a majority interest in Gold and Stock. William Orton, the president Western Union, cited Edison's relationship with Gold and Stock as one of the primary reasons for buying the company, once again proving that the most valuable resources a company can have are human resources. Orton was the usual American success story. He'd had grown up in modest circumstances and had to leave home as a teenager to make his living setting type in a newspaper office. Orton went on to work as a schoolteacher and clerk before getting his first job in the telegraph industry.[362]

Under the control of Western Union, the Gold and Stock Telegraph Company renegotiated with Edison, granting him $35,000 in Western Union stock and a salary and commissions for his ongoing work on behalf of the company.[363] The new contract, like the old one, was non-exclusive, so Edison was able to continue in his role as chief engineer for the American Telegraph works. Edison, who had been hungry and homeless less than two years earlier, was now a prosperous and important man.

His value to Western Union was not the result of a perfect record of success; far from it. Most of the devices he invented during that period, like most of the things he invented throughout his career, were initial failures that required extensive tinkering before they became useful in actual practice. But with endless tenacity and boundless energy he made gadgets like his alphabetic printer and his dual and quad transmission systems gradually evolve into commercially valuable products. Edison's view, as he once expressed it to a recently-hired employee, was "Nothing that's any good works by itself...you got to *make* the damn thing work!" This was his guiding philosophy and it gave him the courage and tenacity to keep trying through numberless failures, in nearly every project he ever took on as an inventor.

The financial success that Edison achieved in the early 1870s didn't dampen his passion for learning. He continued to be a dedicated student of anything and everything related to his chosen field. He read extensively about electrical theory, consuming the works of theoretical scientists like Michael Faraday to gain a deeper understanding of phenomena he observed in his laboratory. And the more theory he learned the faster he could problem-solve in the real world.

In 1876 Edison was wealthy enough to build his own independent research lab. Early that year he built the famous laboratory complex in the tiny hamlet of Menlo Park, New Jersey where he would create some of his most famous inventions. Edison's complex was one of the largest R&D laboratories in the country at that time. Its purpose, in Edison's words, was to produce "a minor invention every 10 days and a big thing every six months or so."[364]

The first move he made as an independent businessman was to lure a few hand-picked men, two in particular, away from his old Gold and Stock and American Telegraph operations. Draftsman Charles Batchelor and machinist John Kruesi, Edison's key players, were both typical self-made men of that era. Batchelor was born in England and spent most of his childhood working in a sweatshop after being abandoned by his father. He came to the United States in 1865 at the age of 20.[365] Kruesi lost both his parents and grew up in an orphanage in Switzerland, and was then apprenticed to a locksmith; he reached the U.S. in 1870.[366] Both men were self-educated, smart, and tireless enough to keep up with the workload that Edison imposed on himself and his team. Both proved so important to Edison's research that Edison eventually started giving them a percentage of the royalties from the inventions they produced.[367]

With facilities of their own, Edison and Batchelor sat down to make a list of things they could invent that would have market value.[368] One of the first things they came up with was a system for making multiple copies of a letter by using an electric pen on layers of chemically treated paper. Within a couple years the electric pen system was selling internationally and making the lab a good deal of money. Many of the other money-making ideas Edison and his lieutenants came up with were improvements to existing telegraph technology. Western Union, as the nation's dominant communications company, continued to be the primary client for these telegraphy-related inventions.

The Race for the Telephone

It's not the size of the dog in the fight,
it's the size of the fight in the dog.

MARK TWAIN

On June 25 of 1876, just a few weeks after Edison's Menlo Park lab opened for business, Alexander Graham Bell gave the first public demonstration of his telephone at the Centennial Exposition in Philadelphia. Edison, who had several of his own inventions on display at the Exposition, showed little interest in the telephone at first, not appreciating its commercial potential. Within a few months, however, Edison and his team were spending much of their time doing telephone-related research for Western Union, as the big conglomerate endeavored to put Bell out of business and dominate the new industry.

The development of the telephone was a wild ride, with many colorful characters battling each other just as hard as they battled the technological challenges they faced. The Goliath in the contest was Western Union, one of the world's largest corporations with a capitalization of 41 million dollars. Cornelius Vanderbilt, the richest man in America, was the company's largest stockholder.[369] Andrew Carnegie was another major stockholder. When the Dow Jones company first published its index of industrial stocks Western Union was one of the 11 companies in the index, along with nine railroad companies.

In the role of David facing off against Goliath was Alexander Graham Bell. Bell was a teacher of deaf students, like his father before him. After immigrating to the United States at the age of 23, he had made a living by teaching part time at Boston University and tutoring deaf children in one room of his little two-room apartment.[370] During the years he spent working on his telephone his apartment did triple duty as home, classroom, and laboratory. His only financial backers were the fathers of two of his students.

Bell's backers didn't pay him a salary, and his telephone research cut into the time he could spend teaching, so he had to live very frugally and manage his time extremely well. While they didn't pay him a salary, his two investors did reimburse him for his tools and equipment and pay the salary of a part time assistant named Thomas

Watson. Watson was the usual American story. His father worked in a livery stable and Thomas went to work to support himself at the age of 14. When Bell hired him late in 1874 he was 22 years old and well known among Boston inventors as a capable assistant.[371]

In 1874 Bell was not the only inventor trying to develop a telephone. He already had a rival named Elisha Gray. When Gray began to focus his efforts on developing a telephone that same year, he was 38 years old and already quite successful. He had patented several significant improvements to telegraph technology and was co-founder and superintendent of a company that employed over a hundred men.[372] Gray was yet another self-made success story; he'd grown up on an Ohio farm and was forced as a youngster to quit school and go to work when his father died.[373] As a youth he made his living as a carpenter while spending every spare minute educating himself about electricity and telegraphy.

On February 14 of 1876 one of Bell's financial backers formally applied for a U.S. patent on Bell's telephone, which at that time was still a work in progress. Later the same day Gray came to the patent office to file a "caveat," a notice of his intent to eventually apply for a patent, for his own version.

The race really heated up four months later, when Bell gave his Centennial Exposition demonstration. Bell became the talk of the nation and Western Union President William Orton began to pay serious attention. Western Union backed Gray's work, expecting that he could come up with a design of his own that wouldn't be covered by Bell's patent, which the company intended to challenge in court at any rate. By the spring of 1877 the company had doubled down by engaging Edison to develop his own telephone. The near-penniless Bell was now competing with two of the most accomplished telegraphy engineers in the nation, both of whom were backed by the nearly unlimited resources of the nation's dominant communications company.

Edison soon developed a transmitter superior to the one Bell was using. Bell's transmitter used the vibrations of the human voice to actually generate a constantly-changing current, which was then translated back into sound waves by his receiver. Edison used direct current from a battery in his telephone system. The variations in current were achieved through the use of a variable resistor that changed its electrical resistance in response to minute changes in air pressure caused by sound vibrations. Edison used carbon as his semi-resistive material, and the small round disc he developed came to be known as the "carbon button."

Soon Western Union was selling telephone contracts all around the nation. The company used technologies that Gray and Edison had developed, but also borrowed heavily from Bell, in violation of his patents. Western Union also fought in court to prove that the original idea for sending the human voice over a wire was Gray's, not Bell's. The Bell Telephone company sued Western Union for patent infringement and went to work marketing its own telephone contracts in competition with the larger company.

When the Bell interests abandoned Bell's original inductive transmitter and started using Edison's carbon button in their phones, Western Union turned the tables on Bell Telephone and sued them for patent infringement. The competing legal cases ground their way through the courts for months. Western Union was able to employ whole teams of high-priced lawyers to represent the company in court, while the Bell partners had only limited resources, but in the end David defeated Goliath. In November of 1879 Western Union was forced to terminate all telephone operations and leave the lucrative business to the Bell Telephone Company. Western Union turned over all of Gray and Edison's telephone-related patents to Bell in exchange for 20 percent of Bell's telephone rental receipts over the next 17 years.[374]

Bell Telephone morphed into AT&T and became, for a time, the largest corporation in the world.[375] Alexander Graham Bell got rich, although not as rich as he would have become if he'd kept all his shares instead of selling most of them way too early. Even Thomas Watson, who was given a five percent share in Bell Telephone at its founding, became a very wealthy man.

THE PHONOGRAPH

Before the legal dispute over the telephone was even resolved Edison had already found a new focus for his team. Edison was always working on more than one invention at a time, and he had a knack for using the lessons he learned from one project to refine his approach to something else. Edison's intensive study of acoustics during the race for the telephone led directly to one of his most famous inventions, the phonograph. In early December of 1877 Edison handed John Kruesi a sketch with the words "Kruesi, build this." The sketch showed a metal cylinder covered in soft tinfoil, with a crank at one end. A metal stylus, connected to an amplifying horn, was mounted on a shaft that ran parallel to the cylinder.

When Kruesi brought the prototype to Edison, the machinist bet his employer two dollars that it wouldn't work. Edison slowly turned the crank while shouting the words to a nursery rhyme into the horn, then re-set the stylus and started turning the crank again. The machine repeated his words back to him, and the recording industry was born.

Initially Edison made little effort to market the phonograph; he only made a serious effort to develop a commercial version after other inventors copied his design and brought it to market successfully. In describing the initial phonograph experiments he later admitted that he "was always afraid of things that worked the first time."[376]

Within a year the Menlo Park crew was working on something even bigger than the carbon button or the phonograph, and important people were paying attention. J.P. Morgan, the nation's most powerful investment banker, alluded to the project in an October 20, 1878 letter to one of his confidants. The banker wrote that he was "very much engaged" in a matter of "the greatest importance" not only to the financial success of the Morgan bank but "to the world at large... Secrecy is so important that I dare not put it on paper...Subject is Edison's electric light."[377]

The development of the electric light was typical of how Edison and his team created most of their miracles. The road to success was paved with failure, with Edison and Batchelor taking copious notes every time another experiment fizzled out or burned up. It took roughly two thousand carefully-documented failures to develop a bulb that would put out enough light and burn long enough to be commercially viable.

Edison's basic idea was to run direct current through a filament of high-resistance material in a vacuum bulb. Initially he assumed that existing technologies for generating power and creating vacuums would allow him to focus on simply finding the right material for his filaments. After a few hundred trials he was forced to admit that no generator on the market was adequate to the job, so Edison focused personally on coming up with a radically new generator, far more efficient than anything else on the market, while other members of his team continued their efforts to find a usable filament. Edison patented his generator and continued to make improvements to it as the experimentation went on.

After more failures the team was forced to admit that any filament material they could find would burn out very quickly if any air at all was present in the bulb when the current was applied. As with the original generators, the existing vacuum pump technology was inadequate. Edison's people combined the best features of the available pumps and patented several additional improvements. Edison hired a fulltime glass blower to manufacture airtight light bulbs that could be evacuated by his new pump. To help with the theoretical side of the research he hired a mathematician with a graduate degree in physics. He hired chemists to help analyze the properties of the different materials that could be used in the making of filaments. The experimentation ground on, with Edison and Batchelor filling up more notebooks with their observations and theories.

By early December of 1879 Edison had a bulb design that worked well enough for a public demonstration. He installed bulbs in several rooms of his own house, and invited some of his biggest financial backers to come and witness what their money had accomplished. While Edison was bringing the investors from the railroad station one of the bulbs in his parlor burst, setting flame to the furniture in the room. When her husband arrived with his investors in tow Mrs. Edison told them that the parlor was closed for renovations. The bulbs in the other rooms of the house performed adequately, so the investors went away satisfied. Four weeks later Edison staged a much larger demonstration for the newspapers, with strings of bulbs glowing indoors and outdoors, and everything went off without a hitch.

Two years later Edison's various electric companies were providing power for lighting to paying customers in downtown New York City and in numerous isolated large facilities including factories, ships at sea, and rich men's mansions. Central plants in other large cities followed quickly. Throughout the decade of the 1880s Edison spent virtually all his time on the electrification of the United States and Europe. He earned hundreds of patents during these years, virtually all of them relating to the generation, distribution, and efficient use of electricity. He earned millions of dollars from patent royalties and from the shares of stock he owned in the various companies he co-founded.[378]

TESLA, EDISON, AND THE BATTLE OF THE CURRENTS

It wasn't long before the money Edison and his partners were making attracted competitors to the field. George Westinghouse, who had made his fortune with the railroad air brake he introduced years earlier, founded a company called Westinghouse Electric and began signing up customers for electrification in 1886. Before long Westinghouse Electric was Edison's biggest rival.

Westinghouse's system used alternating current (AC) in contrast to the direct current (DC) system Edison was using. Throughout the late 1880s the two companies engaged in a marketing struggle known to history as "The Battle of the Currents." The technical differences between AC and DC are not important for the purposes of this book; suffice it to say that AC is what powers our homes and offices today. DC is used today primarily in battery-powered appliances like cell phones, flashlights, and toys. Edison was a notoriously stubborn man, but by the end of 1889 even he had to admit that the DC system he had labored so hard to create was inferior to AC for a number of technical reasons. Edison's companies scrapped DC and began reconnecting their customers with AC service that year.

As the Battle of the Currents was being fought, Westinghouse had one key asset that allowed him to overtake Edison as quickly as he did: a human resource named Nicola Tesla. Tesla was the usual American story. He was born in his family's tiny house in Smiljan, Croatia.[379] Ethnic Serbs were an unpopular minority in Croatia and Nicola's father was a minister in the Serbian Orthodox Church.[380] After immigrating to the United States in 1884 with exactly four cents in his pockets,[381] Nicola Tesla worked in Edison's lab for a while, but the two men couldn't get along and Tesla soon resigned. He would later accuse Edison of cheating him out of a promised bonus.

After leaving the lab Tesla went into business for himself, inventing and patenting new technologies for the use of alternating current, but his business failed, he lost everything, and in 1886 at the age of 30 he had to work as a common laborer to put food on the table.[382] In 1887 he persuaded a Western Union executive to become his financial backer, and began to build an electric company based on his discoveries in the field of AC power.

In 1888 and 1889 Tesla signed a series of contracts with George Westinghouse, effectively merging his company with Westinghouse Electric. It would be a dynamic partnership. Between 1887 and 1897 Tesla patented several game-changing new technologies that made the ascension of AC power inevitable. His polyphase AC motors, generators, and transformers made AC power vastly more efficient and practical than DC and give Westinghouse an insurmountable advantage over Edison's DC system. If Edison had kept Tesla on his payroll through that era, and accepted the Serb's judgment about the superiority of AC, he might have been able to dominate the whole field of electric power throughout the world virtually without competition. Again, as with Gold and Stock's decision to let Edison go years earlier, the loss of a key human resource was extremely costly.

Around the same time Edison and his financial backers made the commitment to switch from DC to AC they re-organized financially, consolidating most of the research, manufacturing, and distribution companies that Edison had founded into one parent company called Edison General Electric. William Vanderbilt and J.P. Morgan were large stockholders, as were other wealthy Americans Morgan represented in his role as the nation's leading investment banker. A few years later Morgan orchestrated a merger between Edison General Electric, in which Edison still held about a 17 percent stake, and a major competitor called Thomson-Houston. The name chosen for the combined company was the General Electric Company; known colloquially today as G.E. (As of this writing G.E. ranks number eight in the Fortune 500 list of America's largest corporations).

The G.E. conglomerate did not include all of the original Edison companies, just those that Morgan and his partners coveted. Independent power-generating companies like Detroit Edison in downtown Detroit were left out of the new company.

When Edison's name was removed from the company, he began to lose interest in its day-to-day operations, and look for other ways to spend his time. Throughout the 1890s he invested most of his time developing technologies for the magnetic separation of iron and other metals from poor-quality ores. The machines he developed worked reasonably well, but the development of nearly unlimited sources of high-quality iron ore in the Messabi Mountain Range, which was acquired by John D. Rockefeller during the economic depression of the mid-nineties and leased to Carnegie Steel on favorable terms, made Edison's new technologies effectively worthless. When his financial backers refused to front him any more capital, Edison spent most of his own fortune on the mining venture before finally giving it up.

An 1890s Edison venture that did prove profitable, so much so that it helped fund his mining project, was the invention of the motion picture camera and projector. Starting in 1894 the movie business was a major success. From 1907 to 1917 royalties from his movie patents earned Edison around a million dollars per year.[383] It goes without saying, of course, that the motion picture industry Edison founded continues to be a money making machine to the present day.

The last really terrific cash cow for Edison and his backers was the alkaline battery he introduced in 1900. Like the movie business, the alkaline battery has proven to be a durable technology. The batteries that we buy in drug and grocery stores today are still based on the technology Edison introduced in 1900. In that year Edison built a battery-powered car for one of the Vanderbilt heirs as a public demonstration of the design's capabilities. The following year he founded an alkaline battery factory with financial backing from Charles Schwab, the Carnegie protégé who had just taken his place as the first president of the United States Steel conglomerate. Edison was able to pay off all his debts from the iron mining venture, and live out his remaining years in the luxury that a multi-million-dollar net worth afforded, primarily because of his movie and battery ventures.

HENRY FORD AND "MR. EDISON"

Just as Benjamin Franklin was a role model for penniless American boys like Thomas Mellon and John D. Rockefeller, Thomas Edison inspired younger Americans through his example. The most famous of Edison's admirers was Henry Ford, and the relationship between Edison and Ford could be the subject of a fascinating book in and of itself.

Henry Ford was born in July of 1863 on his parents' farm near the little town of Greenfield, Michigan. His father William had fled Ireland 20 years earlier during the Potato Famine, arriving in the United States with nothing but some clothes and a small bag of tools. By the time Henry was born William owned his own small farm and was able to provide reasonably well for his family. In Henry's words his parents were "Certainly…not rich, but neither were they poor."[384]

Henry became fascinated with mechanical things at an early age. He made screwdrivers and other tools out of nails and bits of junk, and taught himself to disassemble and repair watches and clocks. At 16 he left his father's farm to make his living working in a machine shop. Henry began to idolize Edison that same year, when the electric light was introduced and stories about the "Wizard of Menlo Park" were in all the newspapers.[385]

In 1891 28-year-old Henry Ford took a job as a mechanic at the Detroit Edison generating plant, responsible for maintaining the large steam engines that drove the company's generators. His admiration for the company's founder may not have had anything to do with his decision to take the job; Ford was a skilled mechanic who was always eager to add to his knowledge, and the generators at the Edison plant represented a new challenge for him. Ford quickly earned a series of raises and promotions, becoming the plant's Chief Engineer within a few years. It was during his time at Detroit Edison that he began working on his first horseless carriage.

Early in 1896, when his first little gasoline powered vehicle was almost complete, Ford saw Edison for the first time, and it was such a memorable event for the younger man that he wrote about it in his journal. Edison was passing through Detroit on his way home after attending his father's funeral and walked past the Detroit Edison plant where Ford was working. The two men didn't meet, but, as Ford related later, "I saw him with a group of men – at least, someone told me that Mr. Edison was in the group, but they passed so quickly that I am by no means sure that I saw the right man."[386] Such was his admiration for Edison that merely seeing the inventor pass by at a distance was a thrill for Ford.

The thing that makes Ford's hero-worship of Edison so remarkable is that Ford was in all other respects an extremely self-reliant, self-directed individualist. Other than his wife Clara, and Edison, with whom Ford eventually formed a close friendship, there was never anyone anywhere whose opinion carried much weight with Henry Ford. From his early, unconventional automobile design to his radically different production methods to his unilateral decision to pay his workers twice as much as most other American factory workers were making, Ford always danced to his own tune. In his autobiography and other writings he often boasts about his life-long willingness to ignore advice and criticism and find success by following his own instincts, and the boast is an accurate one. Yet he openly and unashamedly idolized Edison.

Six months after Edison past through Detroit, Ford got a chance to see his role model at close range. The national convention of the Association of Edison Illuminating Companies was held in New York City in August of that year, and Ford's boss Alexander Dow was scheduled to present a paper. As the plant's Chief Engineer, Ford was important enough be invited to the convention along with Dow. During the course of the convention Ford took take several photographs of his hero relaxing in and around the luxury hotel that hosted the event. When Ford died decades later his personal papers included pictures of Edison, unaware that he was being photographed, chatting with friends and walking down the street near the Oriental Hotel. Ford even took a picture of the great man sleeping in a lounge chair on the hotel veranda.[387]

After the third day of the convention, at a dinner for management personnel, Ford actually got a chance to speak with Edison personally. As the conversation at the table turned to the subject of battery powered vehicles, which at that time were widely viewed as the future of transportation, Dow announced to the group that Ford was working on something different. Edison, to Ford's delight, was interested in hearing all about the car. Ford was invited to move up to the head of the table to sit next to his idol and explain everything in detail. As he talked, Ford grabbed a menu and sketched out his design on the back of it. Finally Edison told Ford that his design looked promising, and encouraged him to continue what he was doing.

Ford went home supercharged with enthusiasm. The man he most admired had told him that he was on the right track, and from then on nothing was going to stop Henry Ford until he'd put the whole nation on wheels. He endured several years of failures and frustrations with Edison-like resolve, and when he finally launched the Ford Motor Company in 1903 the company's sales and profits skyrocketed right away.

Recent start-up companies like Apple and Google, that exploded in value over very short time periods, have got nothing on Ford. One of the early Ford Motor Company stockholders, a schoolteacher named Rosetta Couzens, made a 355,000 percent profit on her investment in just 16 years.[388]

As for Edison, he hardly gave young Ford another thought for the next several years. The first time the two men actually got to know each other was in 1911, when Ford was looking for a battery-powered starter to replace the hand crank on his automobile, and asked Edison to develop one. By this time Ford was richer than Edison and nearly as famous, and of course they had a great deal in common in terms of attitudes and beliefs, so once the acquaintance was renewed they soon became fast friends. When a fire destroyed Edison's factory in 1914 Ford showed up within a couple days and lent Edison $100,000 on the spot.[389]

Over the years after that 1911 meeting Ford and Edison vacationed together, addressed the media together, and even owned adjacent mansions in the Florida resort town of Fort Myers.[390] Their friendship grew closer for the rest of Edison's life, but as various observers who knew the two men during this period have pointed out, it was never a friendship of equals, at least as far as Ford was concerned. Edison addressed the younger man simply as "Ford," but Ford unfailingly addressed his role model as "Mr. Edison."[391]

CHAPTER 13

Diamond Jim Brady

———

James Buchanan ("Diamond Jim") Brady,
the railway-equipment salesman, could have
flourished nowhere save in the U.S.

FORTUNE MAGAZINE, OCTOBER 1954

JAMES BUCHANAN, THE FIFTEENTH PRESIDENT of the United States, does not hold a particularly distinguished place in American history. He is best remembered as the president who tried, without much success, to calm the political tensions that would erupt in civil war shortly after he left office. It is one of those amusing quirks of American history that one of our least successful presidents was the namesake of not one, but two major movers and shakers in the country's economic development.

In 1820, when the future president was still in the House of Representatives, one of his cousins named her newborn son James Buchanan Eads in his honor. This was the same James Buchanan Eads who engineered the trans-Mississippi railroad bridge described in chapters eight and ten. Eads followed up that achievement by engineering a way to clear thousands of years' worth of accumulated silt from the mouth of the Mississippi, opening up the Port of New Orleans to ocean-going ship traffic.

Thirty-six years after Eads was born another baby was named after the politician. In August of 1856, when Buchanan had just been nominated for president, a proud Irish-American Democrat named Dan Brady named his newborn son James Buchanan Brady in honor of his party's nominee. The boy would later be known as "Diamond Jim" Brady, whose exploits would be retold in various books on salesmanship as well as any number of newspaper and magazine articles. Such was his fame during his lifetime that the *New York Times* would cover the event any time he hosted a fancy dinner or took a party of his wealthy friends to the racetrack. *Fortune Magazine* once ran an article about Brady titled "The Greatest Capital Goods Salesman of Them All."[392]

As an Irish Catholic kid growing up in New York before the Civil War, young Jim Brady was starting life in a disadvantaged position. In the 21st century we're used to seeing Irish-Americans in prominent positions in business and politics, but things were different in the 1850s.

Centuries of oppression at the hands of the English had made economic progress all but impossible for the Irish in their home country. An unfair stereotype of being economic losers followed the Irish to the new world in the nineteenth century, along with a reputation for alcoholism and violence that was not entirely unearned. First generation immigrants from the Emerald Isle generally worked as unskilled laborers, often doing the dirtiest, hardest, and most dangerous kinds of work.[393]

When Frederick Law Olmsted was traveling through the Southern states and writing down his observations for publication, Olmsted noticed that Irish immigrants, rather than black slaves, did the most hazardous work. He wrote, for example, about a steamboat terminal at the foot of a tall cliff where 500 lb. bales of cotton were pushed down a steep slide at high speed. Slaves worked at the top of the hill pushing the bales down, and Irishmen waited at the bottom, dodging the hurtling bales and then transporting them onto a waiting steamboat.

Olmsted asked someone to explain the arrangement. "The (slaves) are too valuable to be risked here," said the local, but "if the Paddies are knocked overboard, or get their backs broke, nobody loses anything."[394]

Things were not much better up north. Economist Thomas Sowell has observed that New York landlords and employers of that era were often quite candid in their anti-Irish discrimination.

> Employment advertisements, even for lowly jobs, often used the stock phrase "No Irish need apply." More delicate advertisers would ask for a "Protestant" applicant but others more bluntly said "any color or country except Irish."[395]

During the potato famine that struck Ireland in the 1840s an estimated one million Irish literally starved to death, and another million were able to scrap up enough money for a steerage class ticket off of the island. Many of them landed in the United States in absolutely desperate straits. William Ford, whose son Henry would put America on wheels in the next century, was one of the Irish immigrants who arrived penniless in the U.S. in the 1840s. So were both of Jim Brady's parents.[396]

Some of these immigrants were able to rise above the level of unskilled laborer in the first generation. William Ford worked long hours as a carpenter for 15 years until he'd saved enough money to buy a little patch of farmland, after which he worked full time as a carpenter and spent the rest of his time cultivating his land.[397] By 1850 Dan Brady had scraped together enough money to open a tavern in a low-rent New York neighborhood just outside the notorious Hell's Kitchen slum.

Most of Dan's customers were Irish Catholic immigrants like himself, and political subjects were often discussed over the large schooners of beer he served. Despite now being technically a part of the bourgeoisie, the senior Brady was always happy to join his patrons in complaining about the lowly status of their ethnic group. A common refrain around the bar was that things couldn't get better in the community until the political climate changed.[398]

The senior Brady's philosophy was that "The rich had too much money, the poor had too little. Things would go from bad to worse until there was a more equal distribution of wealth."[399] In the words of one Brady biographer, "To the immigrant Irish it seemed that wealth was as poorly distributed as in the old country, only here it was the Anglo-Saxon Protestant Americans who lapped up all the gravy, while in Ireland it was the Anglo-Saxon Protestant British."[400]

Young Jim loved his father, and enjoyed the convivial atmosphere in the bar (no one in that era would have thought to suggest that the under-age sons of a tavern owner should not be allowed to hang out in the venue where their father made his living), but he never absorbed the resentful attitude so common among his kinsmen. He read Horatio Alger's books about poor boys who rose from rags to riches, and saw no reason why an Irish kid from a poor neighborhood couldn't follow the storyline of the books.[401] Naturally cheerful and outgoing, he didn't group-identify people as poor victimized Irish Catholics or rich mean Anglo Protestants; he saw each person he met as an interesting individual he was probably going to like.

In July of 1863, when Jim was not yet seven years old, anger over the wartime draft fueled several days of rioting in which mostly-Irish mobs burned much of New York City before Union troops finally restored order. Two thousand people died and thousands more were wounded. From in front of his home Jim could see the flames and hear the gunfire. The city's inter-ethnic tensions only got worse as a result.

Soon after the draft riots Jim's father died of natural causes. His mother married a man named John Lucas, who took over the family business. Jim had two siblings, an older brother named Dan Brady Jr. and a younger sister named Hattie, and all three Brady children had a strained relationship with their step-father. In 1867 Dan Jr. ran away from home at age 13 and, overcoming any anti-Irish bigotry that might have gotten in the way, managed to get a job as a bellboy at the St. James Hotel on Broadway.

Three months later Jim left home too, and went to work serving drinks, carrying luggage, and delivering messages at the same hotel. He was 11 years old. His own personal Horatio Alger story had started. Jim did his duties cheerfully and diligently, impressing both his bosses and the hotel's guests. Like the teenage Andrew Carnegie of three decades earlier, he made adults appreciate him both for his work habits and for his likeability. It's good that he did, because the situation back at home went from bad to worse. By the time Jim was 15 years old John Lucas had run the bar's business into the ground and abandoned Jim's mother. There was no home to go back to, even if Jim had wanted to.

One frequent St. James patron who formed a positive impression of young Brady was a railroad executive named John Toucey. Toucey was a self-made man in his own right,[402] and he probably saw a little of himself in the cheerful 15-year-old working man. In 1871 he offered Jim a job as a baggage handler ("baggage smasher" in the vernacular of the era) at the New York Central's famous Grand Central terminal. Jim quickly developed the passion for trains and railroads that would be the defining characteristic of his career.

Toucey soon convinced Jim that if he wanted to follow his mentor's career path he would have to spend his nights improving his mind. Jim went to night school faithfully for the next several years.[403]

Funny as it sounds to a 21st century American, one of the subjects that colleges of that era taught was penmanship. This was an era before smart phones and computer keyboards, and a businessman was judged partly on his skill with a pen. It was at this time that Toucey's protégé stopped signing his name as "Jim Brady," and developed a flowery and distinctive way of writing "James Buchanan Brady" which he showed off every chance he got. (In later years Brady would like nothing better than having a prospective customer suggest that the many diamonds he wore were fake. He would take one off and use it to carve that distinctive signature in large flowing letters in the glass of the Doubting Thomas' office window.)[404]

After eighteen months as a baggage handler Brady got a promotion to ticket agent. The opening was in a ticket office in the Spuyten Duyvil neighborhood in Brooklyn, which at that time was considered a remote back-water of New York. To get there each morning young Brady had to get up at 5:00 AM to take a special train that took employees to similar sites all around the greater New York area.

Few customers got on the trains at this location, so ticket selling was not a constant occupation, and Brady spent his free time productively. In addition to doing his night school homework, he availed himself of the opportunity to improve his value as a human resource by learning Morse code and teaching himself to operate a telegraph key.[405] Toucey was impressed with his initiative.[406]

The crash of 1873 was brutal to America's heavily-leveraged railroads; over a hundred railroad companies had defaulted on their bonds by the end of 1874;[407] but the recession didn't cost Brady his job. Toucey, who by this time was general manager of the New York Central, brought Brady to the head office to work as a clerk in '74. In '77 Brady was promoted to chief clerk at a salary of $50 per week.[408] The labor violence in Pittsburgh that year damaged the Pennsylvania Railroad so badly that the New York Central reigned alone for a while as America's dominant railroad. The recession was over by this time, and business was booming. The future was bright for 21-year-old Jim Brady.

Brady started feeling prosperous enough to spend some of his money and time going to the theater. He acquired a taste for fine clothes, and became quite the dandy, although the diamonds that would eventually earn him his nickname were still out of reach. In choosing his attire he made New York Central president Chauncey Depew his role model. He'd come a long way since his days as a messenger boy at the St. James Hotel.

Things were about to take an interesting turn. After a couple years as chief clerk Brady was suddenly fired. He'd gotten his brother Dan a job with the railroad, and in 1879 Dan committed some offense, whose details are not well known, and John Toucey felt he had no choice but to discharge both Brady boys.

Jim couldn't have known it at the time, but being fired at that juncture was the best thing that could have happened to him. Toucey didn't believe that his protégé had been involved with Dan's misdeeds, and he was sorry to lose such a promising young employee. He also seems to have been genuinely fond of Jim. Toucey discussed the problem with his good friend Charles Arthur Moore of the railroad supply house of Manning, Maxwell and Moore, and Moore offered to give Jim a job interview. The interview went well, and 23-year-old Jim Brady was hired as a railroad equipment salesman. It was a match made in Heaven; a hundred years later book authors would be using Diamond Jim Brady stories to illustrate the principles of salesmanship.

Biographer Parker Morell tells us what Moore saw in Brady:

Jim was no beauty, and his relations with the King's English were of the most democratic, but people liked him instinctively, he knew railroading, he had an intuitive knowledge of psychology and, best of all, supreme confidence in himself and his abilities.[409]

According to another Brady biographer the deciding factor for Moore was that Jim "seemed to know everything about railroad operation and equipment."[410]

Jim spent the rest of 1879 getting some initial training at the company's New York office, and early in '80 Moore was satisfied enough to offer Jim the standard salary-plus-commission compensation package that all his salesmen got. Brady, apparently already believing that he'd found his life's calling, refused the salary and insisted on going to work on a straight commission basis, at a higher commission rate than was originally offered. "We'll both make more money that way," he told his bosses.[411] Moore and his partners agreed to the arrangement, and, after hiring Brady in the first place, it was the smartest thing they ever did.

The youngster spent his life savings on even nicer clothes than he'd been wearing, and on his first piece of diamond jewelry, a one carat ring. He packed up his things and went out on the road in 1880. For someone who had spent his entire life in New York City, he adjusted to a life of nearly constant nation-wide travel with surprising ease. Now, even more than when he worked for the New York Central, trains and railroads would be the center of his life. He traveled by train, slept in hotels near train stations, and ate most of his meals with railroad employees.

And he loved it. Jim Brady loved railroads and everything connected with them.[412] Animated by his passion for the business, he very quickly taught himself to sell his products at a rate his bosses had never seen.

Like any highly effective salesman, Brady liked people and had an easy time making people like him. He "made friends with master mechanics, section foremen, road gang supervisors, station masters, train crews, roundhouse workers."[413] On the outside he was a jolly, happy-go-lucky character who told funny stories and kept everyone laughing. He took full advantage of his expense account, treating his customers to meals and drinks everywhere he went, and the volume of products he sold kept his bosses from complaining about the ever-escalating entertainment expenses.

On the inside he was disciplined, serious-minded, and focused. He knew a great deal about railroading and was always learning more. Brady never drank; he'd made a promise to his mother very early in life to abstain from alcohol and he never broke it.[414] Throughout his career he bought endless rounds of drinks for railroad employees at every level from hammer-swinger to president and, being completely sober at all times, he learned no end of valuable information from lips loosened by liquor, while making himself ever more popular.

From the start of his career, Brady kept meticulous notes on the railroads' prospects, expansion plans, technology, and people. He kept the notes for his own use and sent summaries to his bosses at the head office.[415]

Everything about his approach to business was organized and systematic. Before visiting a purchasing agent he would often enlist the help of a friendly section foreman and visit all the wayside tool shacks in the section on a two-man handcart. The two of them would pump the levers of the handcart to drive it, the foreman pumping on one handle in his work clothes and Brady, looking like a fat Fred Astaire in his silk top-hat and tails, pumping away on the other. Brady would then go to the agent and present a detailed list of the items the agent needed to buy from him, both for routine maintenance and for any special projects in the works, which Brady would of course know all about through his many sources.

Purchasing agents quickly learned that double-checking Brady's claims was not worth the effort. He was scrupulously honest and he knew more about building and maintaining railroads than most railroad employees. Agents learned that it saved time and effort to simply trust Brady and buy what he was selling.[416]

As his commission checks grew ever larger, his spending grew apace. A childhood friend from the mean streets of his old neighborhood had followed his own rags-to-riches path by becoming a skillful tailor, and Brady was his best customer. Jim loved fine food, and indulged himself in huge multi-course meals morning, noon and night. (One Manhattan restaurateur described him as "the best twenty-five customers I ever had.")[417] His spending on diamonds and other jewels grew even faster than that on fine clothing. It was an era when successful men often wore expensive jewelry, and Jim was determined to look more successful than anyone else.

He acquired the "Diamond Jim" moniker in 1884, from another traveling salesman who knew him from the poker games such men often engaged in out on the road.[418] The name caught on immediately, and Jim didn't mind answering to it. Showmanship is part of salesmanship, and he knew that his larger-than-life style made people remember him.

His money didn't all go for clothes and diamonds. He also enjoyed spending money on people he liked, which in Jim's case was almost everyone he ever met. He lived to have fun, and the more money he earned the more fun he could afford to have. Most of the meals, drinks, and gifts that he lavished on customers were paid for from his expense account, but as his income continued to grow he could spend his personal funds being just as generous to non-customers. He developed a love of the theater and would often give flowers and candy, and later diamonds and rubies, to actresses and chorus girls. Male actors who gave good performances would get gifts of food and liquor.

It was in 1881 that Brady struck up his famous friendship with up-and-coming singer/actress Lillian Russell, who was soon to become the biggest star of the American stage. When they first met she was 22 years old, and had just recently gotten her first starring role in a musical on Broadway. From the first meal they had together the two of them greatly enjoyed each other's company. He dated many beautiful women around this time, and in later years would have a long term relationship with a younger woman named Edna McCauley, but between Brady and Lillian Russell the relationship was always platonic. Both of them wanted it that way. Their friendship started as a casual acquaintance and grew stronger and deeper through the years. (It is celebrated in a very entertaining and readable 1972 book titled *Duet in Diamonds*, by John Burke, which was one of the sources for this chapter.)

Lillian Russell's real name was Helen Louise Leonard, and as their friendship grew stronger Jim started addressing her by her childhood nickname of Nell, but in public he continued to refer to her as Lillian or Miss Russell. Their friendship would survive several marriages on Russell's part and all of Brady's romantic adventures, ending only with Brady's death in 1917. They found comfort in each other's friendship in 1906 when McCauley, the love of Jim's life with whom he had lived for 10 years, ran away with Lillian's fiancé.

Russell was not the only theater star who enjoyed a friendship with Diamond Jim. As his affluence grew Brady indulged this passion for the theater with style. He became known as "Mister First Nighter," attending the opening night of each new Broadway play from the center of the first row. His generosity and charm made him so popular with actors and singers that they would often step out of character to greet Brady from the stage, to the delight of the customers who were frequently Jim's front row guests.[419] When Brady was vacationing in Europe in 1898 American stage star Nat Goodwin, who was headlining a show in London, shocked his British audience when he recognized Diamond Jim in the audience and interrupted the show long enough to make a dinner date with him![420]

By 1888 Jim Brady was on top of the world. He spent the better part of each year traveling around the country, living large on his unlimited expense account, and he always came back to New York in time for the theater season. His unparalleled success as a salesman financed a lifestyle that was all his.

Things were about to get better. In 1888 Jim's unique skills opened the door to a whole new level of success.

Freight cars of the 1880s consisted of a wooden car body mounted on an "undertruck" constructed of massive wooden beams held together with enormous iron bolts. The axels and wheels were fastened to the undertruck with more heavy-duty iron hardware. In 1886 an English company called the Leeds Ironworks developed a lighter and stronger truck made of pressed steel. Called the "Fox undertruck," after the company's founder, this truck was not only much stronger than the wooden version, it was so much lighter that it saved money by reducing a train's fuel requirements.

After two years of successfully marketing this revolutionary new product in England Sampson Fox, the founder and president of the company, traveled to the United States to sell his breakthrough to American companies. America's railroad industry was several times the size of England's, and Fox saw America as the promised land that would make Leeds Ironworks' business grow exponentially. For two months he travelled around the U.S. pitching his new technology to executives at all the country's railroads, but he couldn't persuade any of them to buy his product, even on a trial basis.

Fox had several things going against him as he tried to crack the American market. One was the high cost of his truck. Another was the inherent conservatism of American railroad executives. The decision-makers at the roads were very reluctant to take a chance on what they regarded as an unproven and expensive product when they already had years of satisfactory experience with something more affordable. Fox, of course, would boast of the success his British customers had using his truck, but he was viewed as a less than objective source. Also the rigors of American railroading put greater demands on equipment than in England. The cars and loads were heavier, the grades were steeper, and the distances traveled were far greater. Even if his truck were as satisfactory as he claimed when used on English roads, that would not be regarded as proof that it could perform as well on U.S.

roads. It was going to take more salesmanship than Fox could muster to sell his product to the American railroads.

Fox was a very frustrated man when he returned to New York on his way back to Britain. On the day before his ship sailed he visited Charles Arthur Moore, who had refused to represent his company during an earlier meeting. Moore was still unwilling to make Manning, Maxwell and Moore the U.S. agent for Fox's company, but he offered to introduce Fox to Brady, and graciously said that if the salesman wanted to promote Fox undertrucks as a sideline to the Manning, Maxwell and Moore product line he would raise no objection.

Fox and Brady spent most of the evening together at a table in one of Brady's favorite restaurants. As he looked at the drawings Fox showed him, Brady peppered the executive with questions until he was convinced that the product would work as advertised. Brady, confident as ever in his own abilities, convinced Fox that he could sell the revolutionary new truck where Fox had failed. Understanding how badly Fox wanted to enter the American market, he negotiated from a position of strength.

He convinced Fox that the American railroads wouldn't buy such a crucial piece of hardware from a foreign manufacturer. Leeds would have to build a factory in the United States and start manufacturing trucks before they had any customers. Fox agreed to invest the necessary capital to do this. Next came the issue of Brady's compensation. For selling the Fox truck to American railroads Brady demanded a commission of 33 percent of the gross for every truck he sold, an outrageous commission rate by any standard.[421] Fox accepted his terms.

Four weeks later a Leeds Ironworks engineer arrived to set up the American factory. Brady took him to Joliet, Illinois, where he had already rented a blacksmith shop and stocked it with all the tools and materials the engineer would need to start making undertrucks. He'd purchased everything on his Leeds expense account, with many of the materials purchased from Manning, Maxwell and Moore and subject to Brady's usual commission rate. Soon the new factory was building and warehousing undertrucks and it was up to Brady to sell them.

Full of his usual self-confidence, he decided to start with one of the two biggest and most powerful railroad companies in the country. He made an appointment with the executive in charge of rolling stock for the New York Central, a man whose name, ironically enough, was James Buchanan, although he was no relation to the politician after whom Brady had been named. Buchanan had already made up his mind about the Fox undertruck; he'd told Fox a couple months earlier that the New York Central had no use for it. But his door was always open to Brady, so Brady had no trouble getting an appointment. The hard part would be changing Buchanan's mind about the Fox truck.

It's an old cliché that "a good salesman can sell anything," and the cliché is true. Anyone with a reasonably pleasant personality, who has learned the fundamental principles of the buying process, can move from one industry or product line to another and, after taking the time to absorb sufficient product-specific knowledge, earn a good living selling. America has always had an ample supply of salesmen of this caliber.[422] But truly great sellers are qualitatively different. The difference is a passionate love of the product that a great seller sells. It can't be faked, and there's no substitute for it. Brady was decidedly not a "good salesman" who could have sold anything. He was a great salesman, and he could only be who he was by selling railroad equipment. No other career would have allowed him to fulfill his potential. His meeting with Buchanan is illustrative.

When Buchanan found out why Jim was there, he explained all his reasons for believing a Fox undertruck wouldn't stand up to the rigors of American railroading. Jim's response was something that would have gotten a mere "good salesman" thrown out of the office. "The hell you say!" he shouted, "Well, let me tell you this – I know just as much about freight cars as you do, and I say they will work."

Contradicting a prospective customer at the top of your lungs is not something they teach you in sales training courses. Neither is threatening to embarrass the prospect, but that's what Brady did next. "If you won't let me prove it to you, I'll go to the Pennsy, and when I prove it there, you'll be the laughing stock of the business."

The respect that Brady had earned from Buchanan over the previous few years is the reason Buchanan put his ego aside and gave serious consideration to what Jim was saying. He didn't contradict the statement about Brady knowing just as much as he did; he knew it was true. He also knew that Brady had never been known to say anything to anyone in the business that he didn't absolutely believe. And it would indeed have been an embarrassment to be scooped by the New York Central's biggest and bitterest rival.

With perfect timing, Brady removed the last obstacle in his way. He asked Buchanan to put freight cars on 20 Fox undertrucks, load them with ballast, and run them on a trial basis. If they failed the test, he said, he'd pay the full cost of the trial run himself.

Between his reputation and his perfect-pitch understanding of the prospect's thinking, Diamond Jim Brady had come within a successful trial run of selling Fox's product to one of the two preeminent railroad companies in America. Now all that remained was for the product to pass muster, which of course it did, with flying colors. Buchanan paid for the 20 trucks and ordered more. Jim immediately made an appointment with the president of the Pennsy.

Within a few months both of the nation's leading railroads were using Fox trucks with great success, and buying new ones as fast as Leeds' American factory could turn them out. Fox sent more technicians from England, bought more Illinois property, and expanded the factory as fast as possible in an attempt to keep up with the demand his high-caliber agent was creating. Within two years of that first New York Central order his American works had expanded from one small building to three huge ones on a two and a half acre campus.

By this time virtually every railroad in the nation was ordering Fox undertrucks, and Diamond Jim's commission checks were growing so large that even he had a hard time spending all the money. His generosity to his friends moved to a whole new level, as did his jewelry collection.

Charles Arthur Moore, understanding how lucrative the undertruck business was for his onetime protégé, quite graciously suggested that if the great peddler wanted to resign his position with Manning, Maxwell and Moore, he would understand. Jim remained loyal. "You gave me the chance to make good," he told Moore. "And now, just when I've got every railroad in the country eating out of my hand, you want me to resign…I'll be damned if I'll quit now!" He promised to repay Moore for his earlier support by leveraging his position as the only American agent of the Leeds Ironworks to keep the orders for Manning, Maxwell and Moore products flowing in faster than ever.[423]

To keep their American factory supplied with raw materials, Fox and Brady formed a partnership with a couple of American investors and started operating a steel mill. When the new company's engineers developed a method for rolling sheet steel that could be used for locomotive boilers, Brady went to work selling this product to locomotive builders. As always he insisted on being compensated on a straight commission basis.[424]

By the early 90s New York boasted enough luxury hotels, five star restaurants, and high class theaters that executives from around the country looked for excuses to go there. At the same time the city was becoming the nation's acknowledged business center, the London of the New World. Carnegie and Rockefeller moved their respective headquarters to the Big Apple, recognizing that it was the place were high level business was conducted. What all this meant for Jim Brady was that he could spend lots of time with his customers without having to spend as much of his time on the road as he had in the 80s.

Railroad presidents would travel frequently to Brady's town to mix business with pleasure, and Brady was always the best tour guide for trips like this. Things were going nowhere but up for Brady, right up until the stock market crash that initiated the Great Depression of 1893.

When the depression struck, the railroad business slowed to a crawl, and even Brady couldn't sell anything to the roads. Railroads started laying off their workers, defaulting on their debts, and going into receivership. Brady acknowledged the reality of it; he cut one of his business trips short and returned to New York. Many people were making dire predictions about a permanent end to the prosperity, but Brady didn't believe it. "There's nothing wrong with this country," said Diamond Jim, "that ain't only just temporary." His stock market holdings had taken a beating, but he still had a fortune in cash in several different banks, and he resolved to ride out the recession having a good time and spreading the cheer. He believed that the depression would end before his money ran out. If it didn't, he said, "I can always start over."[425]

With no sales in sight Jim was no longer able to use his expense accounts to pay for gifts and entertainment for the railroad men who had once been his customers, so he decided to spend his personal funds on them, "building good will" as he called it.

With more time on his hands, Brady was able to find new ways of keeping himself entertained during the depression years. He spent a few weeks in the fall of '93 at the World's Fair (aka Columbian Exposition) in Chicago, dinning with Lillian Russell and buying expensive furniture and art. At the exposition he developed a taste for French cooking, so early the next year he traveled to Europe. He cut short his European vacation and came rushing home to New York when he learned by wire that the horseless carriage he'd ordered, which was to be the first one ever seen in New York, was ready for delivery.

In addition to his automobile Brady maintained a stable of three plush coaches in different colors, with color-coordinated uniforms for his driver and footmen.[426] The stable housed his carriages, the color-coordinated teams of horses to pull them, several saddle horses, and over a dozen immaculate bicycles that he would lend out to friends for Sunday afternoon outings.

Jim had wanted solid gold bikes, but the builder explained to him that gold was too heavy and soft for bicycle frames, so he'd had to settle for gold-plated steel bikes with tiny diamonds sparkling on the handlebars and wheels.[427]

In 1896 the depression ended and Jim's friends in the railroad business became customers again. The resurgence came while he still had money in the bank, so the party continued uninterrupted. Soon the commission checks were fattening his bank accounts faster than ever. In December of '96 he decided to celebrate the return of good times by sending Christmas packages to friends and customers. For non-customers he prepared 117 complete turkey dinners in large boxes packed in ice. Each package included a 20 pound turkey with all the trimmings, not neglecting dessert. Jim had his personal secretary and servants do much of the work, but he was directly involved in it himself. He personally picked out all 117 turkeys by hand, not trusting anyone else with that critical job.

Most of the turkey dinners went to working class individuals and families. Diamond Jim sent them to secretaries, railroad engineers, conductors, and anyone else he could think of who had earned his appreciation in some way. Many of the recipients didn't even realize that he knew their names. To actual customers he sent more expensive gifts. He had so much fun with his Christmas gift project that he did it every Christmas thereafter for the rest of his life.

In 1901 Brady came up with a new way to give treats to his friends. He bought a 30-room mansion on three hundred acres of farmland near Trenton, NJ, roughly halfway between New York and Philadelphia, the two cities where America's largest railroads were headquartered. He had the house extravagantly furnished, hired a team of servants, and used the place as a weekend getaway for himself, his customers, and his other friends. In addition to the feasting and drinking, his guests could enjoy horseback riding and other outdoor pursuits.

It was a working farm, though not a profitable one. Brady spent a fortune on fertilizer, irrigation, and farm labor to insure that his soil produced bigger and better fruits and vegetables than anything on the market. A small army of pampered hens produced eggs by the dozens, and the world's most spoiled cows produced milk that was home-churned into butter. A staff of farm hands did the outdoor work and domestic servants ran the house and kitchen.

Brady's chef used the fresh meat and produce to prepare gourmet meals for his guests, but there was always a surplus, and Brady had no interest in selling his crops on the open market, so he directed his staff to start shipping fresh food to a long list of friends in large zinc-plated, insulated ice boxes that he'd procured somewhere. The recipient list included actors, actresses and chorus girls, policemen, working class railroad employees, and just about anyone else Jim liked. The beneficiaries were instructed to return the empty ice boxes to the farm for refilling, all through the harvest season.

All of this largesse was in addition to the candy, clothing, theater tickets, etc. that Diamond Jim was always giving away. He actually employed a full-time clerk to organize and dispense all the gifts. He delighted in giving expensive jewelry to girlfriends, female friends like Lillian Russell, wives of customers, and any female actress or singer who gave an especially inspiring performance in a Broadway play. Not all jewelry recipients were female; Jim once gave his tailor a diamond-studded gold watch that had previously belonged to Napoleon Bonaparte.[428]

Brady had an easy time paying for all the things he gave his many friends. As the twentieth century dawned his income continued to increase. In 1899 Brady, Sampson Fox, and a few new partners formed a company that built whole freight cars from steel. The value of the company's shares went up and up for two years, and Fox sold his shares for a fortune in cash and retired. In 1901 Morgan acquired the company for his United States Steel conglomerate, and Brady, who had never been fond of Morgan and didn't like the new management of the car company, sold all his shares and turned in his resignation. Job offers poured in, of course, but before he made a decision about his next job John Hansen, the chief engineer of the steel car company he'd just left, approached him with a proposition.[429] Hansen turned in his resignation, and the two of them decided to go into business for themselves. With this much human capital the company had little trouble raising financial capital; Andrew Mellon and his brother Dick were happy to provide start-up funding.[430]

Soon the new company, called the Standard Steel Car Company, was building and selling cars in competition with Jim's previous employer. The growth rate was tremendous. Jim's customers gave him multi-million dollar purchase orders one after another.[431]

In 1912 a surgeon named Hugh Young had the great good fortune to be the man who saved Jim Brady's life. A lifetime of too much rich food had caught up with the 56-year-old Brady. He had diabetes and high blood pressure among other ills, and when an inflamed prostate threatened his life his doctors told him that the surgery he needed could not be performed because his other health problems made general anesthesia unviable. Brady was too sick to eat and getting worse by the day. He prepared himself for the end. People naturally tended to take advantage of Brady's generosity by asking him for loans, and as he was putting his affairs in order his secretary told him that the IOUs in his safe added up to some $200,000, the equivalent of nearly four million in 2015 dollars. He ordered the secretary to gather up all the IOUs and burn them.

As he was making his end-of-life arrangements he heard of a doctor named Young who worked at a relatively new and small institution called Johns Hopkins Hospital. Dr. Young was by all accounts a brilliant doctor, one of a handful of medical men around the world who were at that time doing the initial work in developing the science of urology. Brady made an appointment and traveled to Baltimore to see him.

Dr. Young gives an amusing account of their first meeting in his autobiography. He had never seen anything quite like Brady, although he doesn't seem to have appreciated at first just how different his new patient was. To him, the fat man in the silk suit and diamonds was just another patient. A little more colorful than his other patients perhaps, but fundamentally just another sick person who needed his help. Young's life revolved around medical science, and it doesn't seem to have even occurred to him that he had a material interest in getting on the good side of this particular patient. He told Brady that he had developed a way to perform the necessary surgery with instruments of his own invention, using only local anesthetic, but he was reluctant to take Brady's case because he was scheduled to leave in a few days for a medical conference in England, and wouldn't be available to provide his usual oversight during the patient's convalescence.

Brady told him that he was willing to trust Dr. Young's assistants to look after him while Young was out of the country, and Young agreed to schedule the surgery almost immediately. The surgery was a success, but an infection set in and Brady's convalescence was difficult and dangerous. When Young and his family left Baltimore the patient was still fighting for his life.

Dr. Young had not shared any of the details of his travel plans with his patient, so he and his family were greatly surprised to see Brady's secretary and driver waiting for them when they got off the train in New York the day before their ship was to leave. They were quickly conducted to the Vanderbilt Hotel, where the hotel manager, with a large retinue of staff, met them personally. The manager told them that "as friends of Mr. Brady" they were to have the best of everything the Vanderbilt could offer. He took them to the best suite in the place, where maids under the supervision of the "hotel matron" took care of their every need. Young and his wife were given front-row tickets to the Broadway play *Robin Hood*. The secretary gave them eight tickets because Brady had thought they might have friends in New York who would like to go with them. For the children and their nanny, Brady's secretary had arranged tickets to a different play.

When the Brady people took them to their ship the next day the Youngs learned that their transatlantic passage had been given the same treatment as their night in New York. They had the best state-rooms on the ship, and each room was abundantly stocked with every luxury, from expensive wines and liquors to boxes of Cuban cigars ("small, medium, and large"), to fresh flowers and expensive candy, right down to little details like the latest issues of various newspapers and magazines. The family must have been sorry to leave the ship when they got to England. "All of this," said Dr. Young, "from a man whom I had known only a few days and who was in Baltimore so sick that I was not sure he would recover."[432] When the doctor got back to Baltimore he learned that each of Johns Hopkins' 50 nurses had received a two carat diamond ring from Diamond Jim.[433]

Brady did recover. His hearty appetite came back to him, and soon he was hosting and enjoying feasts with his customers again. According to the *New York Times* article about one of those 1912 dinner parties, the great peddler had now been "put into condition to name what he wanted to eat and have all he wanted."[434] Brady was back on his feet and doing what he loved. He still had diabetes and other medical problems, but for the next few years he was able to enjoy an active lifestyle, thanks to Dr. Young. He decided to express his gratitude in a large way.

If Young had been a different kind of man, Diamond Jim might have bought him a mansion on Chesapeake Bay and staffed it with pretty French maids, but that was not the doctor's style. Dr. Young lived to heal the sick and further medical science. He told Brady that he had long dreamed of having access to a hospital dedicated specifically to the new science of urology, and Diamond Jim made that dream come true. He built Johns Hopkins an eight-story state-of-the-art urological hospital, which has now been in continuous operation for over a hundred years.

When Diamond Jim Brady died in 1917 he was mourned by the small and the great. When his funeral was held at a Catholic church in New York the throng of people who came to pay their respects was so large that the police department had to send officers to the area for crowd control. Lillian Russell spoke for everyone assembled. "Big, genial Diamond Jim Brady," she said. "We're all going to miss you."[435] That's not a bad epitaph for a poor Irish-Catholic kid from a New York slum.

CHAPTER 14

How They Did It

———

"Let them do what I have done."

CORNELIUS VANDERBILT

THE PEOPLE DESCRIBED IN THE pages of this book achieved their remarkable success because of the principles they lived by; principles that anyone living in a free country can follow. None of the things that made these people so successful are out of the reach of any ordinary American today. The principles are not easy, but they are simple.

PRINCIPLE #1: BELIEVE IN THE EFFICACY OF YOUR OWN EFFORTS.

Of all the persons living on Earth, there is only one person who has the power to cast the deciding vote to kill your dream. That person is you.

FOOTBALL COACH DON JAMES

The people profiled in this book, like millions of other self-made Americans with similar stories, worked hard pursuing their dreams because they believed in the power of their own efforts to achieve the results they wanted. People who go from rags to riches in this country are able to do it because they understand that their own actions are more important than their circumstances.

Bad things happened to all of us, and life is quite often unfair, but hard work guided by wise decision-making can overcome virtually anything. It was bad luck that James Buchanan Brady grew up in a New York slum. It was worse luck that his father died when Jim was seven years old, and that his stepfather mistreated him. It was unfair that nineteenth century Americans were biased against Irish-Catholic immigrants. But Brady didn't wallow in self-pity over the unfair hand that life had dealt him. Rather than dwell on the unfairness of life, he took charge of his own life at age 11, overcame all the obstacles in his way, and made himself the immortal Diamond Jim Brady.

Life was unfair to Benjamin Franklin when it made him the indentured servant of an older brother who beat him. A few years later, when he'd escaped from his brother's tyranny, it was unfair that the colonial governor filled his head with lies and persuaded him to give up everything he had to go to London. Nonetheless Franklin never doubted that he could make his own fate by his own efforts, and because he believed he could, he could and did.

Life was unfair to John D. Rockefeller. It's unfair that his father abandoned the family for months at a time. It's unfair that John and his brother were the only children in their class excluded from the class picture. It's unfair that John had to drop out of high school to get a job so he could support his mother and siblings. But Rockefeller always believed that what he did would be more important in deciding his fate than the things life threw at him, and he was right.

Success in a free country is a matter of making the right choices and exerting the necessary effort, not some special blessing bestowed on a lucky few before they are born. In explaining his own success, Thomas Edison said "Any bright-minded fellow can accomplish just as much if he will stick like hell and realize that nothing that's any good works by itself."[436] Edison didn't say that a bright-minded fellow *could* accomplish just as much, he said *"can* accomplish." He wasn't just making a hypothetical statement. He was making the point that any fairly intelligent person living in a free country *can* do as much as Edison did, if he will use Edison's methods and work as hard as Edison did. Clearly the Wizard of Menlo Park was right. During Edison's own lifetime Henry Ford studied and emulated Edison, with a few new ideas of his own thrown in, and by following those principles transformed the world and made himself a billionaire. The internal resources necessary for success are something we all have, something that any of us can choose to utilize.

THE CREATOR'S ROLE

For those who can accept it, the Bible describes the unlimited resources with which every human being is born. According to Genesis chapter 1, verse 27, "God created man in His own image, in the image of God He created him; male and female He created them." Atheist readers are welcome to come up with their own explanations for the stories in this book, but if the words of Genesis 1:27 are true, each human being is made in the image of The Infinite. The reason America is the place where poor individuals have achieved the most is quite simply that all humans everywhere are endowed by their Creator with unlimited potential, and America is the place where government has interfered least in people's efforts to develop themselves as individuals. Allowed to make full use of the resources God gives them, American individuals have worked miracles.

Consider the complexity of the universe God designed and built. Protons, neutrons and electrons dance around each other, in ways that our brightest physicists still don't fully understand, to create perpetual motion machines we call atoms. The atoms of certain elements are perfectly designed to form stable bonds with the atoms of specific other elements to create molecules that function in precisely the right ways to allow life to exist. The matter and energy of the universe is further organized into stars and planets, with something like a hundred billion stars in our own galaxy alone. There are on the order of a hundred billion other galaxies in the known universe, all neatly organized into galaxy filaments according to some grand master plan.

If the Designer of all that has truly created us in His own image, it's easy to see how an Andrew Carnegie or a John Jacob Astor, or the person reading this book, could find sufficient resources inside himself to achieve great things.

Resources, however, are not success. Resources have to be utilized, and utilizing the potential that God gives us requires good decision-making along with learning and hard work. A person who doesn't believe in the power of his own efforts will not expend the kind of effort that made self-made men like Carnegie and Astor so successful. The absolutely essential and indispensable element of success in a free country is believing in the value of your own efforts. The truth that must be embraced is that *what you do* is always going to be more important than what happens to you.

Principle #2: Be a Human Resource.

*The secret of success is to do the common
things uncommonly well.*

Rockefeller

The starting point for virtually every career is working at some sort of job for a paycheck, and the time to start excelling in your career is the day you get your first job. The best way to make yourself more valuable *to yourself* is by making yourself more valuable to your employer.

When someone makes himself an extremely valuable human resource, one of two things will happen. Either his employer will recognize his value and reward him with raises and promotions, or his employer will be too short-sighted and foolish to do this, and the worker will have to go to the trouble of finding a better job. A mediocre employee does not have the luxury of being able to shop around for an employer that suits him, but workers with skills and habits that give them superior value can do just that.

An example of the first scenario, where the employer is wise enough to know how to treat a valuable human resource, is the managers of Detroit Edison in the 1890s. They recognized Henry Ford's value to the company, compensated him accordingly, and kept him on the payroll for eight years before Ford left to start his own company. If Detroit Edison had done otherwise, Ford certainly would not have wasted any time whining about being "exploited." Henry Ford was not the sort of man who responds to life's problems by wallowing in self-pity. He would have taken his superior skills to an employer who appreciated them.

Sam Walton's autobiography offers several examples of the second scenario. Walton would often lure highly talented and motivated people away from employers who didn't fully appreciate them.

The hotel that employed young Jim Brady didn't give him a promotion during the four years he worked there, but a railroad executive named John Toucey was impressed enough with his hustle and his cheerful attitude to offer him a better job. The only mistake 15-year-old Brady made was waiting to be asked before he left the hotel. When Brady was a little older he learned that it's a good idea to ask for what you want instead of waiting to be invited. Seventeen years later, when Samson Fox came to believe that Diamond Jim Brady was the only man who could sell his Fox undertruck to the American railroads,

Brady asked for the outrageous commission rate of 33 percent of gross, and Fox agreed to pay it. Brady knew he was an extremely valuable human resource, and he negotiated for what he was worth.

When Thomas Gibbons died and his son William inherited his business and became Cornelius Vanderbilt's employer, Vanderbilt was so valuable to the company that he was able to shut it down just by leaving.

The critical thing is to become one of those extremely valuable employees that smart business managers are always looking for. Being a much-desired resource will always open doors. The things that make an employee special are superior skills, superior effort, and superior attitude. Effort is the most fundamental thing because by effort a person who doesn't have them can learn valuable skills and develop a winning attitude. ("A sunny disposition...can be cultivated," said Carnegie in his autobiography; "the mind like the body can be moved from the shade into the sunshine.")[437] None of the characters in this book were born smart and skillful; they all labored hard to turn themselves into human resources, using methods that any ambitious person can copy.

The role models offered up in this book all self-educated aggressively, both in job-specific skills and in more general studies aimed at building what advertising giant David Ogilvy used to call "a well-furnished mind." When Edison, for example, was a young telegraph operator, he spent much of his spare time practicing with a telegraph key, often right at the office where he'd just completed a full day of telegraphing; sharpening the skills his employers paid him for. In addition to the time he spent honing his job-specific skills, he read books on science and technology and experimented with chemicals and electrical apparatus. For pure recreation he read classic novels by writers like Victor Hugo. Trashy television shows were not an option in that era, but if they had been available to him he wouldn't have wasted any time on them.

When Benjamin Franklin was a boy he spent nearly every dime he could get on books, and he continued to be a voracious reader throughout his life. He only got a couple years of formal schooling but he self-educated so well that he became one of the great scientists of his era. Mellon and Carnegie, following Franklin's example, were similarly obsessed with getting their hands on books; Mellon even kept a book in his hat while plowing his father's fields, and stole a few seconds of reading every time his horses were turning around at the end of a furrow. Carnegie wrote letters to the editor of the local newspaper to lobby for access to "the treasures of the world which books contain," and succeeded in getting the access he wanted.

Franklin organized a debating club, or "Junta" as he called it, to further sharpen his own mind and the minds of a few literate friends. Carnegie, apparently inspired by Franklin's example, organized a similar club when he was a youth.

Carnegie and Brady honed their mental powers by going to night school while working full time, in an era when "full time" meant 60 hours a week. Both of them took advantage of slow hours at the office to self-educate in telegraphy.

Earning a bigger paycheck boils down to two things: make yourself more valuable to your employer; and ask for what you're worth, either from your current employer or from a new one.

PRINCIPLE #3: KEEP TRYING.

It is always too soon to quit.

HENRY FORD

All great American success stories have a lot of failure in them. One of the defining characteristics of successful people is that they refuse to accept defeat. Failure and frustration are part of life, especially for people who try to do great things, and one of the key principles of success in life is refusing to be discouraged by your own failures. Examples are legion.

Chuck Yeager, the world famous test pilot who first broke the sound barrier, threw up all over himself the first time he went up in an airplane. When the army offered him an opportunity to earn a promotion to sergeant by qualifying as a pilot he signed up without hesitation. It took him several more flights to overcome his airsickness, but eventually he did, and the rest is history.[438]

When 16-year-old John D. Rockefeller was looking for a job he didn't just mail out a few resumes and wait for someone to hire him. He worked hard every day walking the streets of Cleveland, going to every business office and asking in person for the chance to apply for a job. He never gave up despite being rejected several times a day, six days a week, for six weeks. Eventually he got that first job and got his career underway. Throughout his career he demonstrated the same bulldog tenacity that had gotten him that first job. When his Cleveland refinery burned down he was penciling out plans for a new one before the flames were out.[439]

Eli Whitney didn't quit when Southern plantation owners violated his patent rights and denied him the royalties that his cotton gin should have earned for him. He labored for years, living on a shoestring, before he managed to make his system of mass-producing firearms work well enough to make him a rich man.

Cyrus Hall McCormick grew up on his father's Virginia farm in the early nineteenth century, and spent his teen years trying to build a mechanical grain harvester. He demonstrated a working model of his harvester in 1831 at the age of 22. He continued to improve on his design and two years after that first public demonstration he started running newspaper advertisements in an attempt to sell reapers to Virginia wheat farmers. He failed to sell a single machine that year and for seven more years after that. McCormick supported himself by building and operating a furnace for smelting iron ore, and spent every dollar he could spare working on and patenting his harvester and trying to persuade farmers to buy it.

McCormick finally sold two machines in 1840, when he was 31 years old, for 50 dollars apiece. He failed to sell any the following year, but in 1842 he sold seven harvesters for a hundred dollars each. He sold 29 harvesters the following year and 50 the year after that.[440] His business continued to grow, and he moved his operation to Chicago in 1847. By 1866 he was a millionaire.[441] In 1902 his heirs joined the ranks of the super-rich when J.P. Morgan merged McCormick's company with several competitors to form International Harvester, which survives today under the name Navistar International.

Henry Ford's tenacity was legendary. One Ford biographer observed that Ford, early in his career, taught himself "certain habits of mind," one of which was "a cheerfulness about failure."[442] That cheerful attitude stood him in good stead when, in his late 30s, he started up a car company that quickly failed. Ford then persuaded investors to back a second car company, which was on the verge of failure when the stockholders kicked Ford out. Just before his fortieth birthday he managed to found his third company, the Ford Motor Company, which succeeded so wildly that Ford became a billionaire.

It's not surprising that Ford, who idolized Thomas Edison, would teach himself this attitude; Edison was the world's all-time king of mental toughness in the face of repeated failures. Edison spent years working and studying, spending every dime on books and living hand-to-mouth, before he began to make a decent living as an inventor. And throughout his long career his most significant successes were usually achieved only after hundreds or even thousands of unsuccessful trials. Edison failed more times and in more ways than anyone else in human history, by a wide margin, and he never let it bother him.

Edison was always too closely focused on his work to waste time feeling bad about his failures. Every new failure taught him something he could use in his pursuit of ultimate success, and that was the only thing that ever mattered to him. Fortunately for him, the world-changing innovations he succeeded in creating carry more weight with historians than his manifold failures.

People who succeed greatly are people who keep working hard in pursuit of their goals, undaunted by failures and setbacks.

PRINCIPLE #4: MEET A NEED.

> *I have always served the public to the best*
> *of my ability. Why? Because, like every*
> *other man, it is to my interest to do so.*

CORNELIUS VANDERBILT

Third world dictators can take people's money by force, but in America's free enterprise system a person can only succeed by persuading other people to pay him for something they want. An American succeeds by meeting other people's needs.

William Carnegie didn't understand this principle, but his son Andrew did. The elder Carnegie had a special skill that had once been valuable, and he refused to admit that his skill had become obsolete. Rather than learn new skills that would have greater value in a changing world, he kept on making a product that virtually no one wanted to buy, and by the time he died he was depending on his teenage son to support him. Andrew became the world's richest man because he took the opposite approach. As a teenager he taught himself people skills and telegraphy to increase his value to his employers. As a businessman he always focused his career on products for which the demand was growing: first an express company, then telegraphy, sleeper cars, oil, bridge construction, iron, and finally steel.

Similarly Andrew Mellon achieved his fantastic financial success largely because of his uncanny ability to identify and fund talented entrepreneurs who were developing new products for which the need was soon to become apparent.

Alexander Graham Bell, sadly, had no idea how great a need he was meeting when he made it possible for people to talk with one another over great distances. As the value of his AT&T shares kept rocketing upward, he kept expecting the growth to stop at some point, so he sold most of his shares for a fraction of what they would be worth in just a few years. If Bell had had the foresight of an Andrew Carnegie or an Andrew Mellon he would have held onto all his shares and quickly become one of the wealthiest men in the country. Bell certainly met a need, a huge need, but he failed to profit as greatly as he would have if only he'd understood how important his invention was.

In 1906 a 20-year-old farm boy named Alfred C. Fuller demonstrated how important it is in business to meet customers' needs even in something as mundane as household cleaning products. Alfred had moved to Boston as a teenager and gotten a job selling door-to-door for a small company that manufactured brushes. His customers were early twentieth century housewives who spent a great deal of their time cleaning their homes without any of the time-saving appliances we take for granted today. Fuller was a modest and unassuming young man, and he always listened respectfully when his customers told him about the kinds of brushes they needed. He urged his employers to change the products they were making to better meet the requirements of his customers, but his bosses told him that it was not his place to tell them how to make their products.

After a year Alfred took the risk of leaving his job and striking out on his own. He spent his meager savings on brush-making materials, put together a little workshop in the basement of his sister's house, and went to work making the brushes his customers had told him they needed. The first sales call he made as an independent business-man went well. "Mrs. Angeli," he said to a customer, "I now have that special brush you asked for – the sweeper with protected ends that can't damage woodwork. I made it in my shop just for you." Mrs. Angeli bought the new brush, of course, as did many of her neighbors. Young Alfred's business grew rapidly.

Soon one of his old bosses, a man named Fred Kelly, confronted him and accused him of unethical behavior. Every brush that Alfred sold, said Kelly, deprived Kelly and his partner of a sale. Fuller pointed out that the only brushes he was selling were designs that Kelly and his partner had refused to make, which, in young Fuller's mind, meant that he was not in direct completion with them. Too proud and stubborn to learn anything from the younger man, Kelly walked away in a huff and never spoke to Fuller again.

Fuller sold so many brushes that he soon had to hire production assistants to make the products for him while he was out selling. Soon after that he began to hire salesmen and train them in his own customer-centered approach. Four years after he produced that first brush in his sister's basement he had a staff of over 200 "Fuller Brush Men" peddling his brushes to housewives all across the nation.[443] Fuller quickly became a millionaire. His autobiography *A Foot in the Door* has been an indispensable textbook for self-taught professional sellers for half a century. In the 1940s and 50s a Hollywood studio made movies about his company.[444] No one has ever made movies or written books about Fred Kelly and his partner. After Fuller left them they struggled along doing business in their own foolish way, and lived out their lives in the obscurity that awaits businessmen who ignore their customers' needs.

In the 1840s, when Thomas Mellon had established a reputation as a skillful and diligent lawyer, he learned that providing a good value for the client outweighed social class, and even family loyalties. Mellon had grown up as a poor farm boy, and some of the other lawyers in town came from wealthy and powerful families, but, as Mellon observed, "Litigants will pass by friends and relatives and retain whoever will serve them to the best advantage."[445]

In the 1880s Booker T. Washington demonstrated that even racial bigotry couldn't keep customers away from a business that met their needs. Washington spent the first nine years of his life in slavery before being liberated by the advancing Union Army in 1865. In 1881 he founded the Tuskegee Institute, near the town of Tuskegee, Alabama, to offer remedial and advanced education to Southern blacks, many of whom had, like himself, been born in slavery.

There was no brickyard in the town of Tuskegee, and Washington was able to find clay suitable for brick making on the institute's property, so he and his students set out to teach themselves to make bricks. Being good American entrepreneurs, they failed miserably in their first few attempts but kept trying until they succeeded. When they were able to turn out good quality bricks on a consistent basis they made it known in the town that they had bricks for sale. "The making of these bricks," said Washington, "taught me an important lesson in regard to the relations of the two races in the South. Many white people who had no contact with the school, and perhaps no sympathy with it, came to us to buy bricks because they found out that ours were good bricks."

Given the hostility that Southern whites of that era tended to have toward the whole idea of education for black people, it was probably something of an understatement when Washington said that some of the institute's white neighbors had "no sympathy with it." But Southern roads were primitive and transportation costs were high, especially for bulk commodities like bricks. Faced with the choice of buying their construction materials from a local source at lower prices or paying high prices to import them, the white residents of that part of Alabama put their biases aside and took the best deal available. Later Washington and his students began building and selling wagons and other vehicles with similar success. Washington's final word on the subject is, "The individual who can do something that the world wants done will, in the end, make his way regardless of his race."[446]

PRINCIPLE #5: MAKE GOOD DEALS.

Make the best deal you can, then keep it.

SCOTT ADAMS

Deal making is obviously a central aspect of success in the business world, and it would be hard to find a better example of the art than John D. Rockefeller's 1868 freight rate negotiations with the Lake Shore Railroad. Rockefeller was a very skillful negotiator, and the Lake Shore deal is widely regarded as the breakthrough that launched his company into a dominant position in the American oil industry.

In the 1860s shipping costs could account for more than half the price of a barrel of kerosene sold in New York City. Getting a significantly lower freight rate than the nation's other oil refiners, which is what Rockefeller accomplished with the Lake Shore deal, gave his company a tremendous advantage. As early as 1866 two-thirds of the products Rockefeller's company produced were exported to Europe, which of course meant that Standard had to ship the products to New York or some other deep-water port city where they could be loaded onto oceangoing ships. The Cleveland to New York connection was crucial.

The arrangement Rockefeller made in 1868 gave his company (which would not be known as the Standard Oil Company until two years later) the lowest freight rates in the industry; dramatically increasing the cost advantage that Rockefeller's highly efficient operation already had over its competitors. Critics like Ida Tarbell, who have depicted Rockefeller as a rich and greedy "robber baron" who squeezed excessive profits from his near-monopoly position in the oil business, have often pointed to that 1868 deal as the central factor in making Standard Oil so dominant.[447] The deal didn't happen by accident. It was a brilliant bit of negotiating that any aspiring young businessperson would do well to study.

First, Rockefeller was not trying to "beat" the Lake Shore, he was trying to work with them for mutual benefit. The other refining companies, not the railroad, were the competitors he was trying to defeat. Next, he followed the two great rules of negotiating power: make sure the other party knows that you can walk away if you're not happy, then offer them something they really want.

Rockefeller had the ability to walk away from any transportation deal he didn't like because he'd been smart enough to choose a location for his refineries that gave him options. The management of the Lake Shore knew that if he didn't make a deal with them, he could make it with someone else. From the time he chose a site for his first refinery in 1863, Rockefeller always took care to have more than one transportation option available. His Cleveland refineries always had access to Lake Erie, hence to New York City by ship via the Erie Canal. In addition, Cleveland was served by three competing railroads, giving Rockefeller four viable transportation options.

Knowing that his location gave him bargaining power, Rockefeller did everything he could to make the Lake Shore want to do business with him. He understood the principles of railroad economics very well, and in trying to craft a deal that would be irresistibly sweet, Rockefeller looked at all the relevant issues from the railroad's point of view.

Chapter eight of this book describes the defining problem of American railroads of that era: debt. The railroad companies all raced to build track in new areas, and they could only do it with massive amounts of borrowed money. The Lake Shore was no exception.

The other besetting problem of nineteenth century railroads was the highly seasonal and unpredictable nature of their business. Most of their revenue came from hauling agricultural products,[448] which for obvious reasons was a decentralized, disorganized, and largely seasonal business. Hauling grain and vegetables meant dealing with literally millions of small farmers and brokers, most of whom only had products to ship during the late summer and fall months. Railroad employees had to spend countless man-hours dealing with small customers and soliciting small consignments. When crops weren't being harvested revenues plummeted and the railroads struggled to service their debts.

In his freight rate negotiations Rockefeller offered concessions and incentives tailor-made for a railroad executive struggling with the economic problems of that era. First and foremost, he offered a large volume of guaranteed daily business. He committed to ship 60 carloads of kerosene every day, year round. The 60 car commitment was not something Rockefeller would have taken lightly. It was more product than Rockefeller could produce in his own refineries. He had to make arrangements with other Cleveland refiners to make up the difference until he could expand his manufacturing capabilities sufficiently to fill the contract without outside help.

Kerosene prices were extremely volatile, and before the Lake Shore deal Rockefeller routinely curtailed production during periods when demand and prices were low. By committing to ship the same large volume every day he was promising to run his plants at full capacity, and initially even supplement this with kerosene from rival refiners, regardless of market conditions. While a commitment of this kind created problems for Rockefeller and his partners, it was extremely attractive to the Lake Shore. Because the benefit to the railroad was greater than the pain it caused Rockefeller, Rockefeller agreed to make the commitment.

Rockefeller sweetened the deal further by offering to make expensive infrastructure investments to reduce the up-front costs to the railroad. He agreed to build whole railroad terminals with loading platforms and warehouses to streamline the loading process. The refiner even agreed to accept liability for fire or accidents, thus saving the heavily leveraged railroad the cost of liability insurance.

Rockefeller's company had to pay for these infrastructure projects up front, before it had saved enough money in lowered freight costs to pay for the work. No businessperson likes to spend money up front if he can help it, but once again the benefit to the cash-strapped railroad was greater than the pain Rockefeller's more solvent company suffered. Rockefeller was willing to bargain away something that was less important to him than it was to the other party in order to get something that was of paramount importance to him: the lowest freight rate in the oil business.

It should be added that Rockefeller's rock-solid reputation for always honoring every deal he made was a critical factor in the negotiations. Maintaining a reputation of that kind gives a businessperson bargaining power that others don't have. If someone known for being dishonest or unreliable had tried to make a deal like this, giving the railroad only his verbal promise that he would ship more oil than he was currently able to produce, and do it reliably every day without fail, the Lake Shore management would no doubt have figured a "risk premium" into the freight rate they were willing to extend. Nineteenth century railroad executives had enough uncertainty and risk to worry about without taking on the additional burden of worrying about whether a major customer could be trusted to keep his side of a deal. But the railroad knew Rockefeller's reputation, and trusted him. His reputation was an asset he could trade on, and he took full advantage of it.

Rockefeller's message to the Lake Shore was effectively this: "Here's the sweetest deal a railroad could ask for. It's custom-made for your business model, and you know you can trust me to keep it. I'm either going to make this deal with you, or make it with one of your competitors. Now what will you offer me?"

The president of the Lake Shore agreed to an effective rate of $1.65 per barrel for shipments to New York, a much lower rate than any other refiner got from any railroad in the country.[449] The reduction in transportation costs gave Rockefeller and his partners a tremendous advantage over the other refiners, and over the next several years most of his competitors either went out of business or agreed to merge their companies with Standard Oil.

Deal making, like everything else in business, is a skill that can be learned, and the best way to learn is by studying the masters. Rockefeller's deal with the Lake Shore is a textbook case.

PRINCIPLE #6: BE THRIFTY.

If you would be wealthy, think of
saving as well as getting.

BENJAMIN FRANKLIN

Thrift is one of the most important principles for a poor person who wants to make himself rich. Money saved and invested tends to grow rapidly. On the other hand a poor person who persists in spending too much, and never changes course, can lock himself into poverty for life, because debts grow rapidly too. Early American history is full of examples of the benefits of frugal living and the terrible destructive power of spending too much.

Today far too many Americans allow themselves to buy non-essential things on credit. In the words of financial guru Dave Ramsey, "We buy things we don't need with money we don't have to impress people we don't like." People who dig themselves into a financial hole in this way have more in common with foolish ante-bellum Southern whites than with self-reliant self-made entrepreneurs. One of the perverse cultural values that made the South of that era so backward was conspicuous consumption, financed with borrowed money. Many wealthy plantation owners lost everything they had because of reckless spending. Whenever a planter spent himself into this condition the authorities would seize his plantation and slaves and sell them for the benefit of the planter's creditors, typically Northeastern banks.

People who succeed financially do it by managing their money wisely. During Benjamin Franklin's first several months in London he spent money on theater tickets and other luxuries, and couldn't even save enough money for a ticket home. When he started denying himself these luxuries and saving his money, his life changed dramatically for the better. Within a few years hard work and frugal living had made him the sole owner of a profitable business.

Thomas Mellon learned from Franklin's example that thrift is essential to success, and was able to put himself through college and then complete his law studies, all while working for very small wages. Cornelius Vanderbilt's personal secretary once described his boss as "economical almost to extremes."[450] Virtually all of America's most successful self-made men were wise enough to save their pennies and invest in their own futures. It's true that Rockefeller financed the rapid early growth of his oil business with borrowed money, but the business itself was always profitable. Rockefeller only borrowed so that his successful business could expand faster. And during that early period he took very little money out of the business for his own personal use. The profits the company earned, like the money he borrowed, went back into the business to help it grow. All through his career Rockefeller spent less money on himself than other businessmen in similar financial circumstances.

Even Diamond Jim Brady, the king of the big spenders, never financed his lavish lifestyle with borrowed money. He was not a man who could be described as thrifty, but at least he was smart enough to earn his money first and spend it later.

One of the pillars of financial success is thrift.

Principle #7: Use the Best Human Resources.

Those who came to work for our organization had to be the most brilliant, creative, aggressive people around.

Estee Lauder

A highly successful person will generally have to manage other people at some point; either as a business owner, or while holding a management level job in a large company. There are exceptions to this rule, of course. Jim Brady, to cite one example, never had any management responsibilities in the companies he worked for, even when he was one of the chief stockholders. But most highly successful careers involve management responsibilities. Human resources are the most important resources in any company, and the most successful managers are those who excel at identifying, attracting, retaining, developing, and motivating the best people.

There are many characteristics that make one human resource more valuable than another, but character, intelligence, and adaptability are more important than just about anything else. Workers who lack job-specific experience but have these three key characteristics can be far more valuable to an employer than people who might have relevant experience but lack these characteristics. Henry J. Kaiser's management team provides a useful case study.

Kaiser, of course, was the usual rags-to-riches American story. When he was a child his father made shoes and boots by hand when mass production methods had already made his skills more or less obsolete, so the family was poor. Henry had to drop out of school and go to work in a dry goods store for $1.50 a week at the age of 13.[451] In the early twentieth century Kaiser made his fortune as a construction contractor, building roads and dams. By the 1930s he had assembled a team of dedicated, clever, and open-minded engineers and project managers who delighted in doing the impossible.

In 1938, when a rival company secured the contract for the massive Shasta Dam project that Kaiser had hoped to land for his own company, he decided that if he couldn't build the dam he would cash in on the project another way, by selling his rival the six million barrels of cement that the project required. Kaiser had complete confidence in his team's ability to learn how to build and operate a cement plant in very little time: "I didn't know anything about producing cement… So I sent my boys off East to learn how it was done, how to go about building a plant, and how to get it done in a hurry."[452] His faith in his "boys" was soon vindicated. Construction of their cement plant commenced in June, and by December of the same year the plant was built and in successful operation. After the attack on Pearl Harbor Kaiser made a fortune selling cement to the U.S. Navy for bases in the Pacific.

When the war began Kaiser decided to jump into the shipbuilding business, even though he and his management team had even less experience in that area than they'd had in cement. Once again, his people demonstrated their ability to learn new skills on the fly. In November of 1940 Kaiser took a delegation from Britain to a bare mud flat on near Richmond, California and told them that he would soon have a shipyard built on the site. Five months later the first shipway was built and the keel of the first ship had already been laid. Four months after that the first ship built in Richmond was launched. Soon Kaiser's shipyards were producing freighters and warships at a pace that no other shipbuilder could match.[453]

Soon the biggest problem Kaiser's shipyards faced was the inadequate supply of steel available from America's steelmakers, whose output had been restricted for years by the federal government for political reasons, and who were unable to ramp up production sufficiently to meet wartime demands. The steel industry was as foreign to Kaiser and his people as cement and shipbuilding had been, but Kaiser lobbied the government for permission to go into the steel business. When it was granted he summoned a top hand named George Havas to his office and told him "George, you're going to build me a steel mill." Havas, confident in his own abilities, simply asked the boss what kind of steel mill he wanted.[454] Soon Kaiser was one of the leading steel producers in the nation.

Kaiser's competitors in cement, shipbuilding and steel all had large numbers of experienced people and lots of institutional knowledge, yet Kaiser's team was consistently able to beat those other companies at their own games. Kaiser's people were, quite simply, better all-around human resources than his competitors' people.

Identifying topnotch human resources is an art in itself. Society at large does not always put a high value on the characteristics that make someone a valuable employee. Take Charles Steinmetz, the brilliant engineer who was the General Electric Company's most important asset after Thomas Edison divorced himself from the company. Steinmetz was a four-foot-tall, physically deformed German immigrant who fled Europe to avoid arrest and arrived penniless at Ellis Island, where the authorities very nearly denied him permission to enter the United States. In 1889 an inventor named Rudolph Eickemeyer looked beneath the surface and saw Steinmetz' potential. Working in Eickemeyer's laboratory, Steinmetz developed a method for predicting the efficiency of electric motors mathematically. Steinmetz' work made him so valuable that G.E. management resorted to buying Eickemeyer's company to acquire Steinmetz' services, and Eickemeyer made a pile of money on the deal.

Most of the people profiled in this book were masters at identifying and attracting high quality employees. Carnegie, according to historians Mark Carnes and John Garraty, had "an uncanny knack of choosing topflight subordinates."[455]

Rockefeller's employees marveled at their boss's ability to collect and manage talent. "I have never heard of his equal," said one, "in getting together a lot of the very best men in one team and inspiring each man to do his best for the enterprise." Rockefeller was always on the lookout for the right human resources, and "hired talented people as found, not as needed." Math skills were an important criterion. When Rockefeller was interviewing a man who had applied to be his secretary, he gave the applicant a sheet of figures and told him to total them up, then pulled out his watch and timed the job-seeker. When the young man arrived at the right total "in the required time," Rockefeller hired him on the spot.[456]

A longtime Walmart executive, in explaining the company's rapid early growth, credits Sam Walton's ability to judge prospective employees:

> Sam is very sharp on being able to read people and their personalities, and their integrity, and he didn't make many mistakes back there picking people…He was so good at evaluating and selecting those fellows. He wasn't just looking for store managers. I think he was selecting people he thought he could go forward with.[457]

Unfortunately some of the screening methods that Walton used in the 1960s would be illegal under current federal law. Walton always insisted on meeting the spouses of his prospective store managers, and he would ask husband and wife if they attended church; a question that would quite probably embroil a 21st century business manager in a discrimination lawsuit. Walton also asked prospects about their personal finances, a method of character measurement that was important to him but another tactic that might spell legal trouble for a manager of today. (Under current federal law it is even all but illegal to use I.Q. tests to screen potential employees.)

Henry Ford used even more intrusive methods than Walton's in screening his workers, and not just for management personnel, but even to qualify hourly workers for his factories.

In the early twentieth century the Ford Motor Company was struggling with extremely high absenteeism and turnover among its factory workers. Heavy drinking was a cultural norm among blue collar workers of that era, and all large manufacturers struggled with alcohol related absences among their employees. Illnesses related to unhygienic living conditions also kept workers away from their jobs. To make matters worse, the dull and repetitive nature of the tasks that workers had to do on Ford's assembly lines tended to cause burnout among workers who didn't have the right personality for it, which made the twin problems of absenteeism and turnover even larger for Ford than they were for other manufacturers. In 1913 10 percent of Ford's hourly workforce was absent from work on an average day. Worker turnover during the year was a shocking 370 percent.[458]

Ford management decided to take a two-pronged approach to solving the problem. They would pay their workers twice the wage that other factories were paying, and require verifiable sobriety and cleanliness as a condition of employment. On January 5, 1914, Ford announced that his company would shorten work shifts to eight hours and increase pay for low-skilled workers to an unprecedented five dollars per day. Within a week of the announcement the company had received 14 thousand new job applications. Ten thousand more job hunters lined up outside the company's front gate to apply in person.[459]

To earn that five dollar a day wage a Ford worker had to "demonstrate that he did not drink alcohol or physically mistreat his family or have boarders in his home, and that he deposited money in a savings account, maintained a clean home, and had good moral character."[460]

The company published and distributed pamphlets giving specific instructions for hygienic steps like bathing regularly and keeping garbage and sewage out of the home; things that seem obvious today but that were not widely practiced among immigrant workers of the early twentieth century. To enforce compliance Ford sent inspectors into workers' homes to look at conditions and interview the workers' wives.

Modern day workers would never accept an employer who meddled in their lives in this way, even for higher wages, but the system worked well for the Ford Motor Company in that era. The company was able to fill thousands of new jobs with workers who stayed with the company for long periods and showed up ready for work every day.

Ford paid his workers high fixed hourly wages as a way of making them want to stay with him, but for an employer who wants to spur key people to higher levels of performance, it's important to link the worker's compensation to the company's success and the worker's contributions to it.

Astor, Vanderbilt, Rockefeller, and Carnegie, all made sure their most important employees had a financial interest in their companies. When Carnegie spotted a talented young manager in his organization and wanted to give that person some shares of Carnegie Steel stock, he would find a way to do it even if he had to transfer the shares from his own personal holdings.

Even Edison, who was notorious for his reluctance to pay money he owed to suppliers and financial backers, compensated his top employees well. He motivated key players to excel by giving them shares of stock or shares of the royalties earned by the inventions they helped him develop.

Retaining and motivating good workers takes more than high pay, of course. Money is not the only factor that influences a person to look for a new job or be content with the one he has. Being treated with respect is very important to all workers, and to highly competent and valuable workers in particular.

Rockefeller reportedly knew thousands of Standard Oil employees by name,[461] and he was unfailingly courteous to all of them. He never lost his temper, and he "always had a kind word for everybody." He wouldn't force people to wait for him by showing up late to an appointment because he believed "A man has no right to occupy another man's time unnecessarily." He sought out executives and managers who, like himself, had the ability to work cordially and well with their subordinates, and he was willing to "pay more for that ability than for any other under the sun."[462]

There are many tactics for making employees happy with their jobs while spurring them to greater achievements. A dress code is one. Men who wear neckties at work tend to have higher opinions of their own importance than those who don't, even though most employees would prefer not to have to wear the ties.

Job titles can be another factor contributing to the happiness and confidence of employees. At one time the advertising firm Ogilvy and Mather had eight executive vice presidents, 67 senior vice presidents and 249 vice presidents.[463]

G.E. Management once averted a potential crisis by giving Charles Steinmetz a fancy title. The company had made Steinmetz a department head, and learned the hard way that he was not management material. Demoting him back to his old job might have bruised the ego of the eccentric genius, and management knew that if Steinmetz were to resign it would be a major disaster. His brain power was irreplaceable. By offering him a position as "Consulting Engineer of the General Electric Company" his bosses made a return to the laboratory sound like a promotion, and everybody won.[464]

In addition to attracting and retaining quality employees, top-notch managers help their employees grow. Every human resource, from the most ignorant manual laborer to the most talented engineer, can increase his own skills if he makes the effort. Great managers hone their own skills continually and encourage their subordinates to do the same.

Edison maintained "one of the finest scientific and technical libraries in the world" at his laboratory, and many of his more ambitious employees made full use of it, studying during lunch breaks and after work. The Wizard also sponsored a series of lectures on scientific subjects exclusively for his employees.[465]

One of the key principles Rockefeller taught his employees was "train your subordinate to do your job." Another was learning by trial and error. "Often the best way to develop workers – when you are sure they have character and think they have ability – is to take them to a deep place, throw them in and make them sink or swim."[466]

When John Toucey hired young Jim Brady he immediately persuaded the teenager to improve his mind by going to night school, which Brady did for several years.[467]

Carnegie made people in management positions in his company believe that they could accomplish great things, then he pushed them hard to do just that. He routinely described his more talented subordinates, including young men at lower levels of the organization chart, as his "young geniuses." At the end of a typically excellent year of rapid growth he described the company's performance as "the result of exceptionally able management by the most wonderful organization of young geniuses the world has to show."[468]

Inspiring subordinates to hold a high opinion of their own capabilities is a powerful management tool in any endeavor. Wise leaders in any field who want to get the best from their teams often use methods similar to Carnegie's. When Chuck Yeager was commanding a fighter squadron in the 1950s he confronted the pilots under his command with difficult challenges at every turn, all the while praising and encouraging them so skillfully that they had enormous faith in their own abilities to overcome the challenges. "He made us think," said one, "that we could all fly with his capabilities, which was absolutely crazy."[469]

Estee Lauder, founder of the multi-national cosmetics company of the same name (and a truly great seller of the caliber of a Diamond Jim Brady), personally trained thousands of Estee Lauder saleswomen in department stores all over America, and eventually in parts of Europe. Every time a new Estee Lauder counter opened in an upscale department store anywhere in the world, she would travel to the site and spend roughly a week teaching her skills to her new employees.[470] Being the head of a billion dollar corporation puts heavy demands on a person's time, and it's virtually unheard-of for the chief executive of a company of that size to spend time face-to-face with employees at the bottom of the organization chart, but in Mrs. Lauder's case it was the right thing to do. The company grew and prospered at a phenomenal rate largely because it employed an army of saleswomen personally trained by one of the great sellers of all time.

Any company in any industry is sure to succeed if it employs enough highly motivated high-quality human resources. Putting together a team of this kind is the most powerful thing a business owner or manager can do to ensure his or her success.

Principle #8: Only Principle #1 is Indispensable.

*Always bear in mind that your own resolution to
succeed is more important than any other one thing.*

Abraham Lincoln

A person who believes unreservedly in the power of his own efforts can succeed greatly, even if he doesn't excel in all of the other principles outlined above. Examples are plentiful. Estee Lauder never had to make herself the kind of human resource that an employer would value; she never worked for anyone but herself. She started out in business making face crème on her kitchen stove and selling it from a little table she set up in the beauty salon in her neighborhood, and simply kept selling more and more until she was the leader of a multi-billion-dollar multi-national corporation.

Diamond Jim Brady never managed other people. Charles Steinmetz was a failure the one time his employer tried him in a management position, which shows that he never learned any management skills. Vanderbilt's people skills were never very good.

Edison, to his shame, did not honor business deals as scrupulously as giants like Carnegie, Rockefeller, Vanderbilt and Morgan. As a result, he sometimes struggled to attract investment capital when he needed it.

Edison was never very thrifty, and neither was Brady, yet both of them were able to earn money faster than they spent it.

Steinmetz, who earned his fortune sitting at a desk solving complex engineering problems for his employers, never had to craft clever business deals, or evaluate the market to identify customer needs.

Eli Whitney got next to nothing out of his cotton gin, even as it transformed the Southern economy, because he didn't (at that time) know how to craft a good business deal, but his persistence and his willingness to learn from his mistakes ultimately made him successful and rich.

The decisions a person makes and the effort he exerts are the factors that determine success or failure. The person who embraces this truth will succeed even if he is a little weak in other areas.

CHAPTER 15

Final Word

———

*The progress has been wonderful enough – but when
we compare what has been done with what there is
to do, then our past accomplishments are as nothing.*

HENRY FORD, 1922

As LONG AS AMERICA REMAINS free, young Americans will have to
look no farther than the nearest mirror to find the resources they need
for a successful career. The resources are a gift from God Almighty,
and the freedom to develop and use those resources is a birthright
given to every American by John Locke and the Founding Fathers.
Anyone who tells young Americans from poor families that they are
too "disadvantaged" to overcome life's obstacles and create success for
themselves is poisonous and wrong.

The people profiled in this book all made their contributions in
the eighteenth and nineteenth centuries, when the nation itself was
going from poverty to greatness, but the opportunities are just as great
today as they were in the past, and stories of rags-to-riches success in
America are still common. It's true that the regulatory burdens that
government agencies impose on entrepreneurs are heavier today than
they were in the nation's early days, but in many ways opportunities

are more plentiful today than ever before. Self-education, for one thing, is much easier for modern Americans than it was for those of Andrew Carnegie's generation. Where people like Franklin and Carnegie had to go to extraordinary lengths to get access to a limited supply of books, today "the treasures of the world which books contain," as well as free Internet access, are readily available in public libraries in every city and town in the nation.

The government-mandated racial discrimination that made life so difficult for black Americans in the nineteenth century was all swept away by the end of the 1960's, so for black citizens in particular, there are far more avenues to success available in modern-day America than were in the nation's early days. Immigrants of every race and creed can achieve rapid success in modern-day America, as a stroll down the halls of any Silicon Valley high tech company will attest.

In a free country, anyone who makes wise choices can achieve success that will be limited only by the effort he or she is willing to expend. America is still the land of opportunity, and Americans who believe in themselves and in the power of their own efforts will continue to seize the opportunities they find and achieve great things.

NOTES

FOREWORD: WHY I WROTE THIS BOOK

1. Joseph Frazier Wall, *Andrew Carnegie* (Pittsburgh, PA: University of Pittsburgh Press, 1989), 101-102.

2. Mark C. Carnes and John A. Garraty, *American Destiny, Volume II,* Third Edition (New York: Pearson Longman, 2008), 518.

CHAPTER 1: A NATION OF NONCONFORMISTS

3. Louise Egan, *Thomas Edison: The Great American Inventor* (Hauppauge, NY: Barron's, 1987), 11-13.

4. Alexis de Tocqueville, *Democracy in America* (New York: Bantam Classic, 2000), 350.

5. William J. Rorabaugh, Donald T. Critchlow, & Paula Baker; *America's Promise – A Concise History of the United States, Volume One* (New York: Rowman and Littlefield Publishers Inc., 2004), 44-83.

6. Georgia, North and South Carolina, and Virginia, which was named after Queen Elizabeth I, the so-called "Virgin Queen."

7. "Act of Uniformity 1559," *Wikipedia*, accessed January 10, 2014 http://en.wikipedia.org/wiki/Act_of_Uniformity_1559, "Pilgrims (Plymouth Colony)," *Wikipedia*, accessed January 10, 2014, http://en.wikipedia.org/wiki/Pilgrims_(Plymouth_Colony, "Religion," *Mayflowerhistory.com*, accessed January 10, 2015, http://mayflowerhistory.com/religion.

8. William J. Rorabaugh, Donald T. Critchlow, & Paula Baker; *America's Promise – A Concise History of the United States, Volume One* (New York: Rowman and Littlefield Publishers Inc., 2004), 49.

CHAPTER 2: BENJAMIN FRANKLIN

9. Thomas Mellon, *Thomas Mellon and His Times* (Pittsburgh, PA: University of Pittsburgh Press, 1994), 33.

10. Ron Chernow, *Titan – The Life of John D. Rockefeller, Sr.* (New York: Vintage Books, 1998), 54-55.

11. "Mark Twain's 'The Late Benjamin Franklin,'" *Crummy: The Site*, accessed June 1, 2015, http://www.crummy.com/writing/hosted/The%20Late%20Benjamin%20Franklin.html.

12. Carl Van Doren, *Benjamin Franklin* (New York: Penguin Books, 1991), 1-7.

13. Benjamin Franklin, *The Autobiography of Benjamin Franklin*, (Garden City, NY: Houghton Mifflin Company, 1923), 27.

14. Ibid., 27-33.

15. Ibid., 35.

16. Ibid., 35-37.

17. Ibid., 33.

18. Ibid., 37.

19. Ibid., 37, 38.

20. Ibid., 37, 38.

21. Ibid., 89.

22. Carl Van Doren, *Benjamin Franklin*, 135.

23. C.S. Lewis, *The Screwtape Letters* (San Francisco: Harper Collins, 2001), 127.

24. Benjamin Franklin, *The Autobiography of Benjamin Franklin*, 118-119.

25. Ibid., 117-118.

26. Walter Isaacson, *Benjamin Franklin – An American Life* (New York: Simon and Schuster Paperbacks, 2003), 29.

27. Carl Van Doren, *Benjamin Franklin*, 27.

28. Ibid., 30, 31.

29. Ibid., 31, 32.

30. Benjamin Franklin, *The Autobiography of Benjamin Franklin*, 43.

31. Ibid., 48.

32. Ibid, 49.

33. Ibid., 79.

34. Carl Van Doren, *Benjamin Franklin*, 56-67.

35. Walter Isaacson, *Benjamin Franklin*, 52.

36. Benjamin Franklin, *The Autobiography of Benjamin Franklin*, 87.

37. Walter Isaacson, *Benjamin Franklin*, 64.

38. Benjamin Franklin, *Autobiography of Benjamin Franklin*, 92-93.

39. Carl Van Doren, *Benjamin Franklin*, 74-77.

40. Walter Isaacson, *Benjamin Franklin*, 62.

41. Benjamin Franklin, *Autobiography of Benjamin Franklin*, 171-172.

42. "Benjamin Franklin, Information to Those Who Would Remove to America," *The Founders' Constitution,* 12 December 2015, http://press-pubs.uchicago.edu/founders/documents/v1ch15s27.html.

Chapter 3: John Jacob Astor

43. Paul Jeffers, *Diamond Jim Brady: Prince of the Gilded Age* (New York: Paul Wiley and Sons, 2001), 171; Margaret Cheney, *Tesla: Man out of Time* (New York: Simon and Schuster, 2001), 64; "The Vanderbilts," 1995 episode of the *Biography* series on the A&E Television Network.

44. J.R. Dolan, *The Yankee Peddlers of Early America* (New York: Bramhall House, 1964), 20, 21.

45. "John Jacob Astor" *Harper's New Monthly Magazine*, December 1864 to May 1865 edition: http://books.google.com/books?id=tX8CA AAAIAAJ&pg=PA309&dq=john+jacob+astor+born+%28waldo rf+OR+walldorf%29&hl=en#v=onepage&q=john%20jacob%20 astor%20born%20(waldorf%20OR%20walldorf)&f=false.

46. "John Jacob Astor" 2016 episode of the *Pioneers Turned Millionaires* series on the Smithsonian Channel.

47. John Upton Terrell, *Furs by Astor*, (New York: William Morrow and Company, 1963), 26.

48. Ibid., 32.

49. "John Jacob Astor" *Harper's New Monthly Magazine*, December 1864 to May 1865 edition: http://books.google.com/books?id=tX8CA AAAIAAJ&pg=PA309&dq=john+jacob+astor+born+%28waldo rf+OR+walldorf%29&hl=en#v=onepage&q=john%20jacob%20 astor%20born%20(waldorf%20OR%20walldorf)&f=false.

50. "John Jacob Astor" 2016 episode of the *Pioneers Turned Millionaires* series on the Smithsonian Channel.

51. John Upton Terrell, *Furs by Astor*, 37.

52. Ibid., 47.

53. Ibid., 52.

54. Ibid., 52, 53.

55. Ibid., 108.

56. Ibid., 115-116.

57. Ibid., 46.

CHAPTER 4: ELI WHITNEY
58. Adam Smith, *Wealth of Nations,* (Amherst, NY: Prometheus Books, 1991), 83-84.

59. Thomas Sowell, *Conquests and Cultures – An International History* (New York: Basic Books, 1998), 41.

60. Constance McL. Green, *Eli Whitney and the Birth of American Technology* (New York: Harper Collins, 1956), 20.

61. Ibid., 21.

62. Denison Olmsted, *Memoir of Eli Whitney* (New York: Arno Press, 1972), 9.

63. Ibid., 7.

64. Constance McL. Green, *Eli Whitney and the Birth of American Technology,* 26.

65. Ibid.

66. Denison Olmsted, *Memoir of Eli Whitney,* 10.

67. Constance McL. Green, *Eli Whitney and the Birth of American Technology*, 41.

68. Ibid., 12.

69. Ibid., 16.

70. Ibid., 50.

71. Denison Olmsted, *Memoir of Eli Whitney*, 17.

72. Eric Foner, *Give Me Liberty* (New York: W. W. Norton and Company, 2005), 319.

73. Between 1792 and 1797, for example, U.S. cotton production nearly quadrupled, yet cotton prices actually *increased* by 11 percent. See Constance McL. Green, *Eli Whitney and the Birth of American Technology*, 73.

74. Constance McL. Green, *Eli Whitney and the Birth of American Technology*, 53.

75. Ibid., 116.

76. Ibid. 126.

77. Ibid., 128.

78. Ibid., 187, 188.

79. "The Family" *Eli Whitney Museum and Workshop*, 2014, https://www.eliwhitney.org/7/museum/eli-whitney/family.

80. Philip Anschutz, *Out Where the West Begins* (Denver: Cloud Camp Press, 2015), 277.

Chapter 5: Free States and Free Enterprise

81. Alexis de Tocqueville, *Democracy in America* (New York: Bantam Classic, 2000), 218.

82. Ibid., 493.

83. Ibid., 34.

84. Ibid., 418, 419.

85. Booker T. Washington, *Up from Slavery* (New York: Airmont Publishing, 1967 re-issue), 24.

86. David McCullough, *John Adams* (New York: Simon and Schuster, 2001), 553.

87. Frederick Law Olmsted, *Cotton Kingdom – A Traveler's Observations on Cotton and Slavery in the American Slave States, 1853-1861* (New York: First Da Capo Press, 1996), 10, 21, 590.

88. Ibid., 12.

89. Ibid., 16, quoting U.S. Census data.

90. Ibid.

91. Ibid., 91.

92. Ibid., 305.

93. Ibid., 19.

94. Ibid., 64, 147.

95. Ibid., 257, 290, 578.

96. Ibid., 257.

97. Ibid., 149.

98. Ibid., 426.

99. "Slave Census" *Son of the South*, accessed 3 December 2014, http://www.sonofthesouth.net/slavery/slave-maps/slave-census.htm.

100. Frederick Law Olmsted, *Cotton Kingdom*, 186, 187.

101. Ron Chernow, *Washington – A Life*, (New York: Penguin Books, 2010), 493.

102. "Slaves are prohibited to Read and Write by Law," *History is a Weapon*, accessed 13 November 2014, http://www.history-isaweapon.com/defcon1/slaveprohibit.html and Frederick Law Olmsted, *Cotton Kingdom*, 239.

103. *Narrative of the Life of Frederick Douglass* (New York: Oxford World's Classics, 1999), 38, 39.

104. Franklin Law Olmsted, *Cotton Kingdom*, 100.

105. Ibid., 162.

106. Ibid., 258.

107. Ibid., 527.

108. Ibid., 535.

109. "Southern Commercial Convention" *The History Engine*, accessed April 2014, https://historyengine.richmond.edu/episodes/view/20).

110. The Southern Commercial Convention," New York Times, accessed April 2014, http://query.nytimes.com/mem/archive-free/pdf?res=9D06E7D9153CEE34BC4851DFB3668383649FDE, "'Southern Commercial Convention' What a Fraud to Claim This Represents the South," *Civil War Talk*, accessed April 2015, http://civilwartalk.com/threads/southern-commercial-convention-what-a-fraud-to-claim-this-represents-the-south.8056/.

111. Frederick Law Olmsted, *Cotton Kingdom,* 251, 417.

112. "Southern Commercial Convention," accessed April 2014, http://babel.hathitrust.org/cgi/pt?id=hvd.hx4sk9;view=1up;seq=11.

113. "Market Capitalization of Fortune 500 Companies by State," *Fortune Magazine*, May 2014 edition, http://fortunedotcom.files.wordpress.com/2014/05/mac-06-16-14-map.jpg.

114. "Fortune 500," *Fortune Magazine,* accessed September 2014, http://fortune.com/fortune500.

115. Sam Walton, *Made in America – My Story* (New York: Bantam Books, 1993), 5, 6.

116. Ibid., 20.

117. Ibid., 22.

CHAPTER 6: ROBERT FULTON AND HIS STEAMBOAT

118. "Crime on Roman Roads," *Historum*, November 2014, http://historum.com/ancient-history/78806-crime-roman-roads.html.

119. Thomas Sowell discusses these geographical barriors to African development in detail in the third chapter of his *Conquests and Cultures*, published by Basic Books.

120. Thomas Sowell, *Conquests and Cultures* (New York: Basic Books, 1998), 174-248.

121. Alexis de Tocqueville, *Democracy in America*, (New York: Bantam Classic, 2000), 342.

122. Charles R. Morris, *The Tycoons – How Andrew Carnegie, John D. Rockfeller, Jay Gould, and J.P. Morgan invented the American Supereconomy* (New York: Owl Books, 2005), 100.

123. "John Fitch," *Encyclopedia.com*, accessed January 2015, http://www.encyclopedia.com/topic/John_Fitch.aspx.

124. Kirkpatrick Sale, *The Fire of His Genius, - Robert Fulton and the American Dream* (New York: The Free Press, 2001), 32.

125. Ibid., 33.

126. Ibid., 42.

127. Ibid., 44.

128. Ibid., 90, 91.

129. Ibid., 200.

130. Jean-Paul Rodrigue, Claude Comtois, and Brian Slack, "The Geography of Transport Systems," *Hofstra University*, 1998, accessed March 2015, https://people.hofstra.edu/geotrans/eng/ch3en/conc3en/linertransatlantic.html.

131. Kirkpatrick Sale, *The Fire of His Genius,* 145.

CHAPTER 7: CORNELIUS VANDERBILT

132. "The Vanderbilts," 1995 episode of the *Biography* series on the A&E Television Network.

133. *The Vanderbilts* on A&E; and Edward J. Renehan, *Commodore – The Life of Cornelius Vanderbilt* (New York: Basic Books, 2007), 317.

134. Edward J. Renehan, *Commodore - The Life of Cornelius Vanderbilt*, 15.

135. T.J. Stiles, *The First Tycoon – The Epic Life of Cornelius Vanderbilt.* New York: Alfred A. Knopf, 2009. Kindle version, 7.

136. Ibid., 19, and "The Vanderbilts," 1995 episode of the *Biography* series on the A&E Television Network.

137. Edward J. Renehan, *Commodore*, 19-21; T.J. Stiles, *The First Tycoon - The Epic Life of Cornelius Vanderbilt.* New York: Alfred A. Knopf, 2009. Kindle version, 19-20.

138. Edward J. Renehan, *Commodore*, 26.

139. T.J. Stiles, *The First Tycoon*, 24.

140. Ibid., 24.

141. Edward J. Renehan, *Commodore*, 29.

142. Footnote: Biographer Edward J. Renehan claims that Vanderbilt contracted Syphilis from a prostitute and transmitted it to his wife Sophia, (Edward J. Renehan, *Commodore*, 32, 38, 155, 293.) although this claim has been disputed by at least one other biographer.

143. T.J. Stiles, *The First Tycoon*, 73, 152, 323.

144. Ron Chernow, *Titan – The Life of John D. Rockefeller, Sr.;* (New York: Vintage Books, 1998), 50, 54-55, 68.

145. Ibid., 123.

146. T.J. Stiles, *The First Tycoon*, 24, 28, 46, 82,187; Edward J. Renehan, *Commodore*, 51-52, 308; Edward J. Renehan, *Dark Genius of Wall Street – The Misunderstood Life of Jay Gould,*

King of the Robber Barons (New York: Basic Books, 2005), 100.

147. Ron Chernow, *Titan*, 174-179, 386; Edward J. Renehan, *Commodore*, 119-120.

148. Edward J. Renehan, *Commodore*, 28.

149. T.J. Stiles, *The First Tycoon*, 117.

150. Edward J. Renehan, *Commodore*, 41.

151. Ibid., 42.

152. Ford R. Bryan, *Beyond the Model T* (Detroit: Wayne State University Press, 1997), 33.

153. Edward J. Renehan, *Commodore*, 70.

154. Ibid., 105.

155. T.J. Stiles, *The First Tycoon*, 79 of 561.

156. Edward J. Renehan, *Commodore*, 95.

157. Ibid., 119-120.

158. David Ogilvy, *Ogilvy on Advertising*, (New York, First Vintage Books, 1985), 46-47.

159. Sam Walton, *Made in America – My Story*, (New York, Bantam Books, 1993), 197-198.

160. Ron Chernow, *Titan,* 102.

161. Joseph Frazier Wall, *Andrew Carnegie,* (Pittsburgh, University of Pittsburgh Press, 1989), 149-151.

162. Phillip L. Fradkin, *Stagecoach: Wells Fargo and the American West,* (New York, Simon and Schuster, 2002) Kindle version locations 765-851.

163. Edward J. Renehan, *Commodore,* 45-47.

164. Edward J. Renehan, *Dark Genius of Wall Street* (New York; Basic Books, 2005), 77.

165. T.J. Stiles, *The First Tycoon,* 176.

166. Ibid., 197-209; Edward J. Renehan, *Commodore,* 173-174.

167. T.J. Stiles, *The First Tycoon,* 74, 141; Edward J. Renehan, *Commodore,* 73-75.

168. Edward J. Renehan, *Commodore,* 197-200; "The Vanderbilts," 1995 episode of the *Biography* series on the A&E Television Network.

169. Edward J. Renehan, Commodore, 197-216.

170. John A. Butler, *Atlantic Kingdom – America's Contest with Cunard in the Age of Sail and Steam* (Washington, D.C.: Brassey's Inc., 2001), 208-221.

171. Ibid., 74.

172. Edward J. Renehan, *Commodore*, 221-221.

173. John A. Butler, *Atlantic Kingdom*, 208.

174. Edward J. Renehan, *Commodore*, 221-222.

175. John A. Butler, *Atlantic Kingdom*, 215-217, 225; Edward J. Renehan, *Commodore*, 219.

176. Winston Churchill, *A History of the English Speaking Peoples* (New York: Barnes and Noble, 1995), 398.

177. T.J. Stiles, *The First Tycoon*, 346-363.

178. Edward J. Renehan, *Commodore*, 248-249.

179. Ibid., 249-252.

CHAPTER 8: A BRIEF HISTORY OF RAILROADING IN THE UNITED STATES

180. Herbert N. Casson, *Cyrus Hall McCormick, His Life and Work* (Washington, D.C.: Beard Books, 2001), 64.

181. Chisholm, Jesse, *Texas State Historical Association*, accessed June 5, 2015, https://tshaonline.org/handbook/online/articles/fch32.

182. Edward J. Renehan, *Commodore*, 96.

183. Samuel Smiles, *The Life of George Stephenson* (Honolulu, Hawaii: University Press of the Pacific, 2001), 133.

184. Paul Israel, *Edison: A Life of Invention* (Hoboken, NJ: John Wiley and Sons, 1998), 4.

185. Stephen Ambrose, *Nothing Like It in the World* (New York: Simon and Schuster 2001), 28.

186. "First Transcontinental Railroad is Completed" *History.com*, accessed May 2014, http://www.history.com/this-day-in-history/first-transcontinental-railroad-is-completed.

187. Jean Strouse, *Morgan – American Financier* (New York: Harper Perennial, 2000), 66.

188. Edward J. Renehan, *Commodore,* 145.

189. "First TransAtlantic Telegraph Cable Completed," *History.com*, accessed May 2015, http://www.history.com/this-day-in-history/first-transatlantic-telegraph-cable-completed.

190. Jean Strouse, *Morgan,* 70.

191. Philip Anschutz, *Out Where the West Begins* (Denver: Cloud Camp Press, 2015), 168.

192. Stephen E. Ambrose, *Nothing Like it in the World* (New York: Touchstone, 2000), 99.

193. Joseph Frazier Wall, *Andrew Carnegie* (PittsburghL University of Pittsburgh Press, 1989), 157-168.

194. Jean Strouse, *Morgan,* 131.

195. Benjamin P. Thomas, *Abraham Lincoln* (New York: Barnes and Nobel, 1952), 156-157.

196. Stephen E. Ambrose, *Nothing Like It in the World*, 88.

197. Philip Anshutz, *Out Where the West Begins*, 155.

198. Stephen E. Ambrose, *Nothing Like It in the World*, 85, 97.

199. (("Total Government Spending in the United States 1860," USGovernmentSpending.com, accessed June 2015, http://www.usgovernmentspending.com/total_1860USmt_16ms5n.

200. Stephen E. Ambrose, *Nothing Like It in the World*, 79.

201. Ron Chernow, *Titan*, 115.

202. Joseph Wall, *Andrew Carnegie*, 189-190.

203. T. J. Stiles, *The First Tycoon*, 100.

204. Parker Morell, *Diamond Jim – The Life and Times of James Buchanan Brady* (New York: Simon and Schuster, 1934), 24.

205. Ron Chernow, *Titan*, 201-203.

206. Jean Strouse, *Morgan*, 311.

207. Ibid., 246-249; Joseph Wall, *Andrew Carnegie*, 510-514.

208. Jean Strouse, *Morgan*, 319-320.

209. Joseph Wall, *Andrew Carnegie*, 614-621.

210. Jean Strouse, *Morgan*, 421-422.

211. Jean-Paul Rodrigue, Claude Comtois, and Brian Slack, "The Geography of Transport Systems," *Hofstra University*, 1998, accessed March 2015, http://people.hofstra.edu/geotrans/eng/ch3en/conc3en/usrail18402003.html.

212. Edward J. Renehan, *Commodore*, 125.

213. Joseph Wall, *Andrew Carnegie*, 114.

214. "Woodruff – Central Transportation," *Builders of Wooding Railway Cars*, accessed April 2015, http://www.midcontinent.org/rollingstock/builders/woodruff-central_transportation.htm.

215. Benjamin P. Thomas, *Abraham Lincoln*, 2-40.

216. Philip Anschutz, *Out Where the West Begins*, 144.

217. Stephen E. Ambrose, *Nothing Like it in the World*, 47-48.

218. Ibid. 53.

219. Philip Anschutz, *Out Where the West Begins*, 147.

220. Ibid., 168.

221. Ibid., 154.

222. Stephen E. Ambrose, *Nothing Like it in the World,* 30-31.

223. Edward J. Renehan, *Dark Genius of Wall Street – The Misunderstood Life of Jay Gould, King of the Robber Barons* (New York: Basic Books, 2005), 1-24.

224. Ibid., 106-107.

225. Philip Anschutz, *Out Where the West Begins,* 176.

226. "James Buchanan Eads," *American Society of Civil Engineers,* accessed November 2014, http://www.asce.org/templates/person-bio-detail.aspx?id=11145.

227. "Elijah McCoy," *Biography.com,* accessed October 2015, http://www.biography.com/people/elijah-mccoy-9391300.

Chapter 9: The Mellons

228. David Cannadine, *Mellon – An American Life* (New York: First Vintage Books, 2008), 349.

229. Ibid., 506-585.

230. Ibid., 508.

231. Thomas Mellon, *Thomas Mellon and His Times* (Pittsburgh: University of Pittsburgh Press, 1994), 9.

232. Ibid., 14.

233. David Cannadine, *Mellon – An American Life*, 3.

234. Ibid., 9, 45.

235. Thomas Mellon, *Thomas Mellon and His Times*, 21.

236. Ibid., 25.

237. Ibid., 26-28.

238. David Cannadine, *Mellon – An American Life*, 11.

239. Thomas Mellon, *Thomas Mellon and His Times*, 45-46.

240. Ibid., 45-51.

241. Ibid., 32.

242. Ibid., 33.

243. Ibid., 62-64.

244. Ibid., 64.

245. Ibid., 66.

246. Ibid., 73.

247. Ibid., 91.

248. Ibid., 92.

249. Ibid., 93-94.

250. Ibid., 93.

251. David Ogilvy, *Ogilvy on Advertising* (New York: First Vintage Books, 1985), 7.

252. Thomas Mellon, *Thomas Mellon and His Times*, 95.

253. Benjamin Franklin, *Autobiography of Benjamin Franklin*, 118.

254. Thomas Mellon, *Thomas Mellon and His Times*, 101.

255. Ibid., 152-173.

256. Ibid., 183-204.

257. David Cannadine, *Mellon – An American Life*, 44-45.

258. Ibid.

259. Ibid., 55-56.

260. Robert Conot, *A Streak of Luck* (New York: Da Capo Press, 1979), 249.

261. David Cannadine, *Mellon – An American Life*, 97-99.

262. Ibid., 179.

263. Joseph Frazier Wall, *Andrew Carnegie* (Pittsburgh: University of Pittsburgh Press, 1989), 968.

264. Parker Morell, *Diamond Jim – The Life and Times of James Buchanan Brady* (New York: Simon and Schuster, 1934), 192-199.

CHAPTER 10: ANDREW CARNEGIE

265. Joseph Frazier Wall, *Andrew Carnegie,* 789.

266. Ibid., 45.

267. Ibid., 46.

268. Ibid., 71.

269. Andrew Carnegie, *The Autobiography of Andrew Carnegie* (Boston: Northeastern University Press, 1986), 27.

270. Ibid., 28-29.

271. Ibid., 33.

272. Ibid., 34.

273. Ibid., 35.

274. Ibid., 38.

275. Ibid.

276. Joseph Frazier Wall, *Andrew Carnegie,* 91.

277. Andrew Carnegie, *The Autobiography of Andrew Carnegie,* 40.

278. Ibid., 43.

279. Joseph Frazier Wall, *Andrew Carnegie*, 93.

280. Andrew Carnegie, *The Autobiography of Andrew Carnegie*, 58-59.

281. Joseph Frazier Wall, *Andrew Carnegie*, 95.

282. Ibid., 102.

283. Andrew Carnegie, *The Autobiography of Andrew Carnegie*, 57.

284. Joseph Frazier Wall, *Andrew Carnegie*, 114.

285. Ibid., 125.

286. "Woodruff – Central Transportation," *Builders of Wooding Railway Cars*, accessed April 2015, http://www.midcontinent. org/rollingstock/builders/woodruff-central_transportation.htm.

287. Joseph Frazier Wall, *Andrew Carnegie*, 100.

288. Ibid., 160.

289. Ibid., 167.

290. Andrew Carnegie, *The Autobiography of Andrew Carnegie*, 97.

291. Joseph Frazier Wall, *Andrew Carnegie*, 189-190.

292. Ibid., 291.

293. Philip Anschutz, *Out Where the West Begins*, 176.

294. Andrew Carnegie, *The Autobiography of Andrew Carnegie*, 154-155, 203-207.

295. "James Buchanan Eads," *American Society of Civil Engineers*, http://www.asce.org/templates/person-bio-detail.aspx?id=11145.

296. Joseph Frazier Wall, *Andrew Carnegie*, 314.

297. Ibid., 328.

298. Ibid., 531.

299. Ibid., 318-319.

300. Ibid., 479-480.

301. Charles R. Morris, *The Tycoons – How Andrew Carnegie, John D. Rockfeller, Jay Gould, and J.P. Morgan invented the American Supereconomy* (New York: Owl Books, 2005), 132.))

302. Joseph Frazier Wall, *Andrew Carnegie*, 614-621.

303. Ibid., 1,042-1,043.

304. Ibid., 101-102.

CHAPTER 11: JOHN D. ROCKEFELLER

305. Grant Segall, *John D. Rockefeller- Anointed with Oil* (New York: Oxford Portraits Kindle edition, 2001), 54.

306. Ron Chernow, *Titan – The Life of John D. Rockefeller, Sr.,* (Vintage Books, 1998), 10.

307. Ibid., 12.

308. Ibid., 33.

309. Ibid., 17.

310. Ibid., 33.

311. Grant Segall, *John D. Rockefeller*, 94.

312. Charles R. Morris, *The Tycoons*, 17.

313. Grant Segall, *John D. Rockefeller*, 94.

314. Ibid., 89.

315. Ron Chernow, *Titan*, 19.

316. Alexis de Tocqueville, *Democracy in America*, 350.

317. Ron Chernow, *Titan*, 42.

318. Ibid., 44-45

319. Grant Segall, *John D. Rockefeller*, 748.

320. Ibid., 147.

321. Ron Chernow, *Titan,* 49.

322. Ibid., 83.

323. Ibid., 67.

324. Ibid., 39.

325. Ibid., 50

326. Ibid., 90.

327. Grant Segall, *John D. Rockefeller,* 194.

328. Ibid., 205.

329. Joseph Frazier Wall, *Andrew Carnegie,* 177.

330. Ron Chernow, *Titan,* 76, 283.

331. Ibid., 76.

332. Ibid., 106.

333. "8 Dot-Coms that Spent Millions on Super Bowl Ads and No Longer Exist," *Business Insider,* February 2, 2011, http://www.businessinsider.com/8-dot-com-super-bowl-advertisers-that-no-longer-exist-2011-2.

334. Ron Chernow, *Titan,* 114.

335. Charles R. Morris, *The Tycoons*, 83-84.

336. Ron Chernow, *Titan*, 143.

337. Ibid., 144.

338. Jean Strouse, *Morgan*, 154.

339. David Goldfield, et. al, *The American Journey* (Upper Saddle River, NJ: Pearson/Prentice Hall, 2007), Volume II, 553.

340. Jean Strouse, *Morgan*, 311.

341. Paul Israel, *Edison: A Life of Invention* (New York: John Wiley and Sons, Inc. 1998), 333.

342. Mark C. Carnes and John A. Garraty, *American Destiny, Volume II,* Third Edition (New York: Pearson Longman, 2008), 694.

CHAPTER 12: THOMAS EDISON

343. "Herbert Hoover – Statement on a National Tribute to Thomas Alva Edison," *The American Presidency Project*, accessed October 15, 2015, http://www.presidency.ucsb.edu/ws/?pid=22861.

344. Robert Conot, *Thomas A. Edison: A Streak of Luck* (New York: Da Capo, 1979), 7.

345. Gene Adair, *Edison: Inventing the Electric Age* (New York: Oxford University Press, 1996), 17; several other Edison biographies recount the same story.

346. Paul Israel, *Edison: A Life of Invention* (New York: John Wiley and Sons, Inc., 1998), 6.

347. Ibid.

348. Robert Conot, *A Streak of Luck,* 9-10.

349. Ibid., 10-11.

350. Paul Israel, *Edison: Life of Invention,* 26, 27.

351. Ibid., 28.

352. Ibid., 31, 32, 34.

353. Robert Conot, A *Streak of Luck*, 15.

354. Ibid., 29.

355. Paul Israel, *Edison: Life of Invention,* 28.

356. Robert Conot, A *Streak of Luck*, 22, 24.

357. Ibid., 22.

358. Gene Adair, *Thomas Alva Edison - Inventing the Electric Age,* 42.

359. Ibid.

360. Ron Chernow, *Titan,* 177.

361. Paul Israel, *Edison: Life of Invention,* 50.

362. "Death of William Orton," *New York Times*, April 23, 1878, http://query.nytimes.com/mem/archive-free/pdf?res=9E03E2D B113AE63BBC4B51DFB2668383669FDE.

363. Paul Israel, *Edison: Life of Invention*, 63.

364. Ibid., 120.

365. Robert Conot, *Streak of Luck*, 43.

366. Ibid., 44.

367. Paul Israel, *Edison: Life of Invention*, 105, 199.

368. Ibid., 105.

369. When Cornelius Vanderbilt died on January 4 of 1877 his son William inherited virtually all his fortune, including his Western Union shares.

370. Robert V. Bruce, *Bell – Alexander Graham Bell and the Conquest of Solitude* (Ithaca, New York: Cornell University Press, 1990), 90.

371. Ibid., 132.

372. Ibid., 113-114.

373. Ibid.

374. Ibid., 270.

375. Ibid., 139.

376. "Tinfoil Phonograph," *Rutgers University – The Thomas Edison Papers,* accessed November 11, 2015, http://edison.rutgers.edu/tinfoil.htm.

377. Jean Strouse, *Morgan,* 181.

378. Ibid., 311.

379. Margaret Cheney, *Tesla – Man out of Time* (New York: Simon and Schuster-Touchstone, 2001), 25.

380. Ibid.

381. Ibid., 65.

382. Ibid., 60.

383. Jean Strouse, *Morgan,* 314.

384. Henry Ford, *My Life and Work* (North Stratford, NH: Ayer Company Publishers, 1999), 22.

385. Steven Watts, *The People's Tycoon – Henry Ford and the American Century* (New York: Knopf Publishing Group, Kindle Edition, 2005), 66.

386. Sidney Olson, *Young Henry Ford – A Picture History of the First Forty Years* (Detroit: Wayne State University Press, 1997), 71.

387. Ibid., 85, 86.

388. Ibid., 179-180.

389. Robert Conot, A *Streak of Luck,* 408.

390. "Homepage," *Edison and Ford Winter Estates,* accessed December 12, 2015 http://www.edisonfordwinterestates.org/.

391. James Newton, *Uncommon Friends* (San Diego: Harcourt Brace & Company, 1987), 26.

CHAPTER 13: DIAMOND JIM BRADY

392. "The Greatest Capital Goods Salesman of Them All," *Fortune Magazine,* October 1954, 113-115.

393. Thomas Sowell, *The Economics and Politics of Race* (New York: Quill Publishing, 1983), 68.

394. Frederick Law Olmsted, *Cotton Kingdom,* 215.

395. Thomas Sowell, *The Economics and Politics of Race,* 69.

396. John Burke, *Duet in Diamonds – The Flamboyant Saga of Lilian Russell and Diamond Jim Brady in America's Gilded Age* (New York: G.P. Putnam's Sons, 1972), 53.

397. Sidney Olson, *Young Henry Ford – A Picture History of the First Forty Years* (Detroit: Wayne State University Press, 1997), 9-12.

398. H. Paul Jeffers, *Diamond Jim Brady – Prince of the Gilded Age* (New York: John Wiley and Sons, Inc. 2001), 8.

399. Parker Morell, *Diamond Jim – The Life and Times of James Buchanan Brady* (New York: Simon and Schuster, 1934), 9.

400. John Burke, *Duet in Diamonds*, 55.

401. H. Paul Jeffers, *Diamond Jim Brady*, 10.

402. Ibid., 12; Parker Morell, *Diamond Jim*, 13.

403. Parker Morell, *Diamond Jim*, 14-17.

404. Ibid., 29.

405. Ibid., 15.

406. H. Paul Jeffers, *Diamond Jim Brady*, 15; John Burke, *Duet in Diamonds*, 63.

407. Charles R. Morris, *The Tycoons*, 100.

408. John Burke, *Duet in Diamonds*, 63.

409. Parker Morell, *Diamond Jim*, 20.

410. John Burke, *Duet in Diamonds*, 67.

411. Parker Morell, *Diamond Jim*, 31.

412. Ibid., 26.

413. Ibid., 25.

414. Hugh Young, *Hugh Young - A Surgeon's Autobiography* (New York: Harcourt, Brace and Company, Inc., 1940), 219.

415. Parker Morell, *Diamond Jim*, 30, 31.

416. Ibid., 31-32.

417. H. Paul Jeffers, *Diamond Jim Brady*, 4.

418. Parker Morell, *Diamond Jim*, 30.

419. Ibid., 62.

420. Ibid., 141.

421. Ibid., 44-47.

422. The author of this book happens to be one.

423. The best account of this part of Brady's career is in Morell's book, pages 44 through 52.

424. Parker Morell, *Diamond Jim*, 79, 80.

425. Ibid., 90.

426. Ibid., 91, 92.

427. Ibid., *Diamond Jim*, 118-123.

428. H. Paul Jeffers, *Diamond Jim Brady*, 202.

429. Parker Morell, *Diamond Jim*, 192-199.

430. David Cannadine, *Mellon – An American Life*, 176, 177.

431. Hugh Young, *Hugh Young - A Surgeon's Autobiography* (New York: Harcourt, Brace and Company, Inc.), 220, 221.

432. Ibid., 216-218.

433. H. Paul Jeffers, *Diamond Jim Brady*, 309.

434. *New York Times*, August 13, 1912.

435. H. Paul Jeffers, *Diamond Jim Brady*, 319.

Chapter 14: How They Did It

436. Robert Conot, *Thomas A. Edison*, 468.

437. Andrew Carnegie, *The Autobiography*, 3.

438. Chuck Yeager and Leo Janos, *Yeager* (New York: Bantam Books, 1988), 17.

439. Ron Chernow, *Titan,* 101.

440. Herbert N. Casson, *Cyrus Hall McCormick - His Life and Work* (Washington, D.C.: Beard Books, 2001), 1-62.

441. Ibid., 97.

442. Sidney Olson, *Young Henry Ford*, 58.

443. Alfred Carl Fuller, *A Foot in the Door* (New York: self-published, 1960), 75-114.

444. Columbia Pictures made *The Fuller Brush Man* in 1948 and The *Fuller Brush Girl* in 1950.

445. Thomas Mellon, *Thomas Mellon and His Times*, 95.

446. Booker T. Washington, *Up from Slavery* (New York: Airmont Publishing Company, Inc., 1967), 96-99.

447. Ron Chernow, *Titan*, 114.

448. Charles R. Morris, *The Tycoons*, 87.

449. Ron Chernow, *Titan*, 111-117.

450. T.J. Stiles, *The First Tycoon*, 117.

451. Mark A. Foster, *Henry J. Kaiser* (Austin, TX: University of Texas Press, 1989), 1-11.

452. Albert P. Heiner, *Henry J. Kaiser -Western Colossus* (San Francisco: Halo Books, 1991), 67.

453. Ibid., 117-139.

454. Mark S. Foster, *Henry J. Kaiser – Builder in the American West* (Austin, TX, University of Texas Press, 1989), 95.

455. Mark C. Carnes and John A. Garraty, *American Destiny, Volume II,* Third Edition, (New York: Pearson Longman, 2008), 492.

456. Ron Chernow, *Titan,* 177-179.

457. Sam Walton, *Made in America – My Story,* 69-70.

458. Steven Watts, *The People's Tycoon – Henry Ford and the American Century,* Vintage eBooks Kindle Edition, 220.

459. Ibid., 218.

460. Ibid., 241.

461. Charles R. Morris, *The Tycoons,* 158.

462. Ron Chernow, *Titan,* 173-177.

463. David Ogilvy, *Ogilvy on Advertising,* 46.

464. Dale Carnegie, *How to Win Friends and Influence People* (New York: Simon and Schuster, 1981), 248.

465. Paul Israel, *Edison: A Life of Invention,* 274-275.

466. Ron Chernow, *Titan,* 178.

467. Parker Morell, *Diamond Jim,* 14-17.

468. Joseph Frazier Wall, *Andrew Carnegie,* 666.

469. Chuck Yeager, *Yeager*, 294.

470. Estee Lauder, *Estee – A Success Story* (New York: Random House, 1985), 59-63.

CHAPTER 15: FINAL WORD

INDEX

A Foot in the Door (book), 242

AT&T, 73, 197, 241

d'Abbans, Claude-Francis-
Dorothee Jouffroy, 74

Accessory Transit, 94-98

Aeschines and Demosthenes
(rivalry), 139

Adams, Abigail, 58

Africa, sub-Saharan, 72

Alcoa and the aluminum industry, 146

Alger, Horatio, 211, 212

Alkaline battery, 203

Allen, Margaret, 170

American Express, 111

American Telegraph Works, 192,
193

Anderson, James (distill-
ery manager for George
Washington), 63

Anderson, Colonel James
(philanthropist and library
founder), 151

Andrews, Samuel, 176

Apple (computer company), 206

Aristotle, 171

Astaire, Fred, 216

Astor, Caroline, 30

Astor, Jakob (father of John
Jacob), 32, 33

Astor, John Jacob, 30-40, 65,
234

Astor, George, 33, 34

Astor, Henry, 35

Astor, Sarah, 37, 38

Astor, William Waldorf, 30, 39

Baltimore and Ohio Railroad
(B&O), 121, 165

Batchelor, Charles, 194, 199,
200

Battle of the Currents, 200,
201

Bell, Alexander Graham, 195-
198, 241,

Bessemer, Henry and Bessemer
steel process, 163, 164, 166

Bible, the, 14, 90, 131, 233

Bonaparte, Napoleon, 76, 226

Boston and New York
Transportation Co.
(B&NY), 93

Bowne, Robert, 35, 36

Brady, Dan Sr. (father of
Diamond Jim Brady), 209,
210

Brady, Dan Jr. (brother of Diamond Jim Brady), 212, 214

Brady Hattie (sister of Diamond Jim Brady), 212

Brady, James Buchanan "Diamond Jim," 30, 146, 232, 235, 249, 258, 259, 208-230

Brooks, Noah (steamboat captain), 89, 90

William Jennings Bryan, 68

Buchanan, James (U.S. President), 162, 208

Buchanan, James (railroad executive), 221, 222

Canal construction, 76, 79, 96, 108-110

Carbon Button, 197-198

Carnes, Mark, 253

Carnegie, Andrew, 1, 25, 73, 85, 90, 92, 103, 114, 118-126, 146, 148-167, 168, 171, 175, 177, 181, 183, 195, 203, 212, 223, 234, 236, 237, 240, 241, 252, 255, 257, 259, 261

Carnegie, Tom, 153, 156, 154

Carnegie, William, 148, 149, 151, 240

Carthage, 72

Cato, 72

Centennial Exposition, 195, 196

Central Pacific Railroad, 116, 117, 126

Central Transportation Company, 160, 161

Chernow, Ron, 172

China, 38, 39, 72

Chisholm, Jesse, 107

Chisholm Trail, 107, 119

Christmas gifts of Diamond Jim Brady, 225

Chrystal Palace Exhibition of 1851, 112

Churchill, Winston, 100, 104

Civil Rights Act of 1964, 69

Clark, Maurice, 174-179

Collins steamship line, 99-101

Columbian Exposition of 1893, 224

Connecticut, 5, 46, 48, 49, 51, 55

Corsair (Morgan's yacht), 123, 124

Costa Rica, 98

Cotton gin, 43, 48-50, 55, 80

Couzens, Rosetta (early Ford Motor Company investor), 216

Crocker, Charles, 126

Cromwell, Oliver, 5

Cunard steamship line, 99-100

Deer, John, 108

Deism, 12

Democracy in America (book), 3, 56

Denham, Thomas, 19-21

Depew, Chauncey, 214

Detroit Edison, 202, 204, 205, 235

Dodge, Grenville, 117, 118, 127

Dogood, Silence (fictitious character invented by Benjamin Franklin), 14-15

Dot-Com boom and bust, 179

Douglass, Frederick, 64-65

Dow, Alexander, 205, 206

Dow Jones Company, 122, 195

Drake, "Colonel" Edwin, 113, 176

Drew, Daniel, 73, 93, 111, 118, 125, 127

Durant Thomas C. "Doc," 116, 117, 126

Eads, James Buchanan, 119, 127, 162, 208, 209

Earp, Wyatt, 119

Edison General Electric, 202

Edison, Thomas Alva, 1, 85, 109, 145, 173, 183, 184-207, 233, 236, 239, 240, 252, 255, 257, 259

Edison, Samuel, 185

Egypt, 71, 72

Eickemeyer, Rudolph, 252

Electric light, invention of, 43, 183, 199-200, 204

Erie Canal, 79, 108, 245

Erie Railroad, 118, 119, 125, 127

Faraday, Michael, 193

Financial panic of 1819, 130

Financial panic of 1873, 115, 120, 121, 144, 165, 181, 182, 213

Financial panic of 1893, 115, 124, 203, 224

Fitch, John, 74, 75, 77

Fisk, Jim, 73, 118, 127

Flagler, Henry, 179

Ford, Clara, 205

Ford, Henry, 183, 184, 204-207, 223, 235, 237, 239, 254-255, 260

Ford, William, 85, 210

Fortune 500 list, 69, 202,

Fortune Magazine, 70, 208, 209

Fox, Sampson (inventor of the Fox undertruck), 219, 220-223, 227, 229, 235-236

Frick, Henry Clay, 166-167

Franklin, Benjamin, 8-29, 33, 34, 65, 133-134, 135, 137, 140, 141, 143, 147, 152, 153, 174, 190, 191, 204

Franklin, Deborah (nee Deborah Read), 17, 18, 26, 27, 140

Franklin, James, 10-17, 25

Franklin, Josiah, 9, 10, 18, 23

Freedom Iron Company, 119, 160, 162-164

Fuller, Alfred C., 241-242

Fulton, Robert, 71-79

Garrison, Cornelius, 96-98

Garraty, John, 253

Gates, John "Bet a Million," 146

Gates, William II and Bill, 85

General Electric Company (G.E.), 202, 252, 256

Gibbons, Thomas, 84-88

Gibbons, William, 87

God, 3, 5, 13, 14, 55, 92, 108, 159, 175, 177, 233-234, 260

Gold and Stock Telegraph Company, 191, 192, 194, 202

Goodwin, Nat, 218

Google, 206

Google Earth, 110

Gould, Jay, 73, 115, 118, 119, 127

Government spending, 1860 compared with 2015, 117

Gray, Elisha, 196-197

Greene, Catharine, 46, 47

Half War, 51

Hammond, James Henry (South Carolina Governor), 67

Hansen, John (partner of James Buchanan Brady), 146-147, 227

Harrington, George (partner of Thomas Edison), 192

Havas, George (subordinate of Henry J. Kaiser), 252

Hewitt and Tuttle, 173

Hopkins, Mark, 126

Holley, Alexander, 164

Hoover, President Herbert, 184

Hudson River Steamboat Association, 91

Hudson River steamboating monopoly, 74, 75, 86, 88

Hugo, Victor, 188

Huntington, Collis, 126

Illinois and St. Louis Bridge Co., 162

India, 72

Indus River, 72

Interchangeable parts, 43, 50, 53

Iron Age, the, 41

James, Don (football coach), 231

Japan, 72

Jay Cook and Company, 165

Jefferson, Thomas, 29, 51, 75, 107

Jerome, Leonard, 104

Jerome, Jenny (mother of Winston Churchill), 104

Jim Crow laws, 3, 55, 69

Johns Hopkins Hospital, 228-230

Jones, Captain William, 164, 165

Judah, Theodore, 126

Junta, 24-25, 237

Kloman, Andrew, 164

Kaiser, Henry J., 250-252

Keimer, Samuel, 17-19, 21-27

Kelly, Fred, 242

Keystone Bridge Company, 119, 160-162

Kruesi, John, 194, 198,

Lake Shore Railroad, and Rockefeller's freight deal with it, 180-181, 244-248

Lauder, Estee, ix, 250, 258

Leech, Malcolm, 132

Leeds Ironworks, 219, 220, 223

Leonard, Helen Louise – See Russell, Lillian

Ligonier Valley, 144-145

Lincoln, Abraham, 102, 114, 116, 126, 153, 158-159, 175, 258

Liverpool and Manchester Railway (L&M), 108-109

Livingston, Robert, 75-78, 85, 86, 88

Long Island Railroad, 93, 111

Lucas, John, 211-212

MacKenzie, James, 187

Manning, Maxwell, and Moore (company), 214, 220

Massachusetts State Legislature, 189-190

Masterson, Bat, 119

McCauley, Edna, 217-218

McCormick, Cyrus Hall, 55-56, 106, 108, 112, 238-239

McCoy, Elijah, 120, 127

Mellon, Andrew, 128-147, 167, 227

Mellon, Dick (brother of Andrew), 140, 144-147

Mellon, James (brother of Andrew), 140, 141, 142, 145

Mellon National Bank, 147

Mellon, Judge Thomas Sr., 8, 128-147, 167, 204, 242, 249

Mellon, Thomas Alexander (brother of Andrew and son of Judge Thomas Sr.), 140, 141, 142, 143, 145

Mellon, Sarah Jane (nee Negley – wife of Thomas and mother of Andrew), 140, 142

Melinda Miller (early love interest of John D. Rockefeller), 172

Messabi Mountain Range, 203

Monitor and Merrimack, 100
Moore, Charles Arthur, 214-115, 220, 221, 223
Morell, Parker, 214
Morgan, Charles, 96-98
Morgan, J.P., 115, 122-124, 126, 146, 148, 163, 167, 168, 198-199, 202, 227, 239, 259
Morgan, Junius, 115, 160, 163, 166
Morse, Samuel, 111
Motion picture technology and industry, 43, 203
Miller, Phineas, 46-49
Muskets, 49-53
Napoleon Bonaparte, 76, 226
New England Courant, 14-16
New York Central Railroad, 102, 112-115, 118, 119, 122-125, 154, 161, 180, 212-215, 221-222
New York & Harlem Railroad (NY&H), 101-104
New York Times, 209, 229
Nicaragua, 94-98
Nile River, 71-72
North River, steamboat, 74, 78-79
Northern Pacific Railroad, 120, 125
Ogilvy, David, 90, 139, 236, 256

Ohio River, 57, 59, 106, 107
Olmsted, Frederick Law, 59, 61-63, 80
Orton, William, 192, 196
Pacific Railroad Bill, 116
Panama, 94, 96, 98
Payne, Oliver, 181
Penn, William, 6
Pennsylvania Railroad, aka "Pennsy," 92, 110, 112-115, 118, 119, 121-125, 144, 154-156, 158, 159, 161, 165, 182, 213, 222
Pennsylvania Railroad riots of 1877, 122, 213
Philadelphia and Reading Railroad, 124
Phonograph, 198
Pierce, Franklin, 92
Poor Richard's Almanack, 27, 28
Pope, Franklin, 190-192
Pope, Edison Company, 191-192
"Populist" movement, 68
Pressed Steel Car Company, 146, 227
Pullman, George, 113, 119, 127, 161, 166
Puritans, 5-6, 9, 12
Ramsey, Dave, 248
Read, John (father of Deborah), 18

Rockefeller, Eliza (nee Davison), 168-172
Rockefeller, John D., 9, 54, 73, 82-83, 92, 100, 119, 128, 168-183, 191, 203, 204, 232, 238, 244
Rockefeller, Laura Celestia (nee Spelman), 92, 175
Rockefeller, William A. "Devil Bill," 168-171
Rockefeller, William (brother of John D.), 180
Roman Empire, 72
Roosevelt, Franklin D., 128-129
Russell, Lillian, 217-218, 224, 226, 230
San Juan River, 94-95
Schwab, Charles, 146, 165, 203
Scott, Thomas, 154-156, 158-159, 162, 182
Separatists, 4-5
Severn, sailing ship, 39
Shaler, Charles, 137
Shasta Dam, 251
Shiloh, Battle of, 186
Shinn, William P., 164-1165
Slavery, 6, 47-49, 55-70, 114, 127, 157-160, 175, 209-210, 243, 249
Solid gold bicycles, 223

Southern Commercial Conventions, 67-69
Sowell, Thomas, 210
Standard Oil Co., 54, 73, 119, 121-122, 168-183, 244-248, 256
Standard Steel Car Company, 146-147, 226
Stanford, Leland, 126
Steinmetz, Charles, 252, 256, 259
Stephenson, George, 42, 88, 89, 108
Stevens, John, 75, 77, 88, 89, 91
Tarbell, Ida, 245
Telephone, the race for, 194-198
Tesla, Nicola, 183, 200-202
Thompson, J. Edgar, 112, 115, 119, 121, 126, 154-155, 165
Time zones, origin, 122
Tocqueville, Alexis, 3, 30, 56-59, 69-70, 105, 168, 172
Toucey, John, 212-214, 235, 257
Train wrecks, 91-92
Trans-continental railroad, 115-117, 120, 126, 161
Tuskegee Institute/University, 57, 243-244
Twain, Mark, 9, 71, 194
Tweed, William M. ("Boss Tweed"), 103-104

Union Pacific Railroad, 116-117, 126, 161

United States Congress, 69, 100-101, 190

United States Steel, 146, 148, 165, 203, 227

Vanderbilt, Cornelius, 1, 65, 73, 80-104, 106, 111-112, 114, 115, 118, 119, 122-123, 125, 127, 154, 161, 168, 171, 180, 195, 231, 236, 240, 249, 255, 259

Vanderbilt, Jacob, 89

Vanderbilt, John, 89

Vanderbilt, William, 102, 104, 122, 123

Walker, William, 97-98

Walmart, 69, 90, 253

Walton, Sam, 69-70, 90, 235, 253-254

Washington, Booker T., 57, 243

Washington, George, 63, 65

Watson, Thomas, 195-196, 198

Watt, James, 77

Wells Fargo, 73

Western Union, 160, 165, 192-197, 201

Westinghouse, George, 120, 127, 183, 200-202

Whiskey rebellion, 106-107, 131

White "Crackers," 62-63

Whitney, Eli, 41-54, 55-56, 65, 76, 80, 111, 238, 259

Whitney, Eli Jr., 53-54

Wise, Governor Henry A., 67

Woodruff, Theodore, 112-113, 126, 155-156, 160

Yale, 45-46

Yankee Peddlers, 31-32

Yeager, Chuck, 238, 257-258

Yellow River, 72

Young, Dr. Hugh, 227-230

AUTHOR BIOGRAPHY

Al Fuller is a history buff and part-time author who lives with his beautiful and supportive wife in the Seattle area. In his day job he manages a team of salespeople in the Pacific Northwest. He enjoys the great outdoors, college football, and reading the abundant rags-to-riches success stories that American history provides.

He can be reached at Al.Fuller@HistoryHalf.com or via ASelfMadeNation.com.

www.ingramcontent.com/pod-product-compliance
Lightning Source LLC
Chambersburg PA
CBHW072002060426
42446CB00042B/1366